THE FORTRESS

PARTS III. & IV.

By

HUGH WALPOLE

First published in 1932

Read &' Co.

Copyright © 2022 Read & Co. Classics

This edition is published by Read & Co. Classics,
an imprint of Read & Co.

This book is copyright and may not be reproduced or copied in any
way without the express permission of the publisher in writing.

British Library Cataloguing-in-Publication Data
A catalogue record for this book is available
from the British Library.

Read & Co. is part of Read Books Ltd.
For more information visit
www.readandcobooks.co.uk

FOR MY FRIENDS
GERTRUDE AND MUIRHEAD BONE

CONTENTS

HUGH WALPOLE

Hugh Seymour Walpole was born in Auckland, New Zealand in 1884. He was educated at a series of boarding schools in England, followed by Emmanuel College, Cambridge. Walpole's father hoped he would follow him into the clergy, but after three years as a missionary, in 1909, Walpole resolved to become a man of letters. His first commercial success came in 1911 with the novel *Mr Perrin and Mr. Traill*, after which Walpole made the acquaintance of writers such as Henry James and Joseph Conrad, and declared his ambition to become the greatest writer of his era. For the rest of his life, Walpole wrote prolifically. During the twenties he produced more than a novel a year, with *The Cathedral* (1922) and *Wintersmoon* (1928) proving to be great successes. In 1930, he began his most popular series of novels with the historical romance *Rogue Herries*, following it with *Judith Paris* (1931), *The Fortress* (1932) and *Vanessa* (1933). Eventually, he amassed an oeuvre of 36 novels, five volumes of short stories, two plays and three volumes of memoirs. He died in 1941, aged 57. Despite the fact that Walpole sold enormously well on both sides of the Atlantic, and was praised by many of his contemporaries, he is somewhat forgotten now, in part because he was overshadowed by P. G. Wodehouse and others.

Thy gentlest dreams, thy frailest,
Even those that were
Born and lost in a heart-beat,
Shall meet thee there.
They are become immortal
In shining air.

The unattainable beauty,
The thought of which was pain,
That flickered in eyes and on lips
And vanished again;
That fugitive beauty
Thou shalt attain.

Those lights innumerable
That led thee on and on,
The masque of time ended,
Shall glow into one.
They shall be with thee for ever,
Thy travel done.

A. E.

PART III

CUMBERLAND CHASE

UHLAND'S JOURNAL

IREBY. *January* 5, 1843.

Finished to-night that stuff-and-nonsense book Carlyle's *Heroes.* Wonder that I had the patience to read it on to the end, but I fancy that I was always going further to see whether all his tall words and German sentences would lead to anything. They do not any more than does this damnably silly Journal of mine. There is just this difference. Carlyle is a hypocrite and I am not. He knows he is no hero but says he is one—I know that I can be a hero as suitably as any of his Fredericks and Cromwells, but prefer not to be one. And why do I prefer? Because the world is so crammed with fools and conceited coxcombs that it is a finer thing to sit by and watch—to watch, if you like, the decline and fall of the house of Herries and myself with it. Bang—Bang—Bang—Whiskers—Whiskers—Whiskers. This is nothing but the sound a blind man makes seeing himself to bed with the light of a thick stick and the smell of the candle-end. And it is also, if you like, the noise that my beloved father and Sam Osmaston are making just under this floor of my room, both as drunk as cockchafers in lamplight, on their knees most likely, searching for a goose's feather.

But this Journal is supposed to say what I do. Well, what do I do? Get up, you lamentable cripple, and look at yourself in the glass, examine once again your ugly wry face, your ribs, like an old man's counting-board, and your white bit of twisted bone politely called a leg. Good, good! That's the thing, my boy! That's the way to bring your conceit down and sit on the floor to talk about Heroes. But the soul's the thing, is it not? Does not old

13

Carlyle say so? The soul! The soul! Where may you be, soul? Stuck in that leg of mine? Hiding like a rabbit behind a rib or two? Well, come out for once! Let's have a look at you! Where are you, green, crimson or mulberry; and your shape? Are you tortoise-like with a shell like a snuff-box, or thin and spidery, catching flies for your food, or just a pincushion with pink lace and a blue silk bow?

What a week I've had too!

They've all been here. The Newmarks with all their brood, Phyllis a female Alderman, Newmark the prize prig of the market, Horace as long in the leg as a pair of stilts and as wooden, *dear* little Emily and *dear* little Barnabas. All with the latest news of my good grandfather's new offspring. 'Oh, *what* a sweet infant! the dearest little boy!' until I thought my father would throttle the lot of them. Amery Herries too with eyes like gooseberries, the merriest drunken bachelor, and old Rodney from Polchester, sixty if he's a day, touring the Lakes and Scotland with one eye on his clerical dignity and the other on the destiny of every halfpenny! Lord, how I hate the lot of them and how they hate me! Didn't I make little Emily cry by blowing out the candle, and isn't old Rodney afraid of my humours? A family sinking to rot, my masters, cursed because, between too much money-bag on the one side and too much indecisive dreaming on the other, the way to Salvation is missed every time. Not that there *is* any Salvation, even though you search for it. Nothing but madness or death from over-eating whichever way you go.

But now when the house is silent and every stone in this building can be heard scraping its reproaches, I wonder at my indignation. Indignant? No, I have not blood enough for so bold a word. I sit here, sneezing, rubbing my knees the one against the other, healing Rob's ear in the basket, raising my perpetual theme of hatred of my dear John brother-in-law and do nothing, positively nothing. Neither lust urges me nor greed nor envy nor desire for knowledge: only if I had John's neck here I would twist it until his eyes were in his back, and even that is a fancy—nurtured lust, something bred of years of coddling. It *had* a reason once and now I've fed my brain with so many centuries of imagination that to see him tortured in my fancy is as good as the actual deed.

And yet it could have been otherwise. Only this stupid mutton-faced Journal shall know how otherwise it might have been! Another father, flat-faced Adam for a brother and a pair of legs like anyone's, and I had the power, the wish, the ambition. I could have written a book or two, I fancy, better than Bulwer at any rate, or played in a laboratory and made a discovery, or talked as wittily as any Disraeli or Palmerston of them all. I have more brains in my toe-nail (those on the withered foot have an especial brilliancy) than all my Herries cousins lumped together. But from the very first I was outcast. *That* at least is no imagination. I make no claim for it and I ask for no pity, but to be different from birth, to have the street children mock at you and the dogs bark, and visitors to the house look the other way—it is a kind of allowance for hatred. They say Carlyle has dyspepsia and yet he thinks himself a Hero. Well, am I not a Hero that I sit here and think, and think, and wish myself a villain? And my father still loves me. He thinks me a miracle of brilliance and perversity. All that is left to him, poor man, for his brain is fuddled with drink, the ladies won't call, his fine house is a stony desert, and they flourish at Uldale like the righteous!

Ah! there's the rub! Cousin Judith as lively as a flea, Cousin Dorothy and her children fat as good cattle, John and Elizabeth like sucking-doves. There! He is singing. I can hear him under the floor. And Sam Osmaston with him—a fine out-of-tune chorus . . .

IREBY. *November* 13, 1843.

Rob's ear has this canker again. It's his perversity, I well believe, for he knows truly that once his ear is well, out he'll go, to be stoned by the Keswick boys again, I suppose. And the odd thing is, I shan't care. He's been with me almost a year now. I enjoy his face like the parson's, with its side-whiskers and a slobbery white patch like spilt milk on his nose. He's fonder of me than any dog's ever been, but I hate that sycophancy. I'm near shooting him at times or hanging him from the beam with a rope—yes, even while I wash and clean his ear with the tenderness of a woman.

And now what do you think, O my Journal? What has our dear father done but buy a piece of the moor just above Uldale and build a small cottage on it and into that shove Peach and his dirty brood. There is just one patch, it seems, that great-grandfather David neglected to buy, a measly brown bit that even the sheep neglect. He has done it to vex Aunt Judith of course, and vex her it must to have the filthy little Peaches at her garden gate, and Peach at war with her drunken Rackstraw.

Since she scratched dear father's cheeks last Christmas-time he's been all bent on vexing her, although in my view he thinks her a damnably fine old woman. So she is! She and Adam—another brood from the rest of them.

November 22.

I am just back from Rosthwaite where I have been limping about all day like an old woman looking for eggs. But something or someone (Algebraical formula? $x + y = xy2 = God$?) had put it into my mind of late to be interested in my old Great-great-grandfather, the Rogue. It seems that he spent half his life longing for a gipsy girl (Aunt Judith's mother by oddity) who, when he got her at last, incontinently died. I like the smell of that old man and have picked up a pack of curiosities about him, how he sold a stout mistress at Keswick Fair, was given a scar in a duel, fought for the Pretender outside Carlisle or some such thing, married his gipsy at Rosthwaite and cuffed and kicked the guests down his stairs, how she ran away and he roamed the hills for years looking for her; then, catching her at last, gave her Judith whom she died of. There is something deeply sympathetic to me here, for he was outcast as I am, a rebel as I, if I had the guts, would be, a hater too, I fancy, only he would not play Hamlet by the year as I have done.

His old house is a ruin, some tumbled barns swallowed in weed and swiftly vanishing. I sat on some broken mouldy stairs this afternoon and could have sworn to seeing the old fellow watching me ironically. It's his irony I like the taste of. None of the Herries have irony save Aunt Judith. I would like a picture of him, but father says there is none; however, an old cottager well over ninety years with whom I talked to-day—a lively cursing old man with no teeth, so that he must hiss like a snake when he talks, but his hearing is mighty sharp—he remembers him, how he came striding over the little bridge by Rosthwaite, in a plum-coloured coat with a scar down his cheek, and how he and his gipsy lay both dead in the house together and an old man rode up on a horse and carried the new-born child (Judith, by all that's comic) away on his horse with him. The only man of our family with whom I have any touch, and he dead these seventy years! Grandfather Will must remember him. Next time in London I shall harry his wits over him . . .

I am planning a long London visit. This house is the devil. It is colder than any crypt, and the stone, cover it as you may, breaks through and snarls at you. Every wind in the country whips it and the trees moan like kitchen-maids with the toothache. Also I have the ambition to touch up Cousin John a trifle. I could look in at his window and give him a queasy stomach. What is this hatred? Contempt of his mealy-mouthed propriety? Rage at his impertinent marriage with my sister? Jealousy of his strength and whole limbs? Something taught to me in my cradle by my father? Yes, and more than all this. I hate him because I have always done so, because of what he is and because he is happy and I am not. These are honest reasons, but behind these there is the pleasure of the pursuit. As my old roguish ancestor pursued his gipsy so I pursue my John. We freaks in the Herries stock must have our revenge on the normal ones; there is a warfare there that has necessity in it. And I have no other emotions. I have never lusted after a woman in all my days, nor cared for a human being save Adam. Is that my own fault? I could have asked for quite another destiny, but I had no say in it. So, to my only pleasure, to see him start at the sound of my step and flinch under my hand. My leg aches in sympathy.

12 GRANGER STREET, LONDON.
February 12, 1844.

Three weeks in London. What a folly! Dinner at Richmond or Blackwall, the Cave of Harmony, the Coal Hole and such; the inner sanctities of Meadows' and 'Seven's the main' of the caster, and 'Gentlemen, make your game' of the groom-porter. Cards everywhere and, even without the perils of lansquenet, with a pony on the rubber, five pound points and betting on the odd trick, you are caught before you are hooked. There is scarcely a quiet respectable house in all London where they won't rook you if you give them half a chance.

All the same there's a strange curtain of hypocritical respectability over this town since my last visit. They say it is our good little Queen and our handsome German Prince. No nonsense at Court, they say. All heading now for the Virtues.

Last night a party at my grandfather's where, if you please, we sat round in a circle and a woman with teeth like a grinning hag's read us the poems of Mr. Tennyson. Poor old grandfather would have slumbered happily in his corner had not Mrs. Will in a pink dress with 'volants' almost up to her waist (and there must have been at least eight rows of them) pinched him after every melancholy verse. She had time too for elegant flirtation with a fat young man whose whiskers were as long as a horse's mane! I have never disliked anyone more and her loathing of myself is badly concealed by her extreme endearments. She was frightened of me, I believe and hope. But I perceive that I throw a gloom on to every party that I encounter. All the better. This London is a meeting-place of all the snobs, hypocrites, sharps and idiots of Christendom.

But I remain, for I have my own quiet amusements. One of these is the clearing of Cousin Garth's pockets, for such a juggins at cards deserves clearing.

Another is to listen to the bombast of old James or Carey who both have the fancy that *their* England (*theirs*, mark you) is the most Christian and at the same time the most commercial miracle that this weary planet has ever beheld! To hear them talk of old Pam or of Peel you would fancy that we had no Chartists nor starving populace whatever, and to listen to their contempt of *any* foreign country is to realise to the full *one* side of the beautiful Herries shield!

I listen and then with one remark blow their soap-bubbles to air—and don't they hate me for it too! It is worth the boredom of London to see old James flush his double-chin and stutter: 'But, my dear sir—my *dear* young friend . . . '

I have a deeper pleasure than these mild amusements, though. I have discovered Cousin John's hours: he leaves Bryanston Square five of an evening and for the good of his precious health walks across the Park. Thrice a week at least I see to it that he shall encounter me. We never speak; indeed one glimpse of me is enough to destroy his peace for the rest of the day. He would take a cab were it not that he fights his cowardice, and it has happened twice that when he has taken one I have followed him in another, coming from mine as he issues from his. This game gives me a wild and sensual pleasure. There are certain streets and houses that are marked with the colour of our meetings. Best of all I learnt from Sylvia Herries last week that he and Elizabeth would be at the theatre. They had a box and I in the pit enjoyed my evening to the full. At every meeting it seems to me that we come closer together even as my father grows closer to Uldale. I am contented to bide my time, for there is no pleasure for me in life like this chase. Is this madness? It may be that it is, for it seems to me that I am now two persons and when the one is not with him the other is. I sleep but little and walk the streets at night, hearing my own step in pursuit of myself, that same halting stumble that must, I know, haunt the bowels of Cousin John. I would swear that last night, dressing for grandfather's party, I saw two figures in the mirror and neither shadowy . . .

March 13.

I have had an encounter that has moved me oddly. Yesterday afternoon in the Strand I walked straight into Adam. He was brown and ruddy and sturdy, dressed roughly, books under his arm, his eyes serious and kindly as they ever were. May the Devil forgive me, but I was pleased to see him. Our talk was thus:

'Why, Adam!'

'Why, Uhland!'

'Are you well?'

'And you?'

His hand was on my arm and I felt, for a foolish minute, that I would have followed him anywhere. He is the only one in the world not to glance at my leg, to be perfectly at ease with me, to give me some glimpse of a normal world where men are honest and mean their words. Yet I doubt not he is a prig and thinks highly of his own virtues. Yet he was kind without hypocrisy. He asked me to visit them and he meant it, I think. But I turned away. I could have struck him for moving me as he did. I could have struck him, but I looked back after him as though I were letting my best chance go. He is still on my mind to-day. He has given me his address and I have half an impulse to visit him. But for what? I should but despise his amiability and suspect his seriousness. There is no place where we can move side by side and I do not know that I wish that there should be.

IREBY. *April* 7, 1845.

I am so much better that I can at last get to my Journal again. Not that I hunger for it, but it is at least a testimony to some energy. And to-day has been a day as warm as milk and so still that you can hear the cows munching. There was all morning a mist like thick honey with the light breathing behind it a glorious exultant spirit. The sun has been dim all day and Blencathra and Skiddaw have been like whales, unicorns, blankets of soft down, and this afternoon when the sun came fully out and the air was blue they rolled over in delight as puppies do when, deliciously expectant, they want their stomachs stroked. It is not like me to write of the weather, but I have been ill for so long and have smelt nothing but candle-ends, slops and the horsey grain of my blankets.

Last evening I had an odd talk with my father that needs recording. He came in wobbling a candle, in a bed-gown, his chest exposed, but in spite of this very sober. I have been dimly conscious of him the last months, coming in and out of my fantasies. And *what* fantasies! Myself hanging, bare save for a thin shift, from a beam, my toes turned in, and my second self exuding like milk from an udder out of my left ear—and I was Grandfather Will's infant, guzzling at a bottle and clutching a money-bag, and the room was on fire and myself in the middle of it frying like an acorn, or I hobbled on Stye Head, the mists chasing me until I fell headlong into Eskdale, and once a white horse, flashing up a frozen mountain-side, caught me with its teeth and flung me down into ice. In and out of this, then, has come my good father, but only last evening did we have any serious conversation.

He tells me that he has not had a drop of liquor for the last six months, during my illness. And I can believe him. For once he does not look more than his fifty odd years. His fat is dropped from him—yes, and his spirits have gone too. He is a little crazed, I think, as I am. This house has the seeds of craziness in its bones. For he says that Aunt Judith has poisoned me, some insane story about her bribing the cook to spoil my food! There's real craziness as I told him, for whatever that old lady may be about it will never be poisoning. He tells me, however, that Rackstraw whipped one of the Peach children within an inch of its existence for stealing out of the Uldale kitchen-window and that one of the Uldale barns has been set on fire. He wants to have Aunt Judith in jail, but I tell him that the countryside would burn the jail down to get her out.

When all this loose talk of revenge and the rest had died away he besought me not to leave him. He has a fear, it seems, that I shall steal away just as Elizabeth did. He moved me for he loves me with the strongest mingling of pride, fear and egotism. God knows I don't want his love. I have no regard for him except that it seems to me we are caught in the same trap. My illness has left my head clear and empty. I am imprisoned and cannot be free until some act frees me. Death, perhaps, of which I have no fear. But death liberates only one of myself. The other remains imprisoned.

My father held my body in his arms. How lonely and isolated an act! No one has ever held me close to their breast since I was an infant, and my father is not a man of sentiment, but he sees everything else going—health, reputation, wealth—save his love for me and his hatred of the Uldale lot. I tell you we Herries are lost men if we let our dreams go too far, be they good or bad, and this old folly of hating one another is a dream like the rest, for there is no satisfaction to be found in any egoistic desire. I can see that we are intended to lose ourselves altogether in something impersonal, and once Cousin John, the pretty, were gone I could be lost, I fancy, turning with what relief into the thick honeyed air like a child loosed from school . . . But what a couple the two of us, my gross father straining my bony wasted fretfulness against his bare chest, and our eyes refusing to meet! And myself, round the corner, peering and grinning at the idiocy of the scene from behind the wardrobe.

When he kissed me I shrank into my twitching leg and he felt me shrink and for once I hated my unkindness. He is a very simple man, my father. He meant this Fortress to be a great symbol of Herries power—just as Cousin James and Rodney and Grandfather and Amery are building up their fine Victorian England—but to lay stone upon stone is not enough. That is a thing that the building Herries have never understood. I do not believe in God but I do not think that you can build anything without Him.

My father wishes me to take my proper place here when I am recovered. He is reformed, he says—no more the rake. We will attend to farms and property. Yes, but no Herries has ever wanted to accumulate property. We do not care for it enough. We think too much of ourselves and will not yield our personal conceit to anything, not even to property.

And we must get Aunt Judith out of Uldale, he says. And we must make this house warm, he says. It is always so devilish cold. He does not know that there is a rat eating away the foundations. And, when all is said, he loves me like a dog, not knowing why, and I care for nothing and nobody, not I. It is something though to see the gold light again lying evenly over the hills and to hear the stream running down the hill. I have grown, during my illness, a pale forked beard. I look, in the glass, like a green radish.

LONDON. *January* 14, 1846.

Yesterday I had a half-hour of sanity that is worth recording. I spent it with Grandfather Will. He requested me to pay him a visit. Why? Even now I do not know. Some intention perhaps of compensation because he has thrown my father and myself aside for ever and young Ellis reigns in our stead. (Why Ellis? A dreary, dryas-dust, left-over-from-yesterday pantry kind of name, but its mother has rich cousins thusly.) Nor do I blame him for that. We are not a pair to be proud of, I suppose. And so

I went. Appalling that house in Hill Street. No rain-washed air sweeping Blencathra here, but furniture spawning everywhere, masses of it, heavy and despondent, groaning between thick rep and treading down the thick Turkey. There are pallid sightless statues and old Herries gilt-edged on every wall. I was alone in a vast room with my grandfather, and we crept together for safety. 'Keepsakes' were our only company. But I am modern for my time. I am a hundred years hence. I am sickly with the odour of 1950. He is bent now, his hair white, his clothes fitting him, black and stiff, as though they were made in a Bank. But in his old age he is kind and eager. I should judge that this baby is the only human soul for whom he has ever cared, although he spoke of Elizabeth's beauty and seeing her alone in this room one day in the past 'like a vision.' He meant, I fancy, that it could not be true that she was my sister. He thinks me misshapen and dangerous and cannot understand that I should be descended from his loins. Something has gone wrong somewhere and he is bewildered because he has always done the sensible thing. But he intended to be kind, sat close to me although I made him creep, and by not looking at my twitching leg he only looked the more intently. He asked me how I did. He had heard that I had been ill. He feared that he would never see Cumberland again although in his youth he had seen eagles sailing over Glaramara. He has a trick of fingering his coat-buttons as though they were counting-house money. He wanted me to tell him something. But what? That things have not turned out as they should do, his brother Francis a suicide, his son a drunken fool, his grandson a deformity? Well, there is little Ellis, and I see as though under glass his heart beat up again and his old eyes, weary with gazing on figures, open out at the new hope. Then he is proud of England. It is as though he had made it, put a hump on Skiddaw here, added a tomb to Westminster, straightened the Strand, bidden the sea halt in Norfolk, and run the railway to Newcastle. He is tired, he explains to me, and then with great courage lays his hot bony hand on mine.

'For I am seventy-five,' he tells me, 'and have worked hard all my days.'

He hopes that we are all now reconciled, for there was once a silly quarrel. Something about a fan. His wife, 'your grandmother,' was concerned. But that is all so old, so very very long ago, and he hopes that now all is well. Do I see Judith Paris often? A remarkable woman with much spirit and character. And I think of the little Peach children setting a match to Aunt Judith's parlour, and Aunt Judith slapping my father's face.

But he hopes that all is well. We must be friends, all of us. Our family must stand together. They mean something to England. He talks of Palmerston and Peel and the Corn Law crisis and says the 'rotten potatoes have done it,' and how angry the Duke is and that Melbourne told the Queen 'that it was a damned dishonest act,' and that John Russell has come out of it all 'damned poorly,' but they are all dim figures to him now. Ellis aged three has swallowed up the firmament. He has a little rheumatism in his legs, he tells me, but otherwise he is well enough, and so he pulls himself up and slowly, slowly, very stiff and straight, stamps from the room. And I go down into the street to meet my waiting double . . .

IREBY. *October* 9, 1846.

I have seen the 'Barguest.' I am a haunted man. I was lost yesterday afternoon in the wilds between Blencathra and Skiddaw, Skiddaw Forest way. I do not know where exactly I was. I could not find the same place again. I had plunged upward, limping and running and limping again in my own ridiculous fashion, treading down the dried bracken that in certain lights has almost a glow of fire running through it. I had looked back and seen Ireby with its stone turrets, its frowning eyebrow, squat like a discontented image staring down at Uldale. I looked forward and the rocks closed me in. They have that fashion here. They move forward of their own will; you can see them almost scratching their craggy sides. A moment before there had been the long swinging slope of bracken, fields below marked off and smelling rain, the stone wall running straight up into air, a round tufted tree holding the light, cottages and farms—and now only this pressing crowding observant rock, the ridge of the hill black against the October sky save for some little white clouds that like spies crowded to the ridge and looked over down into the amphitheatre. I am noting it down thus minutely because of what then occurred.

I seemed to be able to move neither up nor down; my leg limits me and I felt as though the slope of rock on which I was standing would slide down with me—maliciously, while the rocks round me shook with laughter. And then I saw the Barguest. An old man shaped like a whalebone. He came along towards me on his hands and knees, and once and again he would stop, stare at me, and bite his long finger-nails. But I could see through him; he swayed like water-mist, was at one time so hazily defined that there were wisps of him like clouds about the rock, then so sharp that I could count every button. It was no imagination— or I am mad perhaps with want of sleep. I stayed transfixed, and he came right up to me. I could smell his breath, an odour of mushroom and sodden leaves. He touched me with his long yellow finger-nail and then dispersed into vapour. I know this is so. It is no dream and, if I am crazy, which for some months now I have suspected, what is reality? But I am sure that I shall see this place again and at some fatal time. When the Barguest had vanished I climbed a stone and all the scenery was restored again, the fields green in the October sun, and rain-clouds gathering up above the sea.

WAX FLOWERS
AND THE REVOLUTION

Adam tried, with all the self-control that belonged to his training, to forget what the day after to-morrow meant to him, but, try as he would, again and again something repeated inside himself: 'The day after to-morrow . . . The day after to-morrow. Everything hangs on Monday, my whole life . . . everything I've worked for.'

Margaret, in a brown bonnet, hanging on his arm, caught sight of the magnificent Beadle, whiskered, gold-laced, standing superbly at the door of the Pantheon Bazaar.

'Oh, let us go into the Pantheon . . . I can find something there for poor little Daisy Bain, whose foot was crushed by that wagon last week. It won't occupy us a minute. Do you mind, Adam?'

They were both making a sublime attempt at proving that nothing was toward. To-day was like any other day. And yet, with how many thousands around them, they were, it might be, on the eve of a new era, a new world, a world of light, justice and brotherhood. All London was making preparation for Monday's great Chartist rising. All clerks and officials were ordered to be sworn garrisons. Every gentleman in London was become a constable. (What a very grand carriage outside the Princess Theatre, and what a hideous befrilled Pug in the window!)

After all, what an incredible year! In the month of March alone fearful street fighting in Berlin, flight of the Prince of Prussia, riots in Vienna and Milan, Hungary in revolt, revolution in Austria, and, above all, France tumbling either into a chaos of disaster or a triumph of a new grand order!

And on Monday—Monday, April 10, 1848—England too

27

might see the turning-point of all her history. But Margaret had always a childlike desire for pleasure, and Adam was, nowadays, a great deal more easily pleased than he had once been. They had walked out into the mild spring air that they might quiet some of their almost trembling agitation. How odd it was to see the bird-stuffer's shop with the birds of paradise and parrots, crimson and gold and violent green, a statuary shop with Canova's Graces, the staymaker's, the fitter's shop with the little cork ball bounding up and down on the perpendicular jet of water, the provision shop with the Durham mustard, the Abernethy biscuits, Iceland moss, Narbonne honey, Bologna sausages—these and many many more, and to think that in another two days all these splendours might be at the mercy of the mob, that the poor might have their wrongs righted, the just come to their own . . . It must be truthfully added that any stranger seeing Adam and Margaret as they passed the bowing Beadle at the Pantheon door would have been astonished indeed at such revolutionary sentiments, for never did a pair look more respectable and kindly—Adam, set and solid, with his dark side-whiskers, his handsome high hat and gentlemanly cravat, and Margaret in her brown bonnet and overjacket of white embroidered muslin. Revolutionaries? Surely not this respectable pair!

In fact they did forget for ten minutes inside the Pantheon that they *were* revolutionaries. Margaret was so happy to be alone with Adam for a little that she forgot all else. Adam was changed since that Christmas at Uldale, more thoughtful, more demonstrative, but he was constantly preoccupied with his work, and their rooms were from morning to night crowded with other people. She did not often have him to herself. She was so happy that it had been *his* suggestion that they should take this walk! He did not often suggest that they should go off somewhere alone. She sometimes almost wished that there *was* no Charter, that that flamboyant boastful Feargus O'Connor had never been heard of, that she and Adam and her father need not

28

so continually be considering the wrongs of other people! And the Pantheon, when they were inside it, was enchanting! First they went up to the gallery where they might look down on that exciting coloured maze of babbling children, beautiful ladies, attendant footmen and subservient shopmen. Behind them (and they glanced in for a moment) was that queer neglected little picture-gallery with the dusty twentiethrate pictures and tragic Haydon's enormous spectre-like 'Lazarus' dominating with its fruitless ambition and almost emerging misconceived genius the atmosphere not only of the Pantheon but the street beyond it, the people, the carriages, the houses. Once this was a theatre; here were the Grand Staircase, the Rotunda, the green-room, the conservatories, dressing-rooms. Here were *Ariadne in Naxos, Daphnis and Chloe, Bellerophon, The Cruelty of Nero.* Old Will, a stiff prosperous conceited young man of the City, must here have applauded and Christabel feebly clapped her gloved hands and old Carey have slumbered! Even the lovely radiant Jennifer, with her proud parents, must here have been the beauty of the evening. Judith's Georges must have looked in with a companion to observe the legs of the chorus; Guimard danced in a hoop that reached nearly to her ankles. Those were the pigtail days of Duvernay and Ellsler and Taglioni! Here George III.'s eldest son met the lovely Perdita, and Charles Fox in a domino shouted a tipsy applause!

A church, a wax-work show, an opera, and then one night, in the middle of *Don Giovanni*, twelve demons bearing torches of resin rose to seize the guilty hero, and behold there were *thirteen* demons, one of them carrying *two* torches and disappearing in a flame of real fire while the audience fainted and the manager vanished into a mad-house!

But Margaret and Adam were not thinking of the past: the present and the future were *their* concern! They were very young—Adam young for his almost thirty-three years, Margaret only twenty-eight. Everything was in front of them.

Before they descended from the gallery Adam turned.

'Margaret, are you happy?'

'Very, Adam.'

'You know that you are everything to me now. Whatever happens on Monday, whatever way things go, nothing can alter that.'

'Yes, I know.'

He kissed her and they went down the stairs like a couple of children. To purchase something for little Daisy Bain was no easy task, for the variety of toys was extraordinary and the young ladies at the stalls so *very* polite and superior. Margaret was always easily dashed by patronage and had she been alone would have fled from those elegant young women in dismay, but Adam confronted them so calmly and with so agreeable a smile that they were ready to do anything for him. There was the monkey on a stick, the serpent made of elastic (a compound of glue and treacle), a centipede at the end of an indiarubber string, and many another; but best of all were the wax flowers. Oh! how lovely they were! Margaret clapped her hands when she saw a whole stall of them! She had no eyes then for the tortoise-shell card-cases, the pink scented invitation cards with 'on dansera' in the corner, the muslin slips, the volumes of polkas with chromo-lithographed frontispieces, the sandalwood fans, the mother-of-pearl paper-knives with coral spring handles—all these could be bought at the Pantheon, but she saw only that blazing bank of colour—crimson, orange, violet, silver—the flowers smiling from their stalks—carnations, pansies, roses, lilies-of-the-valley, peonies—their wax petals soft and iridescent, as fresh, as vernal as though but a moment ago they had opened their smiling faces to the sun!

'Oh, Adam, are they not marvellous!' she cried.

Something then touched his heart, as though he had never truly loved her before and as though he were warned that, without realising his treasure, it might be, at a moment, lost to him. He would buy the whole store-load for her! Revolutions, tumbling thrones, the rights of the poor, these things fell down before the wax flowers like pasteboard castles!

She chose an assorted bunch—purple pansies, icily white lilies-of-the-valley, a crimson rose.

'They will live for ever!' she said, smiling into his eyes.

They were packed very carefully into a box, and lying on tissue paper looked, Margaret thought, worthy of the Queen.

'They should be kept under glass to preserve them from the dust,' she said.

The stately young woman who served her smiled with an exquisite dignity.

'That is generally considered wise, madam,' she remarked.

'Oh, Adam, how kind you are!' Margaret whispered as they walked away. 'I shall have these all my life long.' Then dropping her voice, looking at him shyly but with a deep intensity: 'I do love you so.'

They passed the refreshment counter and enjoyed, each, an arrowroot cake. Daisy Bain had been quite forgotten, so hurriedly a doll with flaxen hair was purchased for her. They enjoyed the conservatory with the fountain that contained the gold and silver fish, the exotic plants and gay flowers. But it was very hot in the conservatory, and the parrots and cockatoos made an intolerable screeching. One cockatoo, as Margaret could not help observing, strangely resembled Mr. Feargus O'Connor and, for a moment, a dread caught at Margaret's heart. What would happen on Monday? Was this their last peaceful day? Would they ever be so happy again? She looked at the box that she carried in her hand and sighed. She held Adam's arm yet more closely as they passed out through the waiting-room where some grand ladies were waiting for their carriages, and so into the light and fresh air of Great Marlborough Street.

* * * * *

On their return home they found themselves in another world. Adam discovered suddenly, looking at the room's disorder, the bottles of beer, the smoke from pipes, books thrown on to the floor, that he wanted to be out of it all, that his enthusiasm was dead, that he did not care what happened on Monday, that there was no Cause any longer. As he saw Margaret moving quietly into the farther room, carrying the box that held her precious wax flowers as carefully as though it were glass, he discovered that with her departure all the light seemed to have gone out of his world. He had reached some new relation with her during that half-hour in the Bazaar. She was more precious to him than ever before.

So with that rather stumbling, halting movement that made him seem short-sighted, but that was only in reality because his thoughts were elsewhere, he turned and took in his company. He saw at once that Henry Lunt held the floor. He would of course in any place where he was. He was in no way different from the day when Adam had first met him, still shabby, black, fierce, denunciatory, self-confident. Adam knew that he was brave and honest, but he knew also that he was narrow-visioned, foolishly impetuous, and that his temper was so violent that it was extremely dangerous. He had been twice gaoled for his share in riots and disorders: this had not made him either wiser or more tolerant. He was more conceited than he had been, thought he knew everything and had all the gifts of leadership; to-night he seemed to Adam a noisy, tiresome demagogue. There were now too many of his sort in the movement, and, in fact, the whole impetus seemed to be slipping away from the Chartists. The Irish potato famine, the Anti-Corn Law League, above all the exciting spectacular troubles in Europe, made the Chartist movement a little old-fashioned. Louis Philippe's fall in February still possessed men's minds to the diminution of all else. After all, people said, bad though things were, they were not as bad as in France. We English are too sensible for Revolutions. We are not of that kind. Adam agreed with them. The Chartists, especially men of Lunt's type, appeared now something foreign and affected.

Undoubtedly everyone in the room this evening felt a little of this. Lunt talked the louder because of it, and, sitting on the edge of the table, swinging his stout legs, harangued Kraft, Pider, and Ben Morris and a young Jew, Solomon, as though he were, with wonderful magnanimity, screwing their courage to the striking-point.

Pider, it seemed, had said something mildly deprecatory before Adam came in, and Lunt was all on fire over it.

'Aye,' he was shouting, 'that's just what I was expecting to hear, Pider. There are too many of your sort about, and that's the truth. Here we are slaving for years back to bring this thing about and at last the moment has arrived. The great, magnificent moment, the climax of all our efforts, and what do you do but——'

'Yes, but,' Pider broke in, 'suppose the moment hasn't arrived after all? Suppose Monday's abortive and there's nothing done? Look at O'Connell!'

'Yes, look at O'Connell!' cried Lunt fiercely, jumping from the table and waving his short arms. 'He's dead, isn't he? And deserved to die. They may have given him a fine funeral in Dublin, but we know what he was, a faintheart whose courage failed him just when it was needed. Feargus O'Connor's quite another sort of man——'

'I don't know,' said Pider doubtfully. 'I've heard men say of O'Connor——'

'And what have you heard men say of O'Connor?' Lunt shouted. 'There are always men jealous of their leaders, but I tell you that any man who says O'Connor will fail us is lying in his throat, and so I'd tell him to his face. I know O'Connor. I've eaten and slept with him, and a grander, finer leader of men the world doesn't hold! Answer me that, Pider, and tell me that you know O'Connor better than I do and I'll tell you it's a falsehood.'

Pider, who was not lacking in courage and was in no way afraid of Lunt, started fiercely forward. Kraft came quietly in between them.

'Now, now,' he said, smiling. 'Where's the good of our arguing about what will happen on Monday? Who can say how things will turn? We've done the best we can and must leave the rest to God.'

'God! God!' Lunt shouted fiercely. 'It isn't God we're wanting, but confidence in ourselves. I tell you——'

But Kraft gave a sign to Adam and turned off into a little side-room that he used as a study. Adam followed him and closed the door behind him. He put his arm round Adam and drew him close.

'You look weary,' Adam said.

'Yes, I am weary. Their shouting makes me weary. There are times when I'm sick at heart of the whole thing, times when I wish that I'd never heard of the Cause at all, and had spent my days mending watches or keeping sheep in a field.'

'It's not like you,' Adam said, 'to be down.'

'No, maybe it's not. But to-night I have a kind of foreboding, a sinking of the heart.' He pressed Adam's shoulder. 'What is it, Adam, creeps into all Causes alike, a kind of worm that eats the heart out of them? It's a sort of egotism, I suppose. You grow to think of your own part in it all, to admire your own energy, your fine speeches, to be jealous of others who are praised, to want personal rewards. To be impersonal, to care nothing for yourself, it is the only lesson of life, and no one can learn it!'

'Yes. If there is a lesson!' Adam's dark eyes slowly clouded. 'When you watch the Churches fighting as they are, when you see Jews like Disraeli bringing off their clever fireworks, while you watch a sot like Walter Herries at home trying to frighten women . . . It may be there's no lesson, no plan, no future, no God——'

Kraft shook his head.

'I feel my immortality,' he said. 'I cannot doubt it, but it is perhaps a poor kind of immortality. God *may* be a sort of flash Jew like Disraeli or a dandy like D'Orsay or a story-teller like Charles Dickens or a ranter like Lunt—it may be one long swindle—but it goes on, I *know* that it goes on.'

'Yes,' Adam continued, nodding his head, 'and emotions like my present love of Margaret. That's no present from a cheap Jew; or walking down by Sour Milk Ghyll on a summer evening when the water is whiter than snow and the hills clouds— D'Orsay couldn't make *such* a gift to anyone. But this, Caesar, all this that we have been working for for years—I see no New Heaven and New Earth *this* way. Men don't change. Why do they not change, Caesar, that's what I want to know? Why do *I* not change with all the experience I get? I can remember when I was a tiny boy bathing one evening in a tarn above Hawkshead. My mother was there, and an old fat fellow, my uncle Reuben, a sort of itinerant preacher, who told me stories. He was a wonderful man as I remember—I daresay he was not in reality. He was killed after in a riot when they tried to burn Uldale down, set on by Walter Herries. I owe Walter Herries something, you see. But what was I saying? Oh yes—that night. What was I? Four, five? I don't know. We lit a fire under the trees, there was a dog, and Uncle Reuben told me stories. All beauty, all loveliness is in that night as I look back. Not now. Not here. Not then as I knew it. I was happy, of course, but recognised nothing extraordinary. But looking back I see now that there was something divine in that wood that night. Why,' he burst out, laughing, 'there was something divine in the Pantheon Bazaar this afternoon. My love for Margaret. Hers for me. Let me recognise it now and offer D'Orsay-Disraeli-Dickens-Jupiter my thanks for it.'

Kraft smiled.

'What has happened to you, Adam? You are usually so silent. Words are pouring from you.'

'I know. I'm living at an extra intensity to-night. As though there were only a thin strip of paper between myself and discovery—discovery of what? I don't know. D'Orsay's rouge-pots?'

'I know,' Kraft answered quietly. 'I am the same. It is our

excitement about Monday, I suppose. A Scotsman would say I am "fey." I can see my shroud, Adam.'

* * * * *

Sunday night he slept so little and woke so early that while it was still dark he slipped from Margaret's side, dressed hurriedly, and went out. He walked through the quiet streets for some while without thinking of his direction, then found that he was in the City. Here it was as cool and silent as an oyster. The wall of the Custom House was a dead wall, the Coal Exchange was sleeping, but soon he was down on the wharfs where life was already active and earnest. Here were tubs smelling of oranges, shops—already opened—packed with salt fish, dried herrings, Yarmouth bloaters, mussels and periwinkles, dried sprats and cured pilchards. For he was in Billingsgate. Here the Billingsgate marketeers were drinking from massive blue and white earthen-ware mugs filled to the rough brims with coffee; here porters were busied clearing piles of baskets away, putting forms and stools in order, in eager preparation for the fish auction. The wharf is covered with fish, and the great clock of Billingsgate booms forth five o'clock. The stands are laden with salmon, shoals of fresh herring, baskets full of turbot, while the crowds are gathering thickly, and everyone is shouting and crying at once.

Adam watched with increasing pleasure. Close to him a fine fellow stood, a hat tall and shiny as though he were a habitué of Aldridge's Repository, his sporting neckcloth fastened with a horse-shoe pin, while round his giant stomach was bound the conventional blue apron; he was wearing galligaskins and straight tight boots of sporting cut. Here were the eight auctioneers; here Bowler's, Bacon's and Simpson's, the noisiest taverns (at this hour) in the whole of London. Now was the excited selling of the 'doubles' and the 'dumbarees.' Fish, fish, fish! Plaice, soles, haddocks, skate, cod, ling . . . Suddenly he recollected. My God, this very afternoon, and the gentleman in the galligaskins and blue apron might find all his occupation gone! By five of the evening of this very day, all the soles and cods and haddocks might swim peacefully in the sea for the attention paid to them! This very street, instead of its stream of fish-scales, bones and dirty water, might be running in blood! Instead of gaiety, laughter, money business, there might be death, ruin, a blaze of fire, smoking catastrophe!

There was a sick dismay at his heart. He had been working for years with an earnestness and eagerness that had possessed every energy he had. He had lost in these years much of the fantasy and humour that had been part of his childhood. At this stage he was grimly serious, taking nothing lightly. At that moment in the Billingsgate Market he saw himself as someone fantastically absurd, working like a labourer at piling brick upon brick, and as he laboured the bricks turned, before his eyes, to straw.

A joke, a farce, iridescent fish-scales floating down the teeming gutter. He hurried home.

This morning, Monday, April 10, was a lovely day, the sun streaming down with that soft mild radiance that brings a spring scent of flowers into the London streets. The Chartist detachment to which Kraft and Adam belonged moved off very early to Kennington Common. There was no definite procession to the Common; the Procession, presenting the great Petition, was to march at least a hundred thousand strong, under the leadership of Feargus O'Connor, to the Houses of Parliament.

Here the Petition was to be presented, and what would follow after was the question on everybody's lips. Men like Lunt declared that what would follow would be the greatest Revolution in England since 1688. But how precisely that Revolution would take place, no one precisely knew. It was true that the Queen and her Consort were not supremely popular, but no one had anyone to propose in their place, and even the Lunts of the movement could not claim that the whole of England was at all ready as yet for a President or a Dictator.

The very troubles that the rest of Europe were battling with made many Englishmen proud of their own passivity.

Nevertheless, a Revolution there would be, some sort of a Revolution. What the average man, both Chartist and non-Chartist, feared was that, simply through ill-directed and undisciplined contact, there would be riot and bloodshed, meaning nothing, leading nowhere; men perceived, from the recent Paris example, that one small unexpected event could lead to vast and unexpected consequences. Let fifty thousand shouting Chartists reach Westminster . . . Why, then, both sides being armed, some horrible catastrophe might take the whole civilised world by surprise. No one in London was happy on that lovely spring morning and, if the truth were known, most certainly not Mr. Feargus O'Connor himself, who, in spite of his descent from Irish kings, had no wish to find himself in gaol before the evening.

Neither Adam nor Kraft was happy. They had one last word together before they set out.

'I have the oddest feeling,' Kraft said. 'I dreamt last night, of what I don't know, but I woke saying to myself, "Yes, that's the answer." Now, I know what it all means. I seemed, in that brief dream, to have passed through all experience and to have realised that envy, greed, jealousy, disappointment, lust, bodily sickness—it was not until I had known them all and tranquilly accepted them all, that I began to live. Tranquillity. I tell you, Adam, I am as tranquil this morning as a pond-weed. My anxiety is gone, but my desire too. I cannot imagine what it is that has agitated me so deeply all these years.'

Adam frowned.

'I am not tranquil. I am afraid of what a parcel of fools are likely to do before the day's out.'

It was still very early when the three of them reached the Common. On their way thither they had been impressed by the silence of the town, as of something strongly on its guard. There was little traffic in the streets, very few people about and many of the shops closed. Adam learnt afterwards that many of the important official buildings round Westminster were defended with guns and that Whitehall was in reality an armed camp.

When they arrived at the Common they saw that there was the crowd that had been confidently expected. There were many banners flaunting devices like 'The Charter, the whole Charter, and nothing but the Charter,' 'Justice for All Men and No Favour,' 'Up! Up for O'Connor!' and there were a number of brass bands.

Men, women and children sat and walked about, rather listlessly, dressed, some of them, in their Sunday clothes, while others seemed to boast their poverty. There were many pale, thin, with angry, restless eyes and hungry faces; others appeared to have come to enjoy the sights. There were some booths with food and drinks.

Everything was very quiet, there was a murmur of voices, a sense of expectant waiting as though at any moment a miracle might break out in the sky above their heads.

Soon after their arrival Lunt joined them.

'Not so many as were expected,' Adam said.

'Pooh,' Lunt answered. 'They'll turn up. It will take many of them time to get here. And this is nothing. You wait until the Procession starts for Parliament and see how many join us. You listen to O'Connor when he makes his speech and you'll hear something.'

Soon it happened that everybody began to press together towards the centre of the Common and the crush became uncomfortable; toes were stepped on, umbrellas and sticks poked into innocent faces, women lost their children, and children were crying, pockets were freely picked.

Adam saw that it was towards O'Connor and one or two gentlemen near him that the crowd was thronging, and soon, owing to Kraft's important position in the movement and the badge that he wore, he found that they were enclosed in the magic circle. He was so close to Feargus O'Connor that he could observe him well. A wild theatrical gentleman, he seemed both over-decorated and shabby, for he had on the breast of his blue coat a number of ribbons and medals, but his pantaloons were older than they ought to be and stained with mud. His hair fell in untidy ringlets from under his high hat, and he waved with a great deal of excited gesture the cane that he was carrying. In the other hand he had a stout roll of paper that was supposed by everyone to be the famous Petition. He was, it was clear, excellently conscious of the attention that he was receiving. Once and again he would put up his hand to his rather soiled cravat, the cane would drop to the ground and be obsequiously lifted by someone. He would dart his head up rather as a suspicious hen might do, stare with proud and melancholy indignation at some small boy who, open-mouthed, was gazing at him with all his eyes.

It appeared that he had some reason for indignation, for it seemed that his pocket had been picked. Had anyone ever heard the like? The leader of the country against tyranny and oppression, and his pocket had been picked! How much had there been in his purse? He could not be sure, but a very considerable sum; also a blue silk handkerchief to which he attached sentimental value.

But Adam quickly realised that Mr. O'Connor was not at all at his ease. While he talked with an excited and incoherent fervour his eyes were for ever searching the horizon and searching it with a kind of terrified preoccupation as though he expected at any moment to see a large scaly dragon, vomiting fire, issue from the Kennington trees.

He greeted Kraft absent-mindedly and shook a finger with Adam (the rest of his hand clutching the sacred roll of paper) without seeing Adam at all.

He became with every moment more deeply agitated. Beside him was a long, thin, cadaverous man who looked like a Methodist clergyman, and a stout, rubicund fellow like a butcher. There was no sign, however, of any organisation or leadership. From time to time someone broke through into the magic circle, whispered mysteriously to O'Connor and vanished again. He on his part would nod his head with great self-importance or shake it or look up to the heavens or wave his cane. He alluded again and again to the fact that his pocket had been picked, and once and again would burst into a fine frenzy, invoking the Deity: 'My God, have I been chosen to lead these people at this great hour? Have they come to me hungry and shall they not be fed?' Then, dropping his voice: 'What is it, Forster? Has Cummin not arrived? Where is Whitstable? Have they got the thief that has my purse? March to Westminster? But where are the others? This is not the half of them! And my toes trodden on and my pocket picked . . . '

The crowd waited with a most exemplary patience. They were, it seemed, ready to picnic on the Common for the day if necessary. Many of them, Adam was convinced, were not Chartists at all. Many were rogues and vagabonds who had come to gather what they might out of so large a crowd. He saw, as he looked about him, many incongruous figures, here a rather shabby young dandy in pea-green gloves and a shirt embroidered with dahlias and race-horses, then a stout serious-looking gentleman with peg-top trousers, chintuft and eye-glass, and close beside him a sturdy fellow who might have come straight from the Billingsgate of the morning, green apron and galligaskins all complete. It could not be said to be a very murderous crowd, and, as Adam looked, his fears of red revolution died away. There would be no revolution here. But for what then all these years had he been working? Not for revolution certainly, but also not for a contented humorous crowd like this. He drew Margaret's arm through his and waited for what might come.

What soon came was an excited stir through the crowd. It whispered like wind through corn. Someone had arrived. Something had occurred. Two men pushed through and spoke to O'Connor; at once his countenance turned red and then white again. He dropped his cane and no one picked it up. He stood, hesitating, his head turning first this way, then that.

The crowd was dividing; it was the Constable, Mr. Mayne, followed by three of his inspectors. Mayne, a fine, resolute-looking man, took his stand a little way from Adam, and sent one of his inspectors forward to O'Connor. It was clear that O'Connor was in a terrible fright. 'Afraid of arrest,' whispered Kraft contemptuously to Adam. O'Connor, after a second's hesitation, clutched his cane and roll of paper and went to meet Mr. Mayne. The two men made a striking contrast, and in that moment of seeing them together, it seemed to Adam that any alarms or hopes on the part of anyone that Revolution would ever again break out in England were finally dissolved.

'Mr. O'Connor,' said Mayne, 'I am here to inform you that the meeting on this Common is permitted, but no procession to Westminster.'

O'Connor said something.

'No. No procession whatever.'

O'Connor spoke again.

'Certainly, Mr. O'Connor, I am very pleased to hear it.'

O'Connor held out his hand; Mr. Mayne shook it.

The Revolution was over.

Mayne, with his inspectors, disappeared, and O'Connor came forward to address the crowd. There were stands with flags and banners for him to appear on, and he did step up on to one of them, attended by some half a dozen gentlemen, but very little that he said could be heard. It appeared that he himself was going to the Home Office that he might present the famous Petition there; there would, however, be no procession; in fact, everything was over, or rather, the Meeting might continue as long as it pleased, but he, Mr. O'Connor, would not appear in it.

He vanished, and there followed an extraordinary scene. Many of the more peaceful citizens, laughing and jeering, turned to leave the Common, but at the same time crowds of roughs and hooligans, urged on by the more violent Chartists, drove their way towards the stands with shouts and threats. Women were screaming, children crying, men shouting, no one seemed to be in command, someone tore down two of the banners.

'We had best be out of this,' Adam said, turning to Margaret. Then he saw Lunt. The man seemed to be in a frenzy and was orating, waving his hands, his hat off, his face congested with anger. In his hand he carried a short, thick club.

'Come,' said Kraft sadly. 'The curtain is down. The play is over.'

They turned together, but at the same moment Lunt caught sight of them. Like a madman he rushed at them, stopped in front of Kraft and shouted:

'Now where are you? You white, shaking coward! You and your friends! This is your work, with your psalm-singing, chicken-hearted caution! You have brought England to her knees, sold us like slaves!'

Kraft said quietly: 'Come, Henry. This is a farce.'

'Farce!' Lunt screamed. 'Yes! and who has turned it into a farce?'

'You and others like you,' Kraft answered sternly, his voice ringing out so that all heard him. 'I have warned you again and again, but you would not listen. With your violence you have frightened most decent men away. Aye, and lost most of our battles before they were even fought.'

Lunt's shouts had drawn a large crowd about them. Some excited men pressed forward, shouting incoherently, some laughed, some agreed with Kraft. But Lunt was beside himself; he moved in a whirlwind of passion in which he could distinguish nothing but his own disappointment, the failure of all that his egotism, yes, and his melodramatic self-sacrifice had for years been planning. He closed up to Kraft, who did not move.

'By heaven!' he shouted, 'I will show you who is a traitor! I'll teach your dirty cowardice!'

Kraft caught his arm.

'Be ashamed, man!' he cried. 'Go home to your wife and children!'

The touch infuriated Lunt, who thrust himself free, swung his club and brought it crashing on to Kraft's head. Kraft fell, his hand catching at Margaret's dress as he went down. Instantly there was silence. It was as though a hand caught the Common, the crowd, the sunlight, and, crushing it all into nothing, flung it away. There was emptiness and the sun shining on Kraft's white shirt and his twisted hand.

Adam was on his knees, his arm under Kraft's head that was crooked and veiled in blood. He looked up. 'A surgeon!' he said. 'For God's sake, someone, quickly, a surgeon.'

But he knew that Kraft was dead—the finest man in the world was gone. Tears blinded his sight as he bent again to the ground.

CHILDE ROLAND
TO THE DARK TOWER

This was one of Judith's good days. This year, 1850, had not opened too well for her. For one thing in January she had had a splendid quarrel with Dorothy, had slapped Amabel (now a big stout girl of eleven) for riding one of the calves, had ordered Dorothy out of the house, had been told by Dorothy that she would not go, had discovered old Peach talking to one of her maids, had dismissed the maid and been of a mind to go up to the Fortress and tell Walter what she thought of him.

When this lively afternoon was over she had gone to bed, lain on her back and laughed aloud at her own bad temper. Dorothy had come in later to make the peace and discovered the old lady sitting up in bed, her lace cap a little askew on her snow-white hair, laughing and doing household accounts. They had embraced, as they always did after a quarrel, and Judith had settled down to the reading of Mr. Thackeray's *Vanity Fair*. She had a passion now for novels, although she considered Thackeray too sentimental and something of a hypocrite. Becky, however, she could thoroughly enjoy and considered that there, but for the grace of God, went Judith Paris. Amelia and Dobbin she could not abide, but Rawdon had quite a deal in common with her dear Georges, who was as close to her still as he had been in 1790.

At the end of a chapter she had blown out the candle and lain down to sleep. She had slept for an hour or so and then woken suddenly to a sharp pain in the side. It was the first sharp pain she had ever known and she greeted it humorously as much as to say, 'Well, I knew you would come sometime. Now that you are here, behave as a gentleman.' The pain behaved badly at first and then, like a new acquaintance, having left his card, departed. But in the morning she felt very unwell indeed, tried to get up but could not, was finally in bed for a week. She was attended by Dr. Fairchild from Keswick, a little wizened sarcastic man of middle age. They got on very well, were rude to one another, gossiped a good deal, and found that they had much in common.

He told her that she had the rheumatics and he put her on a diet. It was from this moment that she began to care about food. Food had never, all her life, been very important to her. She had always had a healthy appetite and took what came. But now that she was forbidden, she lusted. She liked to forbid herself, but hated that anyone else should forbid her anything. Moreover, Dr. Fairchild, with a deliberate maliciousness, as it seemed to her, forbade her the very things for which she cared the most, and especially meat. She had encountered at odd times cranky persons who pretended to live entirely on vegetables. There was poor young Ivison, son of Mr. Ivison the bookseller in Keswick, whose pale earnest countenance both amused and irritated her. It was said that he ate nothing but carrots and cabbage, and once, when she met the poor thin boy beside Mr. Flintoft's Model of the Lake District, he had incontinently fainted there at her feet! So much for carrots and cabbages.

Nevertheless, she did on the whole as she was told, and now, at the beginning of March, was in fine vigour again. Her spirits were all the livelier, because just at this time John was given a holiday and came up with Elizabeth on a visit. It was a year and a half since they had been at Uldale. The house was very full and she adored it to be full. Dorothy's children were growing— Timothy was thirteen, Veronica twelve, Amabel eleven, and Jane (Judith's especial pet) was nine. Old Rackstraw taught Timothy Latin, and there was a governess, Miss Meredith. Miss Meredith Judith did not like at all, but she could not deny that she was an excellent governess. Miss Meredith, who was round and plump like a barrel, had all the present popular conventionalities. It was

Judith's constant delight to shock her, for Judith could not in the least understand this great wave of propriety that had swept over the country. To allude to legs or bosoms or ardent young men or any of the processes of human creation seemed to Miss Meredith like death, and Judith perceived that not only Dorothy but the little girls themselves approved of these reticences.

'But, my dear Dorothy,' Judith would say, 'what is there shocking about being born? Why, I remember at Stone Ends when I was a girl——'

'When you were a girl, Aunt Judith,' Dorothy answered firmly, 'the world was a very different place. Not civilised at all.'

'I am sure,' Judith retorted, 'I can't say about being civilised, but babies are born in exactly the same way now as they were then. It would do Miss Meredith all the good in the world to be flung into a hedge by a tramp——'

But Dorothy was so greatly distressed that Judith desisted.

'*Please*, Aunt Judith,' Dorothy said. 'Do not offend Miss Meredith. She is the best governess in the world. Exactly right for the children. I don't know where we'd ever find such another.'

So Judith refrained, and only teased Miss Meredith when the temptation was quite irresistible.

She loved the house to be full, for she knew that she was a miracle for her age. Dorothy, with all her energy and obstinacy, had no say whatever in the running of the house. And Judith was not at all the conventional tyrannical old woman so common in works of fiction from the days of the Egyptians and maybe long before them. Everyone loved her. She was cared for now as she had never been in all her life before. How in the past she had longed to be liked! How it had hurt her when Will had disapproved and Will's mother hated her and Jennifer plotted against her! But now, when she had all the love that she could possibly desire, she did not greatly care for it. She hated sentiment and always preferred common sense.

Adam, of course, was a thing apart; she was deeply fond of John and Elizabeth, had an affection for Dorothy and the children, but, with the possible exception of little Jane, Adam was the only human being in the world whom she loved.

She certainly did not love herself, but she was proud of her age, her strength, her capability and, above all, her scorn for and successful battles over everyone at Ireby.

Of late Walter had been trying to irritate her in every way that he knew. Things were stolen, her house was spied upon, her servants were bribed, if there was any malicious story possible about anyone at Uldale it was spread in every direction. But Judith and Dorothy were exactly the women to fight a campaign like Walter's. They had much common sense and a strong feeling for the ludicrous. Dorothy was lacking in a sense of humour, but her sense of fun was so strong that to see a gentleman slip on the ice or a lady lose her bonnet in the wind made her stout sides ache with laughter.

So Walter seemed to her silly and Uhland unwholesome.

On this sunny day in March the weather was so warm that John and Elizabeth could walk comfortably up and down the lawn together. Judith, looking at them for a moment out of the parlour window, smiled with approval. John the night before had been most entertaining. If not of Parliament he was near it enough to have plenty of inside information. Both Judith and Dorothy were thrilled with interest as he told them of the hatred that the Queen and Prince Albert felt for Palmerston. Palmerston was John's hero, so he was a trifle malicious about the Queen and the Prince. Lord Clarendon, it seemed, had, a few weeks ago, dined at the Palace, and now it was all over the Town that the Queen in the drawing-room after dinner had lost all control and spoken with so much vehement bitterness that Lord Clarendon had not known where to look; and when she had done the Prince had begun and, when Clarendon had visited him next day, had orated about Palmerston for two hours without stopping.

This gave the two ladies great pleasure to hear, not because they wished the Queen or Palmerston or anyone else any harm;

simply that it brought the lawns and hedges of Uldale straight into the Palace.

So Judith looked out of the window at John and nodded her approval. It was so fine a morning that she had put on a new dress for the first time, a dress made especially for her by Miss Sampson in Keswick. She wore more sombre colours now, although she still loved a touch of brightness here and there. As she was wearing long drawers trimmed with lace, a flannel petticoat, an under-petticoat, a white starched petticoat, and two muslin petticoats under the dress, she had, for an old lady, a good deal to carry. Very soon now the stiff bands of the crinoline were to relieve ladies of their outrageous burden. Judith was wearing a dress of grey taffeta with twelve flounces all of a dark shade of green. Out of this 'like a lily-stem out of a flower-tub' rose her dark-green bodice with pagoda sleeves and a very lovely white lace collar (this last a present from Sylvia Herries the preceding Christmas). Her only concession to her years was her white lace cap. Her small, alert, vigorous body carried its cumbrous clothes with grace and ease; her eyes sparkled like little fires. She had, as she had always had, an air of crystalline spotlessness. The muslins, the collar, the cap were new minted as though direct, that minute, from some most perfect laundry. And so in fact they were. Everything was laundered in the house and Mrs. Kaplan the housekeeper (Judith's slave) saw that all was perfection.

They were rich now at Uldale. Dorothy had money from Bellairs and her portion of Herries money. Judith's own investments, shares in Liverpool concerns inherited from David Herries, land and property round Uldale excellently supervised for many years by Rackstraw, all mounted to an income well beyond their needs. Judith had no desire for wealth, but she liked to have everything handsome about her. Everything *was* handsome. On this lovely March morning Uldale glistened like a jewel.

She went her rounds of the house, tapping with her stick and humming a tune. She visited everything, the high-ceilinged kitchen, pantry, servants' hall, housekeeper's room complete with black cat, work-basket and flowered footstool. Then, perhaps after the dairy the place that she loved best, the still-room. Here were cakes, jams, preserves made; here was the china washed and the dessert set out. Then the lamp-room, the store-room, the meat-larder where were the weighing machine and the great pickling jars. Then the wood and coal stores, the laundry, the pump-room and the dairy. She stayed for an especial time this morning in the kitchen, for its brick-floored spaciousness bathed in sun was exceedingly pleasant. She stood there, smiling at the maids, leaning on her stick, looking at the roasting-spits, the Dutch oven, the chopping-block, the sugar-nippers, the coffee-grinder, the pot and pan racks, everything shining, gleaming, glittering as though active and happy with conscious, individual life.

All was good; all was well; still humming her tune she went out on to the sunlit lawn to find John and Elizabeth.

For a moment she looked back at the house—dear house to whose safety and comfort she had, through all her long life, returned again and again. There had been terrible hours here. She could see David Herries fallen, stricken on this very lawn, she could catch again Sarah Herries' distracted glance, could see Jennifer waiting for her lover, Francis' mad return and frantic exit, the rioters and poor Reuben's slaughter, her own tragic surrender of Watendlath, the Christmas party and the fracas with Walter. There had been every kind of tragedy, farce, drama here; birth, death, ruin, love, humour, light easy days, pain and laughter. She had come through it all, as one always did come through if one kept on patiently enough, did not take oneself too seriously, saw the sequence of event, of change, decay and birth in proper proportion. One came through to this sunlight, to this lovely landscape, this quiet English calm; then, turning, she saw that John was walking towards her and, with that quick intuition that she always had, wondered instantly whether after all the tale was told, whether there were not a number more of chapters to be added.

For John was alone and, she saw at once, in trouble. She had never quite understood John. She had loved Francis, his father, but had never understood him either. The alarms, fears, superstitions, doubts of those two were foreign to her direct sensible nature. The part of her that had shared them she had deliberately killed.

John's slim, upright body, his pale hair, beautiful almost feminine features, had always marked him apart from other men. She thought, as she saw him approach her: 'John will never be out of trouble. He will never know what it is to rest.'

He came straight up to her and, his voice quivering a little, said:

'Aunt Judith. I have told Elizabeth I am going up to Ireby.'

She was astonished. A long grey shadow seemed to fall across the sunny lawn.

'Yes. Didn't you know? He has written her a letter: that scoundrel Peach brought it half an hour ago.'

'A letter?'

'Yes. Here it is.'

He handed her a large sheet of paper scrawled over in Walter's big clumsy hand.

Dear Elizabeth—

As a dutiful daughter you are to pay me a visit. If you don't come of yourself I shall fetch you.—Your loving father,

Walter Herries.

'Loving father!' said Judith, her voice shaking with anger. 'What impertinence!'

'Yes. But of course Elizabeth mustn't go. She wished it, and I forbade her even to think of it. But *I* am going—and at once.'

51

As she looked at him he was again the small boy when the nurse had thrown the rabbit out of the window. He stood there, his head up, his nostrils quivering (exaggerated pictures of him, she thought, but spiritually true), like a high-bred horse, defiant but afraid of the whip because of the catastrophe that a contact might bring. She, too, was afraid of some disaster. She knew, as she looked at him, that she had always been afraid of it for him.

'No. Don't you go, John. I'll pay him a visit. I've been wishing to for weeks.'

'Nonsense,' John said roughly. Then, recovering himself, added: 'Pardon me, Aunt Judith. I didn't intend to be rude, but this is *my* affair. You must see that it is——'

She did not attempt to stop him after this, but only sighed to herself as she saw him mount his bay, wave his riding-whip to her, turning with that charming, rather weak, altogether lovable smile that was so like his father's that it always made her heart ache.

Where would this thing end, she thought, as she entered the house. When had it begun?—back, back, maybe to the days when her father had been a wild young man and sold his woman at the Fair, an old eternal quarrel between beauty and ugliness, normality and abnormality, sense and nonsense—a quarrel born, as all quarrels are in this world, of jealousy and fear. But she did not care for philosophy; she took things as they came, and what immediately came now when she entered the house was a quarrel with Dorothy, who wished to buy a sofa covered with wool-work and fringed with beads that she had seen in Carlisle. To buy this monstrosity and place it in the parlour instead of the lovely old one that had the red apples.

'But it's all the mode!' cried Dorothy. 'The Osmastons have wool-work everywhere.'

'They may,' said Judith grimly, 'but so long as I'm up and about that sofa remains in the parlour. Why, I was resting my hand on it when I came to the most important decision of my life.' Then she added as she tapped away on her stick: 'It's all

Prince Albert and his German taste. I detest the man.'

Meanwhile John rode down the road towards Ireby. It suited his mood that the sky became overcast as he reached the bottom of the Ireby hill. On his left a bubble of seething little white clouds rose on the Skiddaw ridge, and other clouds rushed up to the sun and, with gestures of sulky annoyance, swallowed it. He *hated* himself for this fear that had seized all his bones like water. The very thought of Uhland made him sick. But perhaps Uhland would not be there. He did not mind Walter at all; he was simply a gross, quarrelsome, bad-mannered fool. His thoughts went back to that day in his childhood when, with Adam, he had watched Walter on the moor. He had been afraid then, but he saw now that it had been Uhland's shadow behind Walter that had, like a prophecy, frightened him. He had been afraid of Uhland before he was born.

He tried now, as he rode slowly up the hill, to formulate that fear, to bring it into the open. But it would not come. That was the awful thing about it. When he forced himself to think of Uhland, or was compelled to do so, he saw him as a shapeless, boneless animal emitting some sickening odour, as one sees a creature in a dream, lurking in shadow in a dank cave or the corner of a cellar, or behind a stone. The hide-and-seek that Uhland had played with him now for so long had introduced into his own soul and body some sickly element, so that, at times, he believed that Uhland was some part of himself—that part we all have, hidden, shameful, lurking. There was nothing shameful in his life except this one cowardice. In everything else he was brave, and so all the more did he feel this one exception to be real.

He raised his head as he saw the grey stone house squatting, in its trees, on the top of the hill. To-day he would force this thing into the open; it should skulk, just out of touch and feeling, no longer.

He tied his horse to the wall outside the garden and walked up the flagged path to the door. Stone frowned at him everywhere.

The gardens were trim but dead. It was late March, and the daffodils were in full golden flood under the rosy Uldale walls. Here, too, beneath the dark trees beyond the flower-beds they flamed in little cups of fire, but the garden itself was black and gritty. As John stood there banging the knocker of the door, the whole place leered down on him.

It was not that it was so large, but that it was so dead. The windows had no faces, the stone turrets were like clenched fists, and worst of all, there was no sound at all anywhere.

At Uldale there was always sound—laughter, singing, running water and the light chatter of birds. He wondered, above the beating of his heart, that there was not a bird singing in the Ireby gardens.

At last there was a creaking of bolts and the door slowly opened. An old bent man whom John had never seen before stood there; he had bow legs and was dressed in the style of thirty years earlier, black worsted stockings, black kneebreeches, a rather soiled neckerchief, and a dull brown tye-wig that cocked a little over one eye. He had a tooth missing, and his words whistled through his lips.

'Is Mr. Walter Herries at home?' John asked.

'If you'll wait I'll see,' said the old man, looking out into the garden as though he expected to see a lion rooting up the bulbs. 'What name shall I say?'

'Mr. John Herries.'

His mind seemed to be on other things as he ambled away, leaving John in the hall. The hall was stony and bare. There was a fireplace with grinning fire-dogs and a large stand hung with heavy coats and stacked with whips. There was no carpet on the stone that struck the feet icily. He stood there, wondering whether the old man would not forget him, when a green baize door to his left opened and a woman came out. She was not young but not old either, and very extravagantly dressed in a Russian short jacket of gold brocade figured with bunches of flowers in coloured silks. Her skirt had so many flounces that she appeared to be robed ten times over. She wore a bonnet lined with rosebuds, and her cheeks were rosebuds too, only extremely artificial, for John had never seen a lady more brightly painted. This brilliant person brushed past him as though he were not there, and she was swearing like a trooper. She turned towards the stairs and shouted:

'Hell take your meanness, Walter!'

She was so angry that she stared at John without seeing him.

As though from nowhere a very large stout man in a night-cap and a rich flowered dressing-gown appeared on the stairs. He was grinning, his nightshirt was open at the neck and he carried a very small brown hairy dog in one hand by the scruff of its neck. Very good-humouredly he called out, leaning with his free hand on the banister: 'Au revoir, my dearest,' and threw the dog to the lady. John started forward, but the lady was quicker, caught the dog with wonderful dexterity, and rushed from the house, banging the door behind her.

Walter wiped his large hands in a handkerchief that very deliberately he took from his dressing-gown. He was about to vanish when John called out:

'Cousin Walter.'

He peered forward down into the dark hall.

'Hullo. Who's there?' he asked.

'John Herries. I wish to have a word with you.'

Walter came slowly down the stairs, drawing his dressing-gown about him, his slippers tip-tapping. He came right up to John and bent forward, peering at him.

'Oh, it's you, is it?' he said at last. 'Where's my daughter?'

He was very clean-shaved, and his cheeks, round and rosy, shone like a baby's and smelt freshly of some scent. His face was fat, but his neck and exposed chest were white and firm. His mouth, eyes, and thin hair protruding from the night-cap gave him the look of age, for he was only fifteen years older than John in reality, but looked quite of another generation. His body was of great size and had a balloon-like appearance under the dressing-gown.

'May I speak to you?' asked John.

'You may,' said Walter quite amiably. 'Come upstairs.'

John mounted after him, and Walter led the way into a room that was as untidy and uncomfortable as a room could be. There was a spitting, smoky little fire in the grate; a carpet, red with a buff pattern and a large tear, in front of the fireplace; two pier-glasses; a wool-work ottoman and a large harp leaning against the wall. The room smelt of caraway-seed and was very close.

Walter, his legs stretched, stood in front of the fireplace and motioned John to a seat.

'If you're cold,' he said, 'I can't help it. Didn't know you were coming. Have a brandy.'

'No, thank you,' said John, turning his hat round and round in his hands.

'Well, what do you want now that you are here?'

'You wrote a letter to my wife. I am here to answer it.'

Walter scratched his head under his night-cap and grinned. Then he sat down in a large faded green leather chair and stretched out his thick hairy legs, kicking off one slipper and crinkling up his toes.

'Forgive my attire, Cousin John,' he said. 'That bitch of a woman put me out this morning—and now I've put *her* out.' He threw his head back and laughed. 'Have a brandy. Pray, have a brandy,' he said again.

'No, I thank you,' said John very ceremoniously.

'Well, I will.' He pulled an old red worsted bell-rope and so still was the house that the clang of the bell could be heard echoing, echoing into eternity. 'Now then,' he said, 'why isn't my daughter here?'

'She is not here, neither is she coming.'

'Well, that's straight enough. But she *is* coming if I want her.'

'You have no sort of right to her,' John answered hotly. He was glad if he was getting angry. That made him less conscious of the silent house, less aware of his own anticipation of

Uhland's entrance.

'And why have I no right? I'm her father, aren't I?'

'You ill-treated her, and then when she ran away because she was so miserable you made no kind of inquiry as to her whereabouts. She might have died for all you cared.'

Walter yawned, scratched his breast, leaned forward, shaking a fist.

'Look you here, Cousin John. Let me tell you something. You are in danger, you are. It began with your mother, who was impertinent to my mother. I gave her a warning, but she wouldn't listen, and I frightened her into her grave. When she was gone I warned you that you'd better be after her—all of you. But you wouldn't take the warning, and, more than that, you have the damned impertinence to marry my daughter—'gainst my wishes too. I don't bear you a grudge. I don't bear anyone in this world a grudge except my old father who goes cohabiting with a woman young enough to be his daughter and gets a child by her. Disgustin'—simply disgustin'. No, I don't wish you ill, but I've been telling the lot of you these years back to move out of Uldale, and you will not listen. You are in danger, Cousin John, and if you won't drink a brandy like a gentleman you'd better be off. I've had an irritating time already this morning, and I don't want another.'

'You needn't think,' said John, getting up, 'that we are afraid of you. We know all the dirty little games you've been playing, putting Peach on to rob and spy, bribing the servants, but it doesn't affect us, not an atom.'

'Does it not?' said Walter, cheerfully. 'No, because you've that old woman in the house. She's a hard-plucked one, she is. I've been fighting her for years, and upon my soul there is no one in the world I admire more. But it won't go on for ever, you know. Dear me, no. There'll be a nasty family crisis one of these days. You can tell the old lady so.'

The old bow-legged man with the brown wig arrived with a bottle and two glasses.

Walter filled one tumbler half full and drank it off.

'That's better,' he said. 'And now you'd better be going.'

He got up and shuffled his great body across the room, yawning, scratching his back, his night-cap tilted over one ear.

'Dam' bitch,' he said. 'I wish I'd broken the bones of that dog.' He kicked the harp with the toe of his slipper. 'That was her doing,' he said, jerking his head. 'Thought she could play on it. Forced me to order the thing from Carlisle . . . ' He swung round at the door.

'Uhland hates you, you know,' he said, grinning like a schoolboy. 'Hates you like a poison. Don't know why. Always has.'

John said nothing.

In the passage Walter said:

'Ever been over this house? Chilly place. Draughty as hell.' He threw open a double door. This was the salon where the fine opening Ball had been given. Here were the tapestries, and the decorations, hanging garlands and the dazzling stars of heaven. But the floor was filmed with dust, there was a large patch in the gilded ceiling, a corner of the tapestry flapped drearily against the wall, a chair was overturned, and there were bird-droppings on the long window-sill.

'Fine room,' said Walter. Then, closing the doors behind him, he said: 'There are rooms and rooms in this place. Too many rooms.'

Somewhere a dog was howling and a door banged, monotonously, like a protest.

'Good-bye, then,' said Walter, nodding. 'I am sure I don't know why you came.'

'I came in answer to your letter.'

'Ah, yes. Well, it's my daughter I wish to see. No one else.'

'I came to tell you that. That she will not come.'

'Yes.' He nodded. 'She will, though—if I want her. Damn that dog. There's no peace in this house.' He shuffled off, disappearing quite suddenly. And he was replaced, for John, hearing a sound,

looked to the left, and there on the stone step of a little winding
stair stood Uhland.

He said nothing. He was dressed in black, with a single
flashing diamond in his stock. He said nothing; he turned back
up the staircase, tapping with his stick. And John followed him.
The silence of the house, broken only by the distant yapping of
the dog, compelled him, and the film of dust that seemed to be
floating everywhere in the house compelled him. But he went
because he was ashamed not to go; the fear that so maliciously
squeezed his heart would mock at him all his life long if he did
not go. And he went because Uhland wanted him to go.

* * * * *

At the top of the little stone staircase the tapping stick led him
through an open door into Uhland's room. This was furnished
with a four-poster, a parrot in a cage, a sheep-dog lying on the
floor by the window, a grand view straight down the hillside to
Uldale, a bookcase, a pair of foils and a bare shabby table and
two old brown chairs.

Uhland stood in the middle of the room and looked at him.

'And pray what have you come for?' he asked him.

They faced one another for the first time, as it seemed, for
many years, and even now John could not bring this face and
body to any definite terms. It was indistinct, floating in dust,
wavering into space. The room smelt of animals, the bed was
unmade, the sheets tossed about. The sheep-dog paid them no
attention, but slowly licked a paw that was wrapped in very fresh
white linen.

John was not indistinct to Uhland. He hated, as he looked,
every particle of him; the high aristocratic carriage of his head,
his gentle amiable eyes, his handsome clothes and, most of all,
he both hated and loved his fear of himself. He drew lines with
his stick on the worn dusty carpet.

'What have you come for?' he asked again.

John's words stuck in his throat; he could not help himself. It may have been the close air and animal smell. He forced himself, as though he were beating with his foot on the floor, to speak.

'I came to see your father about a private affair,' he said at last. 'But now I am here I should wish to know what the hell you mean by following me, spying on me in London and elsewhere during these last years?'

'Ah, you've noticed that, have you?' said Uhland.

They both knew that it would need only a gesture, a careless movement, for them to be at one another's throats. If Uhland had not been lame John must have sprung forward, and oh! the relief that that would be, the clearing away, as one sweeps off cobwebs, of years of dreams, nightmares, shame and terror. But he could not touch a cripple, and, more than that, as Uhland drew lines with his stick on the floor, he seemed to place a barrier between them.

'Well,' Uhland said, 'it has amused me to make you uncomfortable. You are such a coward, so poor a creature, that anything can frighten you. And you had the impertinence to marry my sister.'

'If you were not lame,' said John, 'I would show you whether I am a coward or no.'

'Ah, don't allow that to stop you. Lame though I am, I can look after myself. You have always been a coward. Everyone knows it.'

'If you were not Elizabeth's brother——'

'Another excuse.'

John drew a deep breath. He could not help himself, but this thick close air made the room swing about him. Uhland's stick hypnotised him.

'I'll show you——' he began. 'If I am disturbed by you any more I shall forget your weakness and make you sorry you were ever born. I've warned you. I won't warn you again.'

He turned to go. He saw the dog raise its head, heard the parrot scratch the bars, then knew that the closeness of the room gripped his windpipe, darkened his eyes. The floor swirled up like a wave and struck him. He fainted, sinking limply back against the legs of the chair.

Uhland looked at him, hesitated, then went to the washing-basin, fetched the jug and bent down, his arm under John's body, splashing his forehead with the water.

He had John's body in his arms. He put his hand beneath his shirt and felt the smooth firm warm skin above the heart. He drew the body close to his own, and his long thin fingers passed over the face, the neck, the open shirt. His own heart was beating tumultuously. With one hand he very gently bathed the forehead just as he bathed one of his wounded animals, with the other he pressed his fingers on the mouth, felt the warm lips under his touch, stroked the strong throat, looking always into the eyes.

His hand pressed more intently on the mouth; then he shuddered through all his body. He saw that John's eyes were slowly, dazedly opening, so he drew away, letting the other collapse against the chair. He got up, threw a look about the room, and, very quietly, went out.

EXHIBITION

'I am as excited as a child,' said Judith.

'You *are* a child,' answered Dorothy severely. 'Do wrap your shawl more closely or you will catch the most dreadful chill.'

'Chill—pooh!' said Judith, leaning over the edge of Will's most handsome carriage that she might see the better an extraordinary Frenchman in beard, felt hat and full pantaloons.

They had come to London to stay with Will for the opening of the Great Exhibition.

Long before their departure from Cumberland the Exhibition had penetrated their seclusion. For weeks and weeks no one in Keswick, Bassenthwaite, Cockermouth, Buttermere Valley, Penrith or anywhere else had had any other thought but of the Exhibition and the possibilities of a visit to London. Old Bennett, for example, had received from somewhere in London a plan of a monster lodging-house that would be designed to 'put up' at least a thousand souls from the country at one and the same time 'for one and three per night,' and for this small sum each and every person was to be provided 'with bedstead, good wool mattress, sheets, blankets and coverlet; with soap, towels and every accommodation for ablution, a surgeon to attend at nine o'clock every morning and instantly remove all cases of infectious disease'; there was to be 'a smoking-room, detached from the main building, where a band of music was to play every evening, gratis' and 'cold roast and boiled beef and mutton, and ditto ditto sausages and bacon, and pickles, salads and fruit pies (when to be procured) were to be furnished at fixed prices,' all the dormitories were to be 'well lighted with gas'; to secure the complete privacy of the occupants they were 'to be watched over by efficient wardens and police constables,' and finally, 'the proprietor pledged himself that every care should be taken to ensure the comfort, convenience and *strict discipline* of so large a body.'

What could be fairer than that? Everyone was going. On a certain morning almost the whole of Uldale and Ireby villages departed in carts and carriages for the 'Travellers' Train' at Cockermouth. Others journeyed to Carlisle and met the train for London there. For hundreds of persons round and about Judith's little world this was the first real journey of their lives.

And it was, in fact, oddly enough, Dorothy's first train journey too. She was never one to allow her emotions to get the better of her, but she did cry a little as she left Timothy, Veronica, Amabel and Jane to the rotund Miss Meredith. She had never before been absent from them for a single day, but Miss Meredith was 'the safest person in the world,' nothing could have appeared more secure that morning than the Uldale lawns and rosy walls happy under the soft April sun. When, at the station, she beheld the porters in their green velveteen jackets, heard the engines fizzling, and the large bells announcing the coming of a train that soon arrived, bumping and groaning as though in fearful agony; when, safely in their carriage, they were entertained by a stout gentleman with the grandest whiskers who warned them in a voice, husky and urgent, about the perils of London—the cracksmen, the rampsmen, the snorzers and thimble-screwers, all these exciting varieties of pickpockets and murderers—when at last arriving in the Metropolis and waiting outside the station for their luggage to be brought to them, there occurred, 'under their very noses, just as though they were in a theatre,' a 'school of acrobats,' and an 'equilibrist' spun plates high in air, balanced burning paper bags on his chin, and caught cannon-balls in a cup on the top of his head—why, then Dorothy forgot her children entirely and surrendered completely to her adventure.

She had thought that her main occupation in London would be to take care of Judith, but she very quickly discovered that Judith took care not only of her but of everyone else in her company.

During the first evening at the house in Hill Street, Judith put the second Lady Herries in her proper place in exactly five minutes. She laughed at her, pinched her chin and exhorted her thus: 'Now you mustn't mind me, my dear. I'm seventy-seven years of age and nothing ails me. Wonderful, isn't it? I need no looking-after. I came to London as a very young girl and was not at all alarmed by it, so it's most unlikely that I shall be alarmed by it now. I knew Will long before you were born—that is the prettiest Cashmere, my dear; where *did* you discover it?— yes, and Will knows me too, do you not, Will? So you are not to disturb yourself about me. I shall have *everything* I want, I am certain. And now, may I not see little Ellis? I am dying for a sight of him.'

Dorothy perceived that no one in the large cold house had anything of Judith's fire and vitality, and that that same fire burnt only quietly at Uldale. She realised for the first time how much of her personality Judith subdued in the country, and how patient Judith had often been with herself and her children.

'Judith is a marvellous woman,' said Will that evening. 'More marvellous every time I see her.'

'Yes,' said Dorothy meekly.

That was Will's opinion of Judith; Judith's opinion of Will was that he was pathetic. Will was eighty-one years of age and could only go out for an airing, sitting in his carriage, wrapped up like a mummy and with someone at his side to blow his nose, see that his feet were warm and that his hat was on straight. This 'someone' was never Lady Herries, but rather his attendant, Robins, a thin, severe, black-haired man of very religious principles. Lady Herries paid no attention to her husband whatever. She made a sort of a show on the first night of Judith's visit, gave him his pills and wrapped a shawl around his shoulders, but after that the virtuous Robins did everything, cutting his meat for him, pouring him his wine and suddenly remarking sternly: 'No, Sir William. No potatoes. They are forbidden.'

However, Will did not seem greatly to care. Judith was astonished at his subservience. Was this the stern and austere Will who had commanded so implacably poor weak-jointed Christabel? 'Shall I be like that soon?' thought Judith. 'I prefer death.'

But Will did not care, because he had one constant, eager, unceasing preoccupation—'little Ellis.' Little Ellis was now eight years of age and as small and wizened a boy as you would be likely to find. He was accounted exceedingly sharp, had a money-box into which he was constantly putting sixpences, and inquired the price of everything. Will thought him wonderful and quite frankly now spoke of Walter and Uhland as ungrateful wretches. He saw Judith as Walter's principal aggravator and this made him admire her more than ever. He liked to dilate on the riches that he was leaving Ellis—Walter was not to have a penny, nor Uhland, 'that surly peevish cripple,' anything either. John and Elizabeth, however, were to receive a good legacy. Elizabeth he now loved. He had her to the house whenever he was able, and she, better than anyone else, seemed to understand and comfort him.

Of his wife he never spoke, but his allusions to 'poor, good Christabel' gave Judith to understand that ghosts can, once and again, have their proper revenge.

Now that it was clear that Will would not live much longer, visits of members of the Herries family to Hill Street were frequent. It was not that they were greedy: they cared neither for money nor poverty. But Will was now the most important member of their family, and the death of an important Herries was, in their eyes, a world affair. Carey Rockage, James Herries (a most tiresome and pompous old bore of seventy-two), Stephen Newmark (who considered himself a Herries and then something), Amery, Fred Ormerod (cousin by marriage of Monty Cards and a gay, drinking bachelor), Bradley Cards (a nephew of Jennifer's), Tim Trenchard (a busybody cousin of Garth's and Amery's), all these men with wives, daughters and appendages drove up to Hill Street, left cards, came and sat in the long, dreary drawing-room and asked Lady Herries to receptions.

Of them all Judith liked best to see Sylvia. She had loved Sylvia from the moment of their first meeting and she loved her still, although the beautiful, bright, impertinent girl she had first known was now a weary, over-painted, discontented middle-aged woman. Sylvia had been fighting too long the battle of living above your means. Had it been her lot to have married a man of large and assured fortune she would have been a brilliant and successful leader of Society and, at the last, a contentedly reminiscent old lady. But Garth was a cheerful, corruptible vagabond. They had neither of them morals nor honesty. They had stolen, cheated, lied all their lives long, always without any desire to hurt or damage, but hurt and damage they had—first their friends and acquaintances, last of all themselves. Moreover, the London that now surrounded them was not their own; the raffish, speculating, bouncing world of the Thirties was succeeded now by the serious, earnest, virtuous and hypocritical world of the Fifties. To be fair to Sylvia and Garth, they did not know how to be hypocritical, nor did they think it good manners to be earnest. So they were shabby and left-behind and out at heels.

Sylvia wept on Judith's bosom; the paint ran down her cheeks, and before she left she accepted ten pounds from Judith with a readiness that showed that every day of her life she was accepting small sums from someone.

Elizabeth had one talk with Judith that disturbed her greatly. Elizabeth was now thirty-six but was as remotely lovely as she had ever been. That delicate bloom and fragrance belonged to her still. On the afternoon of this talk she was wearing a costume of the new 'crystallised' gauze so that she seemed the floating cloud to which ladies at that time were so fond of comparing themselves. She was quite unaware of her loveliness: Judith, watching her with sharp, practised eyes, thought that it was as though she lived under a glass bell with John, everything and everybody shut away from them. And she was very unhappy about him.

'He cannot sleep at night,' she said. 'He thinks that I am not awake and he talks to himself. He slips out of bed very quietly and goes into the other room and walks about. I am so frightened, Aunt Judith.'

Judith kissed her, held her hand, but there was always something stiffly independent about Elizabeth. She asked for help but refused to accept it. Also she loved John, Judith thought, too deeply for it to be healthy.

'Is he worrying about your father?'

'I suppose so—or rather it is Uhland. Uhland obsesses him, and since he went up to Ireby that day last year it has been worse.'

'Well, my dear child, I've been fighting your father for years and am none the worse. John should see this sensibly.'

'But it seems like something in his blood, something inside himself. As though he were pursued by Uhland. It is a fantasy, Aunt Judith—not real at all. After all, what can Uhland do?'

'His father had the same, and his great-grandfather; something that would never let them alone. Well,' Judith sighed impatiently, 'I cannot understand it. I never could. When there's a difficulty or a danger, face it. Don't run away from it.'

'John does face it,' Elizabeth answered indignantly. 'You must not think he is a coward, Aunt Judith. He's tremendously brave in everything—but this is like a sickness.'

Judith nodded her head; there were two worlds, she knew, and unless you found the connection between them you never found peace. Once she had herself had to make a choice. She had made it and was now the old woman she was in consequence.

Then she found that it was a very fine thing to give cheap advice to others, but that she had her own trouble to face. Her trouble—one that she had never expected nor considered—was that she was plunged, willy-nilly, into a sea of jealousy about Adam. Willy-nilly because, cry out as she might, refuse to be, at her age, so mean and small and petty, there she was in it up to the neck.

Adam had of course been the great central fact of her visit to London. To see the Great Exhibition certainly, but to see it with Adam. To lean on Adam's strong arm everywhere, to have the delicious intimate little talks with him, simply the two of them alone in her room, that had been for many years now her greatest happiness in life, to feel, above all, that no one had the close relationship with him that she herself had. It was not that she wished to shut Margaret out. She was neither so selfish nor so stupid. Moreover, she had fought that battle before and had won a victory. But her later life had been built up on the absolute intimacy of herself and her son, an intimacy that no one and nothing could break. She was, however, becoming greedy, greedy of her vitality, her uniqueness. She was 'Madame,' the most marvellous old lady in Cumberland and, if she wished, the most marvellous old lady in London. This was nothing in her as cheap and petty as conceit, but the sort of amused triumph we all feel when we are clever at a game. All this was on the surface, but her very soul was possessed by her love for Adam. No one knew how deep that went. She had only loved two people in all her life, her husband and her son, but she loved them like a tigress. At the same time she had human enough wisdom and tolerance enough to keep the tigress behind bars.

Never before had her relationship with Adam been threatened as it was now. She perceived at once that the reason of it was the sudden and violent death of Margaret's father. She had not known of the scene between Margaret and Adam that Christmas-time at Uldale. That would have informed her yet further had she been aware of it. But since Caesar Kraft's death she had seen very little of Adam and Margaret. They had paid only one brief visit to Uldale. She was quite unprepared for this change.

It was not that Adam was not as devoted as ever. He was there at Hill Street to meet her on the first evening. When they were alone in her room, he took her in his arms and hugged and kissed her as though he would never let her go.

'Why, how strong you are, Adam!' she cried, laughing and crying and happy as a queen. It was after this that she perceived that his thoughts were always on Margaret. *He* was of course as silent as ever, but her first sight of Margaret told her that there was here a new assurance and certainty. Margaret possessed Adam now and was quietly radiant because of it. They had three rooms in Pimlico. Adam wrote for the papers, knew Dickens and John Forster, Yates and Wilkie Collins. He was not of the writing world, stayed quietly outside it, made few friends, but made those few firmly. He wrote considerably about politics, reviewed books a little, and said cheerfully to his mother that the only things he really wanted to write were fairy-stories.

'Fairy-stories!' Judith cried, looking at Adam's stocky, thick-set frame and ugly unromantic countenance.

'Don't be afraid, mother,' he said, laughing. 'I shall never write them. I must earn our bread and butter, but a good fairy-story—there must be a handsome satisfaction in writing a good fairy-story.'

This was nonsense of course, so she told him sharply, but it annoyed her that Margaret should think it quite a natural thing for him to do. 'Yes,' Margaret explained, 'he has found real life so very absurd.'

'Nonsense,' Judith answered. 'I never listened to such stuff. Fairy-stories! A man like Adam! Why, he has a chest like a bull's!'

She soon discovered that her relations with her son and daughter-in-law were complicated by her advancing years. She was a wonderful old lady, but she could not do as she used to do. She took her breakfast in bed every morning and did not rise until midday. She was forced to confess that she returned to Hill Street exceedingly weary after her shopping expeditions.

It was necessary, therefore, for Adam and Margaret to come to her rather than that she should go to them, and she thought that Margaret accompanied her husband too frequently.

Being direct and honest, she immediately said so.

'My dear boy, I am in London for a very brief visit. I have one foot in the grave. I love Margaret, of course, but I love you more.'

He said nothing (he never did say anything), but he came alone. Then she fancied that he was thinking of Margaret and wishing that he were with her.

She would interrupt some Cumberland piece of gossip with a sharp: 'Now, Adam, you are not attending. You are thinking of Margaret.'

Jealousy began to mount in her as the tide swells a sea-pool. She slept now but badly, and before had not minded that, for she would lie and think of the old days, of Georges and Reuben and Charlie Watson and Warren, Adam's father, until the room seemed crowded with their figures; but now she could think of nothing but Adam, and, with the fantastic exaggeration that the night hours give, she would beat her thin little hands together and cry to herself that she had lost him for ever, that she was a miserable, deserted old woman, and that she might as well die. It was then that her poignant despair at the choice that so many years ago she had made for the sake of Jennifer, John and Dorothy, would strike her like a voice of doom.

'Ah! if I had but gone with Adam to Watendlath he would have been mine for ever!'

But in the daylight she was by far too sensible and blessed with too strong a sense of humour to tolerate such obvious melodrama. She laughed at herself, her fears, her selfishness. Nevertheless her jealousy mounted. She was as sweet as Tennyson's Miller's Daughter to Margaret, but Margaret was not deceived. The trouble with both Margaret and Adam was that they were so quiet. You could not tell what they were truly thinking!

Poor Judith! Jealousy is from the Devil. It was hard for her that she should have to fight her first real battle with him at so advanced an age!

* * * * *

The Great Day approached. The Great Day arrived!

But the whole of London was by this time an Exhibition. Foreigners were everywhere—Germans, Turks, Americans, French and even Chinamen. On every side amusements were springing up, M. Alexis Soyer opened his Restaurant of All the Nations, there was 'the Black Band of His Majesty of Tsjaddi with a hundred additional bones,' the Musicians of Tongoose, the Troubadours of Far Vancouver, the Theban Brothers, and the most celebrated Band of Robbers from the Desert. Barnum provided a splendid entertainment, whereby for a rather costly ticket a guest was provided with 'a bed, a boudoir and a banquet, together with one hour's use per diem of a valet and a private chaplain, free admission to theatrical green-rooms, a seat in the House of Commons, and a cigar on the Bench of Judges.' Mr. Catlin reopened his Indian Exhibition, and Mr. Wyld would take you on the 'Grand Tour of Europe,' or a visit to Australia or New Zealand for threepence a time.

But it was enough for Judith and Dorothy simply to view the crowds in the streets. The road to the Crystal Palace was an amazing scene. Trains of wagons lengthened far away, like an Eastern caravan, each waiting for its turn to be unloaded. Omnibuses, carriages, carts, barrows congested the road. The public-houses, of which there were a great number, hung out gay and patriotic flags, and their doors were crowded with loafers, soldiers, beggars and women with shawls over their heads. Along the pavement were lined the hawkers shouting their wares, trays filled with bright silvery-seeming medals of the Exhibition, pictures of it printed in gold on 'gelatine cards,' many barrows with ginger-beer, oranges and nuts.

Along Rotten Row troops of riders galloped noiselessly over

the loose soft ground at the rear of the Crystal Palace, while in front of it an interminable line of carriages drawled slowly past. Close to the rails were mobs of spectators on tiptoe, their necks outstretched, seeking glimpses of progress. All along the building were ladders with painters perched high upon them and walking on the crystal covering which miraculously sustained them. At the end of the building were steam-engines puffing clouds of steam, and amid the wreckage of thousands of packing-cases were giant blocks of granite, huge lumps of coal, great anchors, the ruins of a prehistoric world. The noise, confusion, turmoil—who, asked Dorothy, could describe them? She was given to platitudes, and irritated Judith by insisting that 'such chaos is an emblem of man's energy working to a just end.' The Exhibition in fact turned her head a little spiritually, and made her so deeply proud of being a Herries that she seemed to walk like a goddess. All the Herries felt the same, that the Exhibition was their especial work and Queen Victoria the head of the family.

On the Great Day itself, the First of May, the heart of London beat with a pride and exaltation that was to affect the country for at least another fifty years.

Judith, Dorothy, Lady Herries, little Ellis, Adam, Margaret, John and Elizabeth had, all of them, thanks to old Will's power and position, splendid seats for the opening ceremony.

They started early, and that was wise, for the carriage was soon involved in a long, wearisome procession of carriages from whose windows every kind of bonnet and hat was poking and shrill feminine voices exclaiming: 'But this is monstrous! We shall miss the Queen! It is really too bad!'

John and Elizabeth were to join the others inside the building and were already there when Lady Herries, dressed in a magnificent purple bonnet and superb Cashmere shawl, her head very much up, led in her little procession. Judith came last, leaning on Adam's arm.

They had excellent places, and the Sight, the Vision, the

Glory—this, as Dorothy remarked, 'exceeded all Expectations and showed what Man could do when guided by the Divine Will.' (Dorothy was not, in her normal Cumberland domesticity, in the least like this. 'You are a little over-excited, my dear,' Judith had told her that morning.)

Yes, it was superb! Their seats were in one of the galleries, the galleries planted like flower-gardens with bonnets of pink, yellow and white. The Great Central Glory was the Glass Fountain. Of this Archdeacon Rodney Herries' son, Captain William Herries, R.N., wrote in his *A Jolly Tar's Capers* (Weston and Mary, 1895): 'This glorious fountain in the centre of the building, shining, as the sun's rays came slanting down upon it through the crystal roof, as if it had been carved out of icicles, or as if the water streaming from the fountain had been made suddenly solid and transfixed into beautiful forms. Although but a rough, careless little Middy at the time, I can remember well that, standing beside my father, at that time Archdeacon of Polchester in Glebeshire, tears welled up into my youthful eyes and pride of my country fired my ambition.

"'It is such families as ours in such a country as ours," I remember my dear father remarking, "that, under God's Grace, can create, for the benefit of the world, such wonders."'

It must be confessed that Judith saw it all less romantically. Rodney Herries she had, incidentally, always detested. But nevertheless she was carried away, forgetting years, jealousies, aches and pains (for this morning she had a little rheumatism). For one thing the noise was terrific. The waiting multitude was quiet enough, but around them, throughout the building, all the machinery had been set in motion—the MACHINERY, key-note of the Exhibition, symbol, relentless, humourless, of the new world that this day, May 1, 1851, was introducing. There were in the machine-room the 'self-acting mules,' the Jacquard lace machines, the envelope machines, the power looms, the model locomotives, centrifugal pumps, the vertical steam-engines, all of these working like mad, while the thousands near by, in their

high hats and bonnets, sat patiently waiting, passive, unwitting
that the Age of Man on this Planet was doomed!

Judith and Adam, John and Elizabeth, were most certainly
unwitting. Judith's little hand was thrust through Adam's
thick arm, while John and Elizabeth were holding hands under
Elizabeth's shawl. Margaret was thinking of her father and
wishing that he were here, Dorothy's mouth was wide open, and
Lady Herries was studying a coarse-grained Chambéry gauze
near to her and wondering whether she could obtain one like it.
Yes, a superb scene! The canopy above the royal seat, adorned
with golden cornice and fringe and a small plume of blue and
white feathers at each angle, the floors clean and matted, at each
corner of the central square stages for illustrious visitors, from
the gallery tops magnificent carpets and tapestries hanging,
here the Spitalfields Trophy with its gorgeous silks, and there,
the supreme triumph for many, the wonderful plaster of Paris
statues, so white, so gleaming, their nudity draped so decently
with red cloth. A sob rose in many throats, too, at the sight of
the splendid equestrian statues of the Prince and the Queen, so
large and life-like that you might imagine that at any moment
the horses might start to charge down the central aisle. (This
was Dorothy's fine whispered thought.) Here, to quote Captain
William once again: 'Behind these was another Fountain' (it
appears that he nourished a passion for fountains!) 'that made
the stream as it rushed up from the centre and divided itself
into a hundred drops, flashing in the sun as they fell, look like
a shower of silver sparks—a kind of firework of water; and
beside this rose the green plumage of the palm trees embedded
in moss, while close at their feet was ranged a bed of flowers,
whose tints seemed to have been dyed by the prismatic hues of
the water-drops of the neighbouring fountain. Then appeared
the old elm trees of the park, looking almost like the lions of
the forest caught in a net of glass; and behind them again was a
screen of iron tracery, so light and delicate that it seemed like a
lace-work of bronze.'

A little later he continues: 'But it was when the retinue of the Court began to assemble that the scene became one— perhaps the most—gorgeous in colouring and ever beheld; for it was seen in the clear light of the transparent roof above. The gold-embroidered bosoms of the officers seemed to be almost alight with the glitter of their ornaments; there stood all the ministers of state in their glittering suits; the ambassadors of every country, some in light blues and silver, others in green and gold, others in white, with their bosoms' (incidentally a favourite word of the Captain's) 'studded with their many-coloured orders. There was the Chinese mandarin in his red cap, with peacocks' feathers dangling behind, and his silken robes with quaint devices painted upon them in front and at the back. There was the turbaned Turk, and the red fez-capped Egyptian; and there were the chocolate-coloured Court suits, with their filigree steel buttons, and long, white embroidered silk waistcoats.

'There was the old DUKE too' (these are the Captain's capital letters) 'with his silver hair and crooked back showing most conspicuous amongst the whole. At the back and sides of the throne stood the gentlemen-at-arms, in their golden helmets, with the long plumes of white ribbon-like feathers drooping over them. Beside these were the portly-looking beef-eaters, in their red suits and black velvet caps; and near them were the trumpeters, in their golden coats and close-fitting jockey-caps, with silver trumpets in their hands.

Near these were the Aldermen, in their red gowns of office, and the Common-Councilmen in their blue silk gowns, and the Recorder in long powdered Judge's wig, the Archbishop in full lawn sleeves and close curly wig, the Musical Director in his white satin-damask robe and quaint-looking black cap, the heralds in their emblazoned robes, the Garter King-at-Arms in his gorgeous red velvet coat becrusted all over in gold—while round all these were ranged sappers and miners, in their red and yellow uniforms; and behind them were seen the dark-blue coats of the police.'

And the brave Captain complacently comments:

'It was a feast of colour and splendour to sit and gloat over—a congress of all the nations for the most hallowed and blessed of objects—one, perhaps, that made the two old soldiers, as they tottered backwards and forwards across the scene, the most noticeable, because in such a gathering for such an object, the mind could hardly help looking upon them as the last of the warriors to whom the nation would owe its future greatness. I could not but reflect,' the Captain adds, 'that my own family that has been proud to call England its mother for so many centuries had, under God's divine direction, helped sensibly by its honest devotion to duty and its consistent patriotism to bring this Great Country into its supreme world-dominating position.'

Then he continues after this little spurt of family pride: 'At a few minutes before the appointed hour the royal carriages with their bright liveries were seen to flash past the windows of the northern entrance; then darted by a troop of the Life Guards, with their steel helmets and breastplates glistening in the sunshine, and immediately after, the glass sides and roof of the Crystal Palace twanged with the flourish of trumpets that announced the arrival of the Queen. At this moment the gates were flung back, and within the crimson vestibule appeared a blaze of gold and bright colours.

'Then advanced the royal retinue, with the ushers and chamberlain in front, bowing as they moved backwards towards the throne; and after them the Prince leading the Princess Royal, and the Queen with the Prince of Wales, and followed by their Court.

'As the Queen moved onwards with her diamond tiara and little crown of brilliants scintillating in the light, the whole assembly rose and, waving their hats and fluttering their handkerchiefs, they shouted forth peal after peal of welcome.'

And here we may leave the excellent Captain in his happy state of obsequious reminiscence. His book is unquestionably of value, quite apart from its Herries interest, and is certainly worthy of a modern reprint. It attained six editions in the 'nineties.

Sad to say, Judith was not at all moved as was Rodney's son. For one thing the seat on which she was sitting was exceedingly hard, for another she was bothered by the noise of the machines, for another she was feeling odd in the head, a little as though she had been drinking. And for another she had never, all her life, been impressed very greatly by domesticity: the Queen, the Prince, and their two children appeared to her so dreadfully domestic. That was on her father's side. On her proper Herries side she would have been undoubtedly more deeply impressed had she been quite at her ease. But she was distressed about John, about Adam, and a very little about herself. Most certainly she felt queer, as though there were a weight pressing on her heart, as though, unless she were careful, she would see double. She thought that, in all probability, this glittering and scintillating glass disturbed her. Absurd to build so large a place entirely of glass!

She could not resist, however, some beating of the heart when, as the Queen moved forward, wearing her diamond tiara and crown of brilliants, everyone rose and, waving hats, fluttering handkerchiefs, shouted their cries of welcome. Judith rose, fluttered her handkerchief, shouted with the rest. For a moment she was deeply stirred. The sturdy figure of Victoria appeared to divorce itself from all the world around it, as though it said: 'I am lonely. I am a Queen. I represent loneliness, austerity and power.'

She had that quality, was to have it all her life, of sudden dignified remoteness, so that she became a symbol, a promise, a prophecy. Judith, old enough to be that same Queen's grandmother, felt that now. The white head and light-blue coat of the Master of the Queen's Music appeared on the rostrum, he raised his baton, and above what Captain Herries called 'the melodious thunder of the organ,' the National Anthem—led by the choristers—filled the glass dome and was caught by the light and glitter and flung into the sunny heavens. The Archbishop asked for a blessing (the Machinery frantically responded), the Queen and Prince walked in procession, and then Her Majesty declared the Exhibition open. And to end once again with Captain William: 'Immediately were heard the booming of the hundred guns without, telling the people of the Metropolis that the Great Exhibition of the Industry of All Nations had been formally inaugurated.'

Judith recovered herself and sat down. That reaction that inevitably follows all climaxes seized her. What, after all, was all this fuss about? It would only make the country and everyone in it exceedingly conceited. And how tiresome the Exhibition had already become! For months in advance of it no one had talked of anything else, and now for months after it no one would have any other topic. She looked down from the gallery, and the mere thought of all the plaster statues, the great organ, the fountain, the machinery, the furniture, the stalls covered with goods, the endless cups of tea, the ferns and plants and blossoming shrubs, the crying children, angry husbands and disappointed wives, all this wearied her beyond measure.

'I think that I will return to Hill Street,' she said to Adam.

'Very well, mother dear, but first you must see just a few of the sights.'

She did not want to see any of the sights. She would like to be seated safely and privately in her armchair in her room at Hill Street.

Says Captain William Herries: 'Well might the nation be proud of its Crystal Palace. No other people in the world could have raised such a building . . . '

That is exactly what Judith thought, straining up her old eyes to the glitter and the shine. 'All this glass,' she thought, 'so ostentatious,' and her dislike of Prince Albert, assuaged for a moment by the National Anthem, returned in full force.

Adam took her by the arm and she walked gaily along, with Dorothy and Lady Herries very patriotic behind her, Margaret on her other side, and John and Elizabeth not exchanging a word. 'Why don't they speak?' she thought. 'Aren't they happy?' She was wearing a soft grey bonnet and a mantilla of shaded grenadine. She walked as though she were twenty, with every once and again a step that was rebellious, originating in some quite other person. She still saw double on occasion, and there was a twinge of pain in her right shoulder.

There were of course a great many things to see, and oh dear! so many people! Bonnets and polkas, polkas and bonnets, green and brown 'wide-awakes' and fluffy beaver hats—and then the People! this time with a capital P! They will be *much* worse on the shilling days, but there seem to be a great many of them, even as it is, many with babies in their arms, many with baskets, many with fat bursting cotton umbrellas.

'There are too many people,' Judith said to Adam. The pain in her shoulder had spread to her arm-pit. 'Really,' she thought, 'Lady Herries is an *idiot*!'

Oh dear, there are a *great* many things to see! Here is a railwayman, family following, his japan pouch by his side, hurrying to see the locomotives; there a carpenter in a yellow fluffy flannel jacket pointing out to two small boys the beauties of a huge top formed of one section of a mahogany tree.

'Ridiculous!' Judith thought. 'No one in the world can wish for a top as big as that!'

Here is a hatless and yellow-stockinged Blue-coat boy mounting the steps of one of the huge prismatic lighthouses to see the way that it is made . . . Look! there is a model of the Italian Opera House, and behold! there is a minute and most extensive model of Liverpool with a looking-glass sea and thousands of cardboard vessels. This last Adam examined with the most serious care. 'Remarkable! Very remarkable indeed!' he repeated again and again.

Judith could not explain it, she was greatly ashamed but she wanted to slap him. As with all mothers in the world there were moments when she wondered whether these very prosaic results were at all worth all the pains that she had taken.

'Did I bring him up for this?' she thought as she watched him so seriously count the cardboard ships. Then she caught Margaret's calm look of devotion and she hated Margaret. There was no doubt but that she was not at all well.

Of course they must see the machinery. For hours Judith had been dreading this moment. Pressed close against the stout limbs of a member of the National Guard—'Really a *childish* costume,' she thought as she looked upwards to his conical hat with its little ball on top, and smelt the rough texture of his red worsted epaulettes and full-plaited trousers—she was compelled to admire the power-looms, and then there was the steam brewery, then the model carriages moving along the new pneumatic railway, the hemispherical lamp-shades made out of a flat sheet of paper, the exceedingly noisy flax-crushing machine, the splashing centrifugal pump, the whirling of the cylindrical steam-press . . .

'Adam,' she whispered, drawing him a little closer to her, 'I am glad that I am an old woman. All these machines—what a very unpleasant world it is going to be!'

She whispered, because Dorothy and Lady Herries were in a state of fluttering ecstasy. 'Stupendous!' 'What an achievement!' 'Do observe those wonderful little wheels!' 'Man's triumph over Nature!' Dorothy was proving herself true Herries. She saw Herries everywhere. If it had not been for the Herries family . . . Strange! Judith must certainly be unwell, for she wanted to slap both Dorothy and Lady Herries.

'Adam,' she whispered, 'I fear that I *must* sit down!'

There was no reply and, looking up, she saw that Adam was not there. Looking further she discovered Adam and Margaret, a distance away, their backs turned to her, close together examining a piece of machinery. That was possibly the worst moment of her life. Absurd—so little a thing! And yet the horror of Georges' death, the tragedy of Francis' suicide, the awful evening of Adam's birth—none had touched the loneliness, the isolation of this neglect. Lady Herries was examining a miniature engine with a great assumption of technical knowledge, Elizabeth and John had disappeared.

Judith proudly, her bonnet up, walked away. As she reached the outer hall pain seized her, her heart was beating strangely. Her limbs trembled. Everyone around her seemed weary. On the steps of the red-cloth-covered pedestals weary women and children were seated, some of them munching thick slices of bread and meat. Around the fountains were gathered exhausted families drinking out of thick mugs. All over the floor were orange-skins, dirty pieces of paper; Judith sat down on one of the crimson steps, resting her head on her hands. Was she going to die in this ridiculous place with all these strangers around her? The noise of the machines rattled and quivered, piercing her very backbone. 'Am I going to die? Is this the end?'

A stout woman near to her, her legs spread, crooking a baby in one arm, was drinking out of a bottle. Strange, Judith thought, to allow such people in on the day of the Queen's first visit. But that was right. All were equal—all women together. She had read somewhere that after a certain hour the general public would be admitted. The sight of the woman strengthened and comforted her. She was herself a vagabond, born of vagabonds. No Herries, but daughter of a gipsy. Even though her son deserted her, even though all the pains in the world attacked her, even though this horrible machinery invaded the world, destroying peace and privacy, no one could touch her, she was independent.

She looked up, and there was John! He was standing quite near to her but did not see her. On his face was a look of pitiable distress. He held himself taut, his hands to his side, as if he were answering some charge. On every side of him the crowd pushed and thrust, but he was as alone as though no one else were in the world.

The sight of someone in trouble always caused her to forget herself. She rose, although her knees trembled, walked over to him and touched his arm. He started; her touch had drawn him from a dream.

'John, dear. Take me home. I am very tired.'

That charming kindly smile that she loved in him so much warmed her heart.

'Why, of course, Aunt Judith. We will find Elizabeth.'

She had her hand lightly on his arm. No one should know how ill she felt.

'Such a noise! So many people! I am realising, my dear John, what a very old woman I am.'

'Nonsense, Aunt Judith,' he said, patting her hand. 'This would be too much for anyone.'

But as he looked at her with so kindly an expression, she realised that it was true: she was an old woman at last.

THE FUNERAL

The last visit to London that she was ever to pay was early in 1854, and the occasion was Will's funeral.

They all said that it was defying Providence for her to go, for she was seventy-nine that Christmas, but she was determined: nothing and no one should stop her. In honest fact they all knew a fearful pride in her resolve. Seventy-nine and going to London! No one but a Herries could have done it, but the Herries always lived to a great age and died in their boots! Look at Will! Eighty-four and in the City three days before his death. It was true that he had been strapped up in his carriage like a mummy, and had held a sort of reception there in Threadneedle Street with clerks and people bowing to him on the steps of his offices: nevertheless, eighty-four and working in the City!

Judith was perfectly conscious of all the things that the different Herries, scattered about the country, would be thinking of her enterprise and, being half Herries herself, she was pleased that they should be pleased. Then of course she insisted that she must pay tribute to Will, for Will was part of her whole life, and now, when her youth was for ever present with her, intermingling with all the current events of her day so that it was often impossible to tell which was past and which was present, Will was perhaps nearer to her than he had ever been before. For as a girl she had never liked him; as a woman she had often despised him; but now, joined as they were in their old age together, she almost loved him.

She had, however, two principal motives for her departure. One was that she would see her beloved Adam, a motive sufficient to carry her *and* her coffin if necessary to the North Pole; and the other (although this she confessed to no one in the

83

world) her desire to show Walter Herries that she was still alive and kicking.

Now, when she could not move about as she had once done, but must sit, either in the garden when it was sunny and warm, or in the parlour before the fire, or in her bed with her lace cap on her head and mittens on her fingers just like any other old lady (although she was not in the least like any other old lady!) events and persons were inclined, if you did not keep them in order, to acquire a gigantic significance.

On the one hand she was tranquil as she had never been in her life before. Old age certainly did that for you; and on the days when there was no pain to bother her (for pains of one sort and another paid her now quite constant visits), when she was neither wildly excited by some pleasure (like an unexpected dish for dinner or a sudden visit of a friend, or something entrancing that little Jane had been doing, or a piece of gossip) nor exasperated by some bit of foolishness or some alarm about Adam, why, then this tranquillity was marvellous! You just sat there, or lay there, and it lapped you round like a radiant sheet of golden light, light within you, above you, around you, while the trees burnt in gold steadily against the sky and the streams ran murmuring to your feet, and all this lovely world stood still for you. It was at such times (and they were many) that the past became the present and the present the future. Then there was no Time. She was a child again, watching them ride the horse up Tom Gauntry's staircase, and she was eating roast goose at the 'Elephant,' she was walking beside dear Charlie Watson at Watendlath—all was alive again, nothing had died, she herself was immortal.

Nevertheless the things that disturbed, disturbed violently, and the thing that disturbed the worst was Walter. No climax had come as yet to their quarrel. That moment when she had turned to Jennifer and said (ah, how many years ago! Poor Jennifer!): 'Do not be distressed, my dear. I am going to remain,' that challenge had as yet reached no climax. But the climax would come. She knew it as though she were a prophetess and could see the future. Already enough unhappiness had been generated by that old, old quarrel. John's life, Elizabeth's life, Jennifer's life, Walter's life, Uhland's life—all these had been damaged by it, as hatred and jealousy and envy always damaged any lives that they touched. Her own life and Adam's had been changed by it, for she would have been in Watendlath long ago but for it, and still there was worse to come. She had stayed in Uldale and protected them all, but Walter was still there, the Fortress was still there, Peach's cottage (there was now a younger Peach in command) was just over her garden wall; Walter was a sot and Uhland a crazy misanthrope—but they were not gone, they still remained.

She had been told, only a week or two ago, that Walter had said of her: 'That old bed-ridden gipsy.' Bed-ridden, was she? She would show him! She would go to London if for no other reason!

Nevertheless, it was Will that she was thinking of as she made her departure. Her heart was soft with tenderness.

Dorothy came with her and was full of matronly care and fuss. After the day of her visit to the Great Exhibition, Judith, to everyone's surprise and offering no reason, abandoned her gay colours and adopted a kind of uniform, black with white ruffles and white lace at the throat. With her hair that had the shining softness of snow and the deep white upon white of an evening cloud, with her small pale face, her exquisite neatness and cleanliness, carrying in her hand her cane, she had the air of some austere Mistress of Ceremonies. But then her whole body and nature laughed at austerity. As she grew older her sense of fun, enjoyment of little things and active consciousness of that enjoyment, her eagerness for news, her avidity for sharing in everything, these things constantly increased in her. Her heart—she was warned that she must be careful of her heart. 'My heart?' she laughed. 'It's as sound as one of Dorothy's muffins' (for Dorothy was a good housekeeper but a heavy-handed cook). Then there was the rheumatism, and sometimes she felt faint. Once indeed she fainted in her bedroom, but no one was there with her and no one was told of it. On many days she was as well and strong as Veronica and Amabel—both very healthy girls. One afternoon she slapped Veronica very heartily indeed because that child, aged now sixteen, told her that God disapproved of reading common books on a Sunday.

'You are a prig, the most dreadful animal in Creation,' Judith cried, and when Veronica, losing her temper, shouted, 'And you're a gipsy,' Judith slapped her. Veronica, who was not a bad child, was appalled at what she had done, and Judith walked all the way upstairs and brought her down a bag of peppermints. (Judith liked peppermints and always kept a store in her bedroom.) All this in one afternoon.

Moreover, with her favourite Jane, now a wisp of a child of thirteen, she would play games by the hour and never tire. They would play backgammon and Pope Joan, and then Jane would read to her—Macaulay's *History*, Ruskin's *Seven Lamps of Architecture*, *Pendennis*, *Hypatia*. Judith thought Ruskin 'a bit of a prig' but didn't say so, because Jane thought him so beautiful. After Adam, Judith loved most in the world this dreaming romantic child who was of the tribe of Francis and Reuben and John. 'I am afraid she will be unhappy,' Judith thought, 'but she will have some of the joys none of the others will know.'

When she set off with Dorothy for London it was Jane who came into her room alone, Jane she held to her heart with all that impetuous feeling that years could not dim, Jane who gave her a parcel of three little handkerchiefs that she had worked, Jane who stood in the road staring long after the carriage had disappeared. Timothy, now a big stout fellow of seventeen, who bore a strange resemblance to the portraits of his great-grandfather David Herries, teased her:

'She's a nice old lady, but whew! what a temper!' he remarked.

Jane gave him a queer look.

'All right,' he said uneasily, pinching her ear. 'I daresay I like her as much as you do, if all the truth were known.'

* * * * *

She was so weary when she, at last, reached Hill Street that she felt as though her whole body had been crushed under the wheels of the train that had conveyed her.

She saw Lady Herries for a moment, and her tenderness for poor Will enveloped the stout painted lady, whom she had never liked, who, however, looked better in her full black silk than she had ever looked in gay colours. She was sitting in the vast dismal drawing-room and wearing a bonnet of velvet and crêpe. Everyone was wearing velvet just then.

'That's one thing,' said Judith to Dorothy as she began to undress. 'I shall never wear velvet, my dear. Never! I shall die first! She added: 'I am dead now, I think. The smell of gas in that train was quite awful. Give me Mr. Thorpe's *Northern Mythology*. It's at the top of my bag. It will send me to sleep if anything will.'

The maid who brought her her breakfast in the morning was full of information. There was nothing that Judith liked better than to have someone with whom she might chat while she was having her breakfast.

It seemed that Will had died quite suddenly of heart failure at three o'clock in the morning. He had not felt well and had gone to his wife's room and had fallen down there dead.

The maid did not know, Judith did not know, no one would ever know of the awful little conversation that had taken place on that last morning.

It was true: he had felt very unwell and had stumbled to Lady Herries' room. He walked with great difficulty, but she had woken to see him standing there, swaying on his feet, a candle in his hand.

'I think I am going to die,' he gasped, his hand at his heart. She had jumped out of bed, found the drops that were to be given to him if there were a heart-attack. He had sunk, blue in the face, into a chair. He recovered a little, looked up into her

87

face, and saw in those pale-blue eyes a look of eagerness.

'You are glad that I am dying,' he said.

'Will! Will!' she cried, sinking on to her knees beside the chair. 'How can you be so cruel?'

'It is very natural,' he replied. 'I don't blame you. It is perfectly right. You never even pretended to love me. No one has ever loved me. Not even Ellis——'

She protested and tried to hold his hand. He waved her away with a gesture of great dignity. Then his face became purple.

'I have wanted the wrong things——' he murmured, and died.

The funeral was to be at twelve. A great many members of the family were expected. Soon Adam came in to see her. She held out her arms and he knelt by the bed, took her small white hand in his and laughed for sheer joy at being with her again. For, when you had said everything, there was something between these two, stronger than life, stronger than death, something that no one shared with them, something that if it could be caught and held, hard and shining in one's hand like a flaming crystal, would explain, quite sufficiently, what everything is about and why we are travelling at all. But of course it can't be caught.

'Isn't this room absurd?' Judith said, laughing. She could never grow accustomed to the fashions of the time. She belonged in taste to the end of the eighteenth century. Looking back, everything of that time seemed to her to have lightness, brilliance and form. Everything in 1854 was huge, heavy and static, wrapped, too, in a sort of damp fog.

In her room there was a sofa covered with red rep, a copper scuttle and scoop (quite gigantic), a huge fender of brass, fire-irons of set steel, a hearthrug of white sheepskin, two great Minton vases with a floral design on a turquoise ground, a picture made out of seaweed in a frame of Tunbridge ware, a work-box—also of Tunbridge ware—that had a lid with a bouquet in mosaic and sides with 'Berlin wool' mosaic, and a vast dressing-table and mirror, trimmed with glazed linen and muslin. All these things and many more jostled one another in the room that was chill with the chill of the grave. In their centre, very bare, very innocent, was a tin bath.

Among these things Adam knelt and held her hand. He was a broad square man now, brown of face. She didn't like his whiskers, although, of course, every man wore them. She loved his eyes, which were bright, shining and most kindly. He had great breadth of shoulders, looked as strong as an ox. He was absent-minded, but not with her. He wrote for one of Dickens' papers, reviewed books. He was happily married. He was thirty-eight years of age. All these things were apparently true. But the only thing that was true for her was that he was a small child running up the path from the Tarn at Watendlath, calling out to her that he had seen a kingfisher.

These glorious moments came to her very seldom, but, after that awful hour at the Exhibition, she had beaten down her jealousy. Killed it? No, perhaps not, but she was nearly eighty years of age and must learn to accept facts. Was there anything else to learn of life?

She stroked his brown cheek, kissed him, chattered, laughed, then sent him away. She must get up and face the family.

* * * * *

It was a moment that they none of them afterwards forgot, her entrance into the big drawing-room where they were all gathered together. The blinds were drawn and the room was lit with gas which giggled like a silly schoolgirl. The gas was, however, the only jester. Everyone was immensely solemn. Lady Herries sat on the sofa, Ellis at her side. All around her were grouped the family. James Herries was the oldest—he was seventy-five. He stood beside the sofa, a vast, swollen, pompous effigy in black. There was Archdeacon Rodney, with his wife Rebecca, one of the Foxes of Ulverston, and their son the naval officer. There was Stephen Newmark, close to him Phyllis, now very stout, and four of their seven offspring, Horace, Mary, Katherine and

Emily; there were, of course, Garth and Sylvia and Amery, that gay bachelor Fred Ormerod, Bradley Cards and his little wife who was like a pincushion in figure, Timothy Trenchard, his wife and two daughters, Carey Rockage, only a year younger than James and almost as stout, with his wife Cecily and their children Roger and Alice. John and Elizabeth stood quietly by themselves in a window. Walter, Will's eldest son, and the new baronet, was not present, nor was his son Uhland. Everyone thought this disgraceful.

When Judith entered, followed by Dorothy and Adam, a wave of emotion swept the whole assembly. Even Lady Herries, who disliked Judith and was eagerly jealous of her position as the centre of this day's ceremony, was moved. For this was what the Herries above all else loved. Survival. Perpetuity. To last longer than anyone else. To have life and vigour when all your contemporaries had failed to last. Even as once upon a time they had made eager bets on the centenary of Great-Aunt Maria, so now their excitement and pride were kindled, for Judith Paris was seventy-nine and yet walked with a firm step, her head up, her eyes shining, the most commanding figure of them all.

But there was more than this. Judith had, in all these years, won a great reputation among them for honesty, kindliness and fair charity. They were not, on the whole, very charitable to one another. No members of any family are very charitable to one another. They know all the wrong things. But Judith, because she had lived in the North, had been outside their squabbles, rivalries and jealousies. They thought her a fine generous-hearted woman. She herself, as she saw all those Herries, so solemn and so black, felt a strange mixture of two quite opposite emotions. She thought them absurd and she felt that she would like to mother them all. They *were* absurd—old James so conscious of his baronetcy, so stout, his black legs like pillows, his grizzled whiskers like cauliflowers; Newmark, his head perched above a high stock and collar so that he resembled a dignified but anxious hen; dear Phyllis, so *fearfully* fat and her dress so voluminous that all her brood could comfortably have nestled beneath it; Sylvia, alas! no longer pretty, badly rouged, the black velvet on her dress cut to resemble pansies; Rockage, with an odd resemblance to dear old Maria, long dead, but living again in her son's untidiness and a kind of shabby goodwill (how well Judith remembered that occasion when she had slapped his face at the house in Wiltshire for his riding to hounds over the drawing-room chairs!); Horace Newmark, now a plump pale-faced man of thirty-five in large spectacles and resembling a little in his air of high discontent Mr. Thackeray—yes, they were absurd and lovable too. How Will would be pleased did he see this great gathering! How he would approve of the black and the dignity and the solemnity! At the memory of him, to her own surprise, a tear stole down her cheek. 'Old ladies cry easily!' she thought, as she kissed the widow's plump cheek.

She walked about among them, and they were all very kind to her. It was all crêpe and black broadcloth. Robins, followed by a thin young footman with a cold, walked around offering sherry and a biscuit.

She sat down in a chair near the darkened windows, and the low-murmured conversation went on around her like a draught creeping in through the walls and the floor. It was late February and very damp. There was a discontented, peevish fire in the huge fireplace, but as is so often the case with English fireplaces the heat went up the chimney and left the room severely alone. Nearly everyone seemed to have colds; the sneezing was prodigious. It was understood that a thin rain was falling outside.

Soon she had John and Elizabeth beside her chair. Elizabeth looked lovely but not, Judith thought, very happy. When Elizabeth moved away to talk to Margaret, Judith caught John's hand in hers and said:

'Well, dear John, how are you?'

They were away from the others. She felt his hand clutch

hers, tightly, and had an impulse to put her arms around him and hold him safe.

'Very well, Aunt Judith, thank you.'

'And the Secretaryship?'

'Oh, splendid! They are so very good to me.'

'And Elizabeth?'

'We are more in love than ever.'

She nodded her head.

'That's right!'

He was the handsomest man in the room by far. But as she looked at him she caught the oddest resemblance in him to his father Francis. Just that way had his father looked at Uldale that night when he had implored her help. Her help against what? Against nightmares, ghosts, his own frustration . . .

'It's odd, isn't it,' John said, 'Walter and Uhland not coming?'

'Very wrong of them.'

'Yes, I suppose so. Have you . . . have you seen them at all?'

'No, my dear.' She smiled grimly. 'They poison our cows once and again. Walter threatened to bring an action against Bennett's boy for stealing his timber. Let him try, that's all!'

'Yes, Aunt Judith . . . You know, Elizabeth wrote a letter to Walter the other day. She thought she ought to. She heard he was ill.'

'Did she, my dear?'

'He never answered her, though.'

The time had arrived. St. Luke's, Chelsea, a church that Will had attended for many years because he liked its Gothic and the length of its sermons, was their destination—a long journey at the pace that their carriages would take them. The hearse had plumes, almost as large as palm trees. The array of carriages was magnificent. Judith accompanied Lady Herries and Ellis in the first carriage.

That is always a problem, the conversation on a funeral journey, but Lady Herries made it no problem at all. First she cried, looking out of the carriage window, pleased and satisfied with the attention that the procession was securing. Then she set about the task of convincing Judith that her life was now at an end, that she had only Ellis to live for, and that she alone, of all God's mortals, had understood Will and given him what he needed. Ellis, who was now eleven years of age, less shrivelled than he had been, but bony, horse-faced like all the Herries, with sharp eyes above a large bony nose, said nothing. Did he care at all, wondered Judith? Did he know that he had been the one comfort and pride of his father's old age? At any rate, he looked like a gentleman. It was extremely difficult for any Herries *not* to look like a gentleman, which was perhaps what was the matter with them. Judith noticed that once and again Ellis stole a sharp look at her. Of what was he thinking? Of her age, in all probability. How old she must seem to him! And yet he had been accustomed to old people! A sudden sympathy for the poor child caught her. She put out her hand and held his. The little hand, in its shiny black glove, was as cold as a sea-shell.

'Will altered,' Lady Herries was saying. 'Altered immensely in the last years. He depended upon me for everything. I say nothing against his first wife—' ('You'd better not,' thought Judith) '—but to pretend that she understood him was absurd. Poor Will! Everyone thought—even those nearest to him' (this with a glance at Judith) 'thought that his great interest was money. Erroneous—quite erroneous. If you had heard the way that he would talk late in the night——'

Judith began to be angry. But she saw her anger coming from a long way off. She had, through many years' practice, trained herself to meet it and turn it back before it reached her heart. Bad for old ladies to be angry, and in any case waste of time. But how she did hate this woman! False and greedy and sham! Poor Will! how lonely in those last years he must have been! Old pictures began to crowd up again—that familiar one when she and Will and Francis had watched the fireworks by the Lake and had prophesied about their lives. Soon she would begin to cry. She *must* not cry. She *would* not before this woman—all scent, whalebone and crêpe. She could not see her face for the heavy black veil that covered it, but she knew how small and mean those eyes were, how tight and hard the little mouth! Those were not the thoughts for a funeral, poor dear Will's funeral, so she looked out of window and saw a French poodle walking beside an old lady; he had a peaked nose, woolly wig, leggings and tail-band, and a horrible shaved, salmon-coloured body. The old lady was younger in years than Judith but not half so vigorous. She walked as though she were a hundred.

They were passing slowly through a mean, shabby street. Groups gathered, children ran, men took off their caps—for this moment the Herries dominated the scene. It did not make them proud. It was their right, now and always—so much their right that they gave it scarcely a thought. Here is a gin-palace, here a seedy French *pension*, children in torn pinafores gazing at the sweet-shop window, here a rag shop with tobacco-pipes crossed in the window and turpentine-infected bundles of firewood. Through all this, drink, poverty, childhood, sweets and tobacco and gin, Will is grandly riding for the last time!

'Without my care and affection I shudder to think what his last years would have been——'

Judith clutched the top of her cane with her two little hands. In all her seventy-nine years, with the single exception of Mrs. Ponder, she had never disliked anyone so much. She heard a sniff, a strange little strangled sniff. Ellis was crying, tears were trickling down his bony nose. She put out her arm and drew him closer to her. He stayed against her as stiff as a whalebone. But she was glad that he was crying. He *had* cared for his father then. He *had* cared! She would do something for Ellis. Ask him to Uldale, let him play with Dorothy's children . . . Then she found that she too, under her veil, was crying, and suddenly she wanted to lean forward and take Lady Herries' hand. Perhaps what the woman said was true. She *had* cared for Will—in her own peculiar undemonstrative way.

They have arrived at the church. Herries wing out of carriages like crows from a nesting-tree. But silent. Immensely solemn. How broad and deep the hat-bands on the black hats, how heavy the whiskers, the stocks, the voluminous black skirts, the umbrellas, the thick black boots! A crowd has gathered about the church-door. The church has all its attendant offices and officers—the stout, self-important beadle, the neatly grained high boxes, the three-decker pulpit, the wizen-faced pew-openers (two of them). The church is icily cold, and the hassock on which little Ellis kneels is hard as iron. He is miserable and feels a sense of aching loss, although loss of what he has really no idea.

Judith, sitting there, watching the big coffin draped in black, wondering about the pew-opener in the black bonnet who had already retired to a corner behind a pillar to count the pennies, thought that the Herries must have multiplied themselves threefold since they entered the church. She thought—for her imagination was fantastic now with weariness and chill—that the ghosts of departed Herries must have joined the living. Maybe if she looked more closely she would see poor Warren there, gazing at her as he used to do with that dog-like devotion, Francis, Jennifer, even David and Sarah, and Deborah Sunwood whom she had loved so dearly in her childhood, and Jennifer's father and mother, and poor Christabel. When you reached her age the dead and the living were all equally alive—no one was dead, no one was living.

Yes, Adam was living! He sat beside her, and sometimes he would look at her to see that all was well with her. Then, quietly, with that solid protection that she loved so in him, he put his strong arm round her: and then, to her shame, to her great disgrace, she fell fast asleep!

She woke hurriedly to find that the coffin was leaving the church and that she, with Lady Herries and Ellis, must immediately follow it. 'Oh, dear! How disgraceful!' she thought. 'I do hope that nobody saw me! 'But she walked down the church, very firmly, all the Herries' eyes upon her. She did not care for the family now. She was thinking only of Will—Will, whose last grand ceremony was over, who would do sums on paper no longer, would be denied potatoes by Robins never again; with the exit of that body out of the church one long chapter of her life as well as his was closed.

* * * * *

Later they were all in the long dining-room. The table was covered with food: drink of every kind was on the vast sideboard that looked as though it had once formed part of a great mahogany mountain and was still marked with the pickaxes of ardent climbers. Judith, dizzy with an almost drunken weariness, sat in a chair near the fireplace. All that she wanted was to go to bed; meanwhile she must listen to the Family. Inhuman furniture and human bodies, high mountains of ham and beef, chickens, pies, great loaves of bread all circled round her together. There was a marble group near the window—'Sir William Herries, Bart., and Lady Herries'—poor Christabel like an early Christian Martyr in a long icy flowing robe. The fender was of painted mahogany. There were six dessert-stands in ormolu with monkeys carrying silver nuts. On the mantelpiece were some towering vases of Copeland ware, gold on a cobalt blue ground.

'Everything is so large,' she thought, and once again had the old, old wish that her own legs were longer. Soon, however, she forgot both her weariness and the furniture in her interest in the conversation that went on around her. They had forgotten her, all save Adam and Margaret. But, more than that, they had already forgotten Will. Gone were those hushed voices, vanished that sad solemnity. As they crowded about the table, eating like wolves and drinking like the damned, their voices rose ever higher and higher, their excitement, with every moment, keener.

For now, liberated from that momentary consciousness of

poor William, aware that he was safely underground and that they could therefore move freely forward with the enterprise and energy that belonged to their Herries blood, they were discussing the War.

It was, she reflected, natural that they should do so, for only yesterday, February 27, England's ultimatum to Russia had been despatched. She herself detested war, any war, every war. She had been in Paris in 1815 and had borne Adam there, seen his father die there, suffered agonies and terrors that had affected her whole life. Why anyone should be *glad* about war she could not imagine, but not only was everyone in the room *glad*, they were *triumphant*.

She saw, too, with that detached observation that came from her mother Mirabell (who had been quite certainly not at all a Herries) that this was for them not an English war but a *Herries* war. It was the Herries who were indignant at the Massacre of Sinope, the Herries who applauded and supported every action of Lord Stratford, the Herries who had advised Lord Palmerston to resign, the Herries who thought Louis Napoleon a hero, the Herries who mocked poor Mr. Cobden and silly Mr. Bright for their support of the Peace Society.

As Judith listened she realised with every moment more fully what it was that separated her from the Herries clan and all the other clans in the world like them—what it was that had separated her father and Francis and Reuben, what it was that gave John his terrors and made little Jane walk apart from her healthy and energetic sisters. Here it was, this quality of the uneasy imagination, this desire for a beauty that was never to be caught, this consciousness, pursuing, relentless, unceasing, of a world *behind* the world. She could have got up from her chair and, stamping her cane on the floor, have cried: 'You fools! You fools! Will nothing teach you?'—but all she did was to smile a little, refuse a plate of ham courteously offered her by the Archdeacon, and consider pensively the silver monkeys with their silver nuts.

So, over Will's dead body, they sang their Song of Triumph.

Old James, whose chest was congested so that he wheezed like a harmonium, coughing over his plate of chicken, cried to anyone who might listen: 'I tell you, sir, these damned Russians must be put down.' He caught the ear of Cecily Rockage, a thin woman of sixty who greatly admired him (as she admired indeed everyone, for she was a humble woman). 'I can tell you for your private ear, my dear Cecily, that in the Club a day or two back Clarendon himself told me that in his opinion Newcastle had managed Palmerston exceedingly well, getting him to withdraw his resignation without any conditions, you know. Of course, the Radicals are disgusted, and so they may be. But in my opinion——'

'That's just what Carey says,' Cecily Rockage murmured, looking about her in her dim, peering way to see that her beloved son Roger was having plenty to eat and was thoroughly happy.

'They are important,' Judith thought. 'They are beginning to cover the country.'

In her Cumberland retreat she had not realised *how* important the Herries had grown. Once upon a time there were but a few of them, a gambler here, someone there riding a horse into a wilderness, an old man and an old woman drinking over the fire, but now the times had favoured them. They believed in England, they believed—almost terribly—in themselves. Oh! how they believed! What unquestioning confidence they had! Everything, everything was right with England from her Government to her furniture, and Judith realised, as she looked about her, as she heard Ormerod's gay laugh, and the Archdeacon's benevolence, and Stephen Newmark's solemn blessing, as she saw the women billowing in happy pride about their men, Sylvia a little elated with wine, Phyllis the proud mother, Rodney's Rebecca the eager listener, that there was something fine and grand in their faith, that these men and women *were* making England what she was, England the dominant Power of the world, the Queen of the Earth!

Only—was it worth the trouble: all this hard work, energy, faith? Queen of the Earth! *Was* that really important?

'I am really very tired, darling,' she whispered to Adam. 'I think I'll go up to bed if no one minds.'

No one minded. Earlier in the day, when William was still above ground, she was of importance. Now she was forgotten; England's Glory had taken her place.

* * * * *

Later Adam came to say good night to his mother. As he climbed the high stairs, leaving the boom and whisper of voices behind him, he felt a great longing to take his mother and Margaret, wrap them in shawls and whisk them off, with himself, to a desert island—a glorious island of burning sun, coral sand, heat and light and colour. The three of them alone, living for ever, always warm, always private, telling one another stories, and making necklaces of shells. He stopped on the landing opposite a dark engraving of Prince Albert and the Queen, and laughed. Two mice heard him laugh and, surprised out of their lives, whisked away.

He entered his mother's room carefully. There was a fire burning; the copper scuttle-scoop, the brass fender, the steel fire-irons shone resplendently. The old lady was lying, her pillows propped up behind her, apparently staring at a large oil painting entitled 'Little Black Sambo,' which showed a small black child daintily covered with the leaf of a palm tree, sitting on the sea-shore sucking his thumb while two little white girls, clad immaculately in muslin and long pantaloons, stared at him with speculation. The firelight danced on the wall; the rain beat against the pane—it was not an uncheerful scene. She did not turn her head nor move when he entered. In spite of his heavy figure he trod very gently, sat down on a chair beside the bed and waited.

Then suddenly an awful fear seized him that she was going

to die. Her face was always pale, but her small hands as they lay on the gay patchwork quilt had a marble pallor. And she lay so very still. She was, after all, of a great age. She should never have made the journey to London; this day must have been of a fearful exhaustion for her.

The thought that he might lose her at any moment now—that she might go out like a candle carelessly blown by the wind—made him catch his breath, constricted his heart. The only three people in the world whom he loved, now that Caesar Kraft was dead, were his mother and Margaret and John. His nature was deeply modest, acutely sensitive. He could not believe that men and women liked him, and it was true that, at present, very few knew him because he was so silent about himself and thought himself a useless, cumbering failure. He had had great ambitions for the good of man and they had all failed. At that moment when Kraft had fallen and died at his feet, all his hope of helping his brother man had died. He had not the confidence nor the power nor the will. He was so shy of thrusting himself forward, so shy of display or self-advertisement, that men thought him proud and arrogant. At the newspaper office, in the little Club to which he belonged, even with a man like Charles Dickens, genial, friendly, exuberant, he could not let himself go. But these two women understood him, his mother and Margaret understood him, and to lose one of them . . .

And there was one more thing. He was only half alive in London. His soul ached for Cumberland, but Margaret did not like it. She was unhappy there. Stones and clouds, clouds and stones . . .

She turned her head and saw him. She put out her hand and caught his.

'Dear me, how nice, Adam! I have been dreaming, I suppose. But I don't know. I never know now whether I am dreaming or not . . . I was very tired, I must say, but bed is most comforting. There is no place like bed. I am sure that I never expected to feel that. I used to be so very energetic. But it's my body that's tired, not my spirit . . . How disgusting old James is, eating such a lot at his age!'

They talked quietly and happily together.

'Mother,' Adam said. 'One thing I hadn't told you. Will Leathwaite is coming to London to be my servant.'

That interested her. 'Is he indeed? What a good thing! I like Will so very much.'

'Of course it's absurd that I should have a servant with the little I make. But he wants to come. He says he doesn't care what I pay him, and it will be a little piece of home.'

'A very big piece,' Judith remarked, chuckling. 'That's nice for you, dear. Are they still guzzling and drinking down there?'

'I suppose so.'

'And what a deal they talk. Chatter, chatter, chatter. They are all delighted there's a war—why, I cannot imagine.' She closed her eyes and dreamt again. She talked as though out of a dream. 'I fancied just now that God was in the room. A God a little like Georges and a little like yourself, Adam. Perhaps that's what God will be—composed of the people we love most. He was so very kind and most reassuring. I have never been a religious woman, you know, Adam. Reuben Sunwood used to be greatly disappointed with me. He was so very certain. But I suppose an old woman may be allowed her fancies. I find that everyone is very certain about God in these days. Quite different from when I was a girl. It's as though they had made Him themselves.'

She sat up, climbing up out of her dream, full of energy again.

'I do hope you are happy, dear Adam,' she said.

'Yes,' he said. 'When I am with you and Margaret, mother. But I'm terribly shy. It grows on me, I'm afraid.'

'Yes, your father was the same. But I shouldn't worry. We are different—you and I and poor John and little Jane. And the Herries family is an awkward family to be different in. All my life I have been fighting them. And now I am not fighting anyone any longer, even Walter. Too much trouble.'

She lay back again, closing her eyes.

'How lovely life is, all of it—having a baby, fighting Walter, pains and aches, food and riding up to Watendlath, poor Jennifer, the garden at Uldale, dear Adam, dear, dear Adam . . . '

She had fallen asleep. He sat there for some while watching her, then bent down and kissed, very gently, her forehead, then stole from the room.

CLIMAX TO
A LONG SEQUENCE

I. JUDITH AND WALTER

Will Leathwaite had come to say farewell. He was going at last, after six months' delay, to London to be Adam's servant. Judith was able to sit on the lawn in the September sunshine, it was so warm. The sun had the shininess of a hot sea and the lawn was like misty waters; the colours seemed gently to roll in shades of pale citron, of silver-grey, from the floor of the little Gothic temple to the walls, faintly pink, of the beloved house. Across the road, beyond the old peach-stained stones, rose the shadowed forms of the mountains, stretching themselves like great luxurious cats in the sunshine. A flight of curlews broke the pale wash of the sky, and you could feel, even though you could not see, the rough grass of the brown moorland, the icy glitter under the warm sun of the running moorland streams. Those green slopes, as yet scarcely purpled with heather, heaped up like a wave above the house answering the plaintive windy cry of the curlews.

In the middle of this peace, listening as always for her delight to the rhythm of running water, water slipping happily under the sunlight, she said good-bye to Will Leathwaite. It was as though she were sending Adam a piece of the North. Will was nearly fifty now and towered above her as he stood, his cap in his hand, staring in front of him. His colouring was very fair and there was a bald patch on the very top of his round bullet-like head. His features were stamped with simplicity, obstinacy, strength and kindliness; his cheeks were russet with good health, and there were little wrinkles at the corners of his very blue eyes that spoke of extreme good-nature. His body was large, broad, clumsy, his shoulders a little bowed. It was plain that he saw only one thing at a time and that once he had an idea in his head, nothing—no earthquake, no thunderbolt—could loosen it. He stood up in the thin Northern sunlight as though he had been created by it.

'Well, Will, you will look after Mr. Adam, will you not?'

'I will, ma'am.'

'Will you like town life, do you think? It is very different from anything you've been used to.'

'So long as Mr. Adam is satisfied, I'm ready,' he answered.

'It will be a great thing for Mr. Adam. He hasn't many friends, you know.'

'Yes. T'nature of him is slow like my own, ma'am.' Then he smiled, a delightful slow, considering smile. 'T'best way, I think, ma'am.'

The children, Amabel and Jane, ran across the lawn, laughing and shouting, with a ball. He turned and watched them with a quiet decorous pleasure.

'Write to me, Will, and tell me how you find everything.'

'Yes, ma'am. Thank you, ma'am.'

He touched his yellow forelock and stepped slowly, steadily away, moving his great body with the ease and dignity of a gentleman in his own right. She sighed happily. It would be nice for Adam to have so trustworthy a man at his side.

She was glad that she was feeling strong and vigorous and that the air was warm, because she had much to think about. Both Margaret and John were staying in the house. Adam had written to say that Margaret was tired with the London air and needed a holiday, so she had been at Uldale a week and, so far, the visit had been a great success.

John had suddenly appeared with only a telegram's warning. No one knew why he had come. Then Elizabeth had written to say that she had sent him because he could not sleep in London.

The summer had been hot: his master was in Switzerland. She herself was going to stay with the Rockages at Grosset. It was better that she and John should be apart for a while. This was sufficiently alarming, but John had said nothing until suddenly last evening, wishing Judith good night, he had told her that Elizabeth was going to have a baby.

'It's all wrong, Aunt Judith,' he burst out. 'I should not have a child.' He was quivering and his face was strained with distress.

'What nonsense!' she said. 'I never heard greater nonsense. Why, it's splendid for dear Elizabeth to have a baby.'

'It will be a coward—as my father was, as I am.'

He left the room without another word. After that she slept very badly. Dream followed dream, and every dream was filled with apprehension. Every part of her past life seemed, in her dreams, to be now connected and to point to some inevitable result. She was once again with Georges at Christabel's Ball, with Charlie Watson in Watendlath, with Warren in Paris, and someone cried in her ear: 'Had it not been thus this would never have come about.'

'But what?' she cried.

But she could not see the event. She struggled, her heart full of love and fear. Adam, approaching her, tried to speak to her but was prevented. John waved to her a despairing hand before he vanished from sight. But she could do nothing. She was held, as one is in dreams, impotent, with no power in her limbs to move. Suddenly the old cruel figure of Mrs. Ponder, Jennifer's servant, appeared. She was on her knees searching Judith's private papers.

'*Now* you will have to leave the house!' she cried, raising her malignant face.

'But I will not!' Judith answered.

And she had not. That was one thing upon which she could look back with pleasure, that in spite of all the odiousness and spying, in spite of Jennifer's lazy treachery, she had faced Mrs. Ponder to the end, seeing the hateful woman at last out of the house. But what had Mrs. Ponder to do with John? Ah, she remembered the little scene when that vile woman had thrown John's rabbit out of window. Was that, too, one link in the chain? Had every event, however slight, its inevitable result? But she must do something about John. She must not allow him to slip into tragedy as his father, Francis, had done. She must do something about John, and then she looked up to see Margaret coming across the grass towards her. She was now thirty-four years of age and a fine strongly built woman with a broad carriage, a calm open countenance and great quietness and repose in all her movements.

'She has grown,' Judith thought, 'like Adam and Adam like her, as many married people do when they have lived much together and love one another.' As she thought this a spasm of the old jealousy bit her as it might be a little animal jumping from the grass, but she brushed it away with her hand.

Margaret was wearing a simple grey muslin with panniers of white taffeta *placed* at the edges. In the bosom of her dress she had a white rose. Her dark hair was brushed back on either side, parted in the middle. She was carrying her hat in her hand. She brought peace and assurance with her.

'I like this woman,' Judith thought, as though she were seeing her for the first time. 'I am friends with her at last.'

The children had tired of their game and had run into the house. The sun was very slowly sinking, and the golden glow moved, travelling from place to place, softening the mountains with a purple flush while the sky faded slowly from bright blue into a translucent amber. Soon there will be a world of grey and silver and the hill will be dark, chill and strong. But that is not yet. The two women have half an hour to talk, the running stream the only sound in the world save their voices.

'You will not be cold, Mother?' Margaret asked, laying her broad strong hand on Judith's black dress.

'Oh no, my dear. And see that the grass is not damp for you.'

Margaret laughed. 'I have so many petticoats,' she said, 'I

could sit in a stream and not be wet.'

Her voluminous grey dress spread out on the green grass and the light transmuted it.

'Have you seen John?' Judith asked.

'No; he has been away all day,' Margaret answered, sighing. 'He seems dreadfully unhappy. He has been so for months. He would talk to Adam at one time, but lately he has avoided him too, and Adam loves him so much. Elizabeth says that he will not talk to her either.'

'Yes—he is as his father was.' Judith beat her small hands impatiently on her lap. 'I can catch hold of *nothing*.'

'Adam thinks,' Margaret began, 'that it all began from the day when someone near here told him about his father and mother. He had a shock then that has weakened him like wafer, and it is of no use to say that he *ought* not, that I would not be like that, that *I* would not let the past touch me. We are all different, and it seems to me that the Herries who *are* weak are weaker than any others, as though someone had said once: "If you are born a Herries and refuse to have common sense you shall suffer as no one else suffers. Have common sense or die." Adam has just enough common sense to save him.'

'Well, he is only half a Herries, my dear,' Judith said briskly. 'His father was only half a Herries and I am only by nature quarter a one, for my father was a wanderer and a vagabond and so was my mother. And here I am as warm and comfortable as a cat, thank goodness. It's more than I have deserved.'

Margaret hesitated. She found words no more easily than Adam, but there was something that she had been wanting for a long while to say, and now was a good time.

'Mother,' she began at last, slowly, in her deep rich voice, looking down at the grass. 'You do not hate me any longer, do you?'

'Hate you? Why, no, my child, I love you.'

'You did hate me once.'

Judith shook her head. 'No, I never hated you, of course.

How could I when Adam loved you?—and besides all my life I must confess that I have found it very difficult to hate anyone. John's mother for a while once, and a horrid servant she had. Walter, perhaps, at odd moments. No. But I was jealous of you, I must confess.'

'Yes, I knew it.' Margaret stroked the grass with her hand. 'And it made me terribly unhappy. But I have never been able to express myself. I am so very shy of feeling, and women are not supposed to have any feelings. It is not thought nice.'

'In my young day,' Judith said, nodding her head vigorously, 'women had plenty of feeling and showed it. I don't know what's come over the world. Women are not supposed to have legs any more, and children are found in gooseberry bushes. Stuff!'

'And you are not jealous any more?'

'No. All my fires have died down. I sit and look on. But I love you, my dear. I do indeed. Adam has been the passion of all my life since my husband died, but a time came when I saw that someone else must do the things for him that I had done—and more things than I could ever do. How fortunate I have been that it was a woman like you, not one of these coarse painted creatures or one of these niminy-piminies all affectation, or one of those good perfect creatures like the woman in Mr. Dickens' *David Copperfield*. What was her name? Agnes. But, of course, Adam would have chosen well. He would have had a whipping from me if he had not.'

'I have wanted to tell you,' Margaret said slowly, 'how grateful I am to you, how dearly I love you. I cannot say things, but I thought that once I must tell you——'

She leant up and put her arms around Judith. The two women kissed, and Judith laid her hand for a moment on Margaret's broad forehead.

'God bless you and keep you in all His ways, dear daughter. And now,' she went on quite sharply, 'I must go in. The sun will soon be down. How nice! I shall read Mrs. Gaskell's *Cranford* over the fire. They say it is all about old ladies who are frightened by cows—like Mrs. Potter at Threlkeld. Give me your arm, my dear. My right foot has gone fast asleep.'

* * * * *

A little later she was sitting in front of the parlour fire, her feet propped up on a worsted stool, a thick woollen shawl round her shoulders, and large spectacles on the end of her small nose. Her trouble was that her nose was *too* small. The spectacles *would* slip off! It was only of late that her eyes had begun to fail her. She was reading *Cranford* with many chuckles.

'How true this is! We are just the same here round Uldale. "*In the first place, Cranford is in possession of the Amazons—all the holders of houses, above a certain rent, are women. If a married couple come to settle in the town, somehow the gentleman disappears; he is either fairly frightened to death by being the only man in the Cranford evening parties, or he is accounted for by being with his regiment, his ship, or closely engaged in business all the week in the great neighbouring commercial town of Drumble, distant only twenty miles on a railroad. In short, whatever does become of the gentlemen, they are not at Cranford; . . . but every man cannot be a surgeon. For keeping the trim gardens full of choice flowers without a weed to speck them; for frightening away little boys who look wistfully at the said flowers through the railings; for rushing out at the geese that occasionally venture into the gardens if the gates are left open; for deciding all questions of literature and politics without troubling themselves with unnecessary reasons or arguments; for obtaining clear and correct knowledge of everybody's affairs in the parish; for keeping their neat maidservants in admirable order; for kindness (somewhat dictatorial) to the poor, and real tender good offices to each other whenever they are in distress—the ladies of Cranford are quite sufficient.*"'

Judith laid the book down on her lap and considered.

'How very excellent! That is exactly Miss Poole and Janet and

Mary Darlington and Mrs. Withers and Mrs. Spooner. We are a world of women. Why? Why is Dorothy so important? She is not very clever nor is she at all beautiful, but she has a kind of kingdom. Now I *never* had a kingdom——'

The door opened. The little maid Eliza, her face twisted from its rosy simplicity with surprise, horror, alarm, excitement and general sense of drama, whispered something.

'What do you say, Eliza?' Judith asked, turning round and pushing her spectacles back on to her nose.

'Sir Walter Herries, ma'am.'

Walter! Her book dropped to the floor. She stayed, for a moment, listening as though she expected to hear some dreadful sound, but all that came to her was the cheerful shrill voice of someone singing in the kitchen. Then, sitting up very straight, she said:

'Ask Sir Walter to come in.'

A moment later he was standing beside the sofa, very stiffly bowing. He was dressed for riding and carried his hat in his hand. His hair was grey now (he was sixty-two) and he was clean-shaven, which was most unusual and gave him an odd babyish appearance. His red face was purple-veined, but he was not so stout as when Judith had last seen him. He was untidy, as though he had no one to look after him. Judith, against her wish, felt sorry for him.

'Well, Walter, how are you? Won't you sit down? Been poisoning any of our cows lately? How are the little Peaches? Humphrey, the stable-man, found one of them in our gooseberry bushes not long ago.'

Walter sat down. He spread his legs, looked gravely at her; she noticed that his mouth was not very steady and that his hands shook.

'You are looking well, Judith,' he said.

'I am very well, thank you.' She took off her spectacles.

She did not intend that he should say that her sight was going. Then sharply, as though to convey to him that she had not all day to waste:

'Why am I honoured?'

'A damned pretty place you've got,' he said, looking about him. 'Everything very fresh and charming.'

'Well—well. That's not what you've come to say.'

'No, it isn't. Sharp as ever you were!'

'Nor have you come to pay me compliments. Do you mind that window? If so, pray close it.' (For the window was open. Judith, unlike her contemporaries, loved fresh air.)

'No matter, thank you.' He hummed and hawed, then began a long rambling statement.

She could not make out what he was after. He had a lot to say about the past. Was it not foolish that they had wasted so much of their lives in quarrelling? He had been a young hot-headed fool, had done many things that he now regretted. Looking back, his ill-temper seemed to him now to have been very aimless, motiveless. But it was his father who, from the time he was a baby, had persuaded him that his mother had been insulted, and then Jennifer and Francis—well, Judith would agree that their conduct . . .

'I will agree to nothing,' Judith said.

But he did not appear to hear her. He went rambling on. He was afraid that he'd taught Uhland the same doctrine. He saw now what a mistake he had made. He saw now that he had been mistaken in many things.

'Well, I'm glad of that anyway,' said Judith. 'But there is no use to go back on the past. If you are asking me to forget and forgive, Walter, frankly I cannot. Too much harm has been done—Francis, Jennifer, Reuben, and Jennifer's children. My own life, too . . .' She coughed. She could not but be sorry for him a little. There were spots on his waistcoat, and his stock was badly tied. 'But what do you *want*, Walter? What have you come here for?'

He hesitated, looked at her as though he were begging her to help him. Then he said an extraordinary thing.

'Hatred, Judith, is a very rare quality in men. One seldom meets it.'

She did not know what to say.

'Very rare,' she answered drily.

'I have never hated you. My mother never hated anybody. Jennifer never hated anyone. You yourself have never hated.'

'Well?'

'What I intend to say is—I am clumsy at expressing myself—but out of all this past quarrelling, not very real, you understand, there has come much unhappiness.' He paused, rubbed his cheek with his hand. 'I myself am not a happy man. All my own fault, I admit it. I have lost my daughter quite through my own fault. There is something bad in our blood which, if it is indulged——'

He stared at her in quite a fuddled way as though he had been drinking, which it was likely that he had. But what was his meaning? What was his intention? For what had he come? She remembered the scene in this very room when she had slapped his face. He was not the kind of man either to condone or forget.

'Hatred, Judith,—real hatred—is a sort of madness.'

'Well?'

He went on again, finding words very difficult.

'You see . . . you know . . . you must understand . . . Upon my word, I am extremely clumsy—you must forgive me—but my boy—Uhland——'

'Yes—Uhland?' she said, more softly, because now, as always when he spoke of his son, there was a new and moving note in his voice.

'I had great hopes for Uhland. I may be a man who has made a mess of his life. When I am sober I am ready to make such an admission—but Uhland was to be different. He had a heavy handicap' (his voice was gathering ardour now that Uhland was his topic) 'his lameness—the sense that he was unlike the others. And then his mother was not strong, and I was not the wisest father. I was anxious to indulge him, too anxious perhaps, and he was unusual, unlike other boys——'

He paused again, and gently, looking at him almost as though she were his friend, Judith said:

'Yes, Walter, I understand. In that at least I have always understood you.'

Encouraged, he went on:

'I am another man when I am in my cups. I will be quite honest with you. I have spoiled many things by my follies, but Uhland I have always kept apart. I saw from the beginning that he was by himself, alone. He has never cared for anyone except your Adam. He has never, I fear, cared in the least for myself, and the knowledge that he did not made me wilder, wilder than perhaps I would otherwise have been. But what I would point out is that all our quarrels, yours and mine and our parents' before us—the events in the life of your own father so many years ago—have found a kind of resting-place in poor Uhland's nature. He was born with a grudge and all his instincts have been twisted. In a fashion he is a scapegoat for the errors of the rest of us.' He stopped once more, wiped his mouth with his hand.

She was, in spite of herself, deeply touched. This was a different Walter from any that she had ever seen. She felt behind his precise, artificial, clumsy speech almost an agony of apprehension, and her own apprehension that she had been so conscious of all day rose to meet his.

She almost cried out:

'Oh, Walter, what is it? What has happened?'

Enemies though they had been all their lives, they were now almost allies.

He went on, staring at her as though that assisted him.

'Uhland has grown ever more strange. Our house is not an agreeable place. I will not pretend that it is agreeable, but of late Uhland's conduct has frightened me greatly——'

'Uhland's conduct?'

'Yes.' He found now the greatest difficulty in choosing his words. 'He is, I fear, most unhappy, but he will speak to no one. He shuts himself in his room. He walks over the house.

113

The servants are afraid to remain where he is. And for myself, I think he hates me.'

She said nothing. He went on more swiftly.

'But it is not of myself that I wanted to speak to you. I came . . . I came because——' He said urgently, leaning towards her: 'You have John staying with you?'

'Yes,' she said.

'You know, of course, that from the time of his childhood Uhland has always especially hated John.'

'Yes,' she said.

'It has been a sort of madness in him. I fear, I greatly fear that I was myself originally responsible for that. It seemed to me in those days unfair—unfair that John should be so handsome while my son——'

'Yes, I know, I know,' Judith said quickly.

'Then I implore you, Judith—I beg of you—send John back to London immediately. Immediately. Uhland knows that he is here. He has, during the last week, been very odd in his behaviour. He talks—he was talking last night—as though that old grudge had reached some kind of climax. We are, all of us, responsible for the past, I more than any, and if anything were to happen——'

'But what could happen?'

'There have been many acts of violence in our family,' he went on. 'It is as though there were an element of violence in our blood . . . No. This is perhaps foolish, unreal. We are, I suppose, the most sober and sensible family in England, and just because of that when we are not sensible——'

He got up and she could see that he was greatly agitated.

'Never mind our family,' he said. 'Damn the family! This is urgent, personal to ourselves. I implore you, send John back to London to-morrow.'

She nodded. She looked up and gave him her hand for the first time for many years.

'Yes, Walter. You are right. Thank you for coming. It could

not have been easy. John shall return to London. In fact this is no new thing. I have been aware of it for many years. John has been under some kind of shadow all his life, as his father was before him. I will see that he goes to-morrow.'

Walter held her hand, looked at her, bowed, then said almost defiantly:

'I have not come here to confess my sins, Judith. I shall be to-morrow as I was yesterday. I shall find myself a fool, I don't doubt, for coming to visit you. But for an hour at least I see sense. Good-bye. I can find my own way out.'

* * * * *

Judith sat on, her hands folded in front of her, looking into the fire, wondering as to which would be the best way to persuade John. This, had she known it, was a waste of energy, for John had heard everything, standing among some flower-pots, his hands scratched unwittingly by the nails of rose-briars fastened to the wall. He had returned from his ride and had seen Walter's horse tied to the gate. A quarter of an hour before he had seen both Walter and Uhland riding down the road from Ireby. He had come round the wing of the house towards the front door when, very clearly through the open window, he had heard the words in Walter's thick ropy voice: 'You know, of course, that from the time of his childhood Uhland has always especially hated John.'

So he stayed there, his body pressed against the wall, his eyes staring out into a sky that swam in frosty September light with one blazing diamond star. He heard everything. He heard Walter say: 'If anything were to happen——', and Judith later: 'Yes, Walter. You are right . . . John has been under some kind of shadow . . .'

So it had come to this! 'Under some kind of shadow! Under some kind of shadow.' And they planned to smuggle him away to London lest anything should happen . . . anything should happen.

He went back to the stable and got out his horse Barnabas. A small terrier, very devoted to him, Mumps by name, little more than a puppy, came rushing across the cobbles when he saw Barnabas let out again. He had thought that the fun was over for the day, but apparently it was not. John went quickly by the gate that bordered the orchard. This brought him straight into the village street and he knew that he would be now ahead of Walter. The sun was just sinking, and hills, fields, pasture and stream lay in a mirror of light; you could fancy that if you swung, lazily, god-like in the sky, you would look down and see your Olympian features reflected in this sea of gold. Almost at once, just out of the village, at the dip in the road before it turned left to Peterfield, he found Uhland, waiting for his father, while his horse cropped the grass.

He knew that he had very little time before Walter came up, and, guiding his horse quite close to Uhland's, he said softly:

'I think that we must end this. It has gone on long enough— and by ourselves where no one can disturb us.'

It was as though because of their connection through so many years they had grown to understand one another like the closest and dearest friends, for Uhland did not appear startled, nor did he ask 'End what?' or 'What has been long enough?' He simply drew his horse a little away from John's and nodded his head.

'Well—if you wish it. As to ending it——' Then he said sharply in his cold rather thin voice: 'What is it you want?'

'That we should have it out, the two of us, once and for all—alone.'

They both heard the tap-tap of a horse on the road. It would be, likely, Walter.

'Yes, I agree.'

They were like two schoolboys arranging a rendezvous for a fight; from the beginning there had been something childlike and something eternal too in their relationship.

Uhland went on, as though to himself: 'Yes, I have had enough of this. I must get rid of this.' He said coldly: 'Well—

what do you propose?'

'To-morrow. I will meet you somewhere.'

Uhland paused. They could see Walter coming down the hill.

'Yes. What do you say to the house opposite Calva in Skiddaw Forest? To-morrow afternoon at four.'

'Yes. I'll be there.'

John turned his horse and a moment later passed Walter without a word or any greeting.

CLIMAX TO
A LONG SEQUENCE

II. SKIDDAW FOREST

On the following day, Uhland, waking very early in his tower, lighted his candle and began to read in a brown stubby volume. It was a translation of Vasari's *Lives of the Italian Painters.* After a while he came to this: '*Whereupon having taken this buckler with him to Florence without telling Leonardo whose it was, Ser Piero asked him to paint something upon it. Leonardo having taken one day this buckler in his hands, and seeing it twisted, ill-made and clumsy, straightened it by the fire, and having given it to a turner, from the rough and clumsy thing that it was, caused it to be made smooth and equal; and afterwards, having covered it with gesso and having prepared it after his own method, he began to think of what he might paint on it, that should be able to terrify all who should come upon it, producing the same effect as once did the head of Medusa. Leonardo therefore, to this end, carried to a room into which no one entered save himself, slow-worms, lizards, field-crickets, snakes, moths, grasshoppers, bats and other kinds of such-like animals, out of the number of which, variously put together, he evolved a most horrible and terrifying creature, which poisoned the air with its breath, and turned it into flame; and he represented it coming out of a dark and jagged rock, belching poison from its open throat, and fire from its eyes, and smoke from its nostrils, in so strange a manner that it seemed altogether a monstrous and horrible thing; and such pains did he take in executing it, that although the smell of the dead animals in the room was very noisome, it was not perceived by Leonardo, so great was the passion that he bore towards his art . . . '*

'So great was the passion that he bore towards his art,' Uhland repeated to himself and closed the book and blew out his candle to let the moth-like colour of the early morning strengthen in the room. So it was to be a great artist, such would he have done had he had the opportunity and the power. He had neither, only the longing. He had done nothing with his life, which now was over. He was certain that it was over and that this was the last time that he would see the early light spread about the room. But to-day he would release something from within himself that had been there since he was conceived. If he could live after that was released—ah! then perhaps he would become an artist.

He always had a headache now when he woke in the morning, a pain that pressed on his forehead like iron, and his eyes for the first hour were misted so that he had read the Vasari with great difficulty, and his lame leg hurt him sorely. But this morning when later he bathed and dressed he felt a glow, a warmth, a deep and burning excitement. That miserable coward had at last faced up to him. He would see him standing in front of him. They would be alone, removed from all the world. He would strike him in the face and see what he would do. This was the moment for which all his life he had been longing, to revenge himself upon the whole world for making him twisted and a cripple, all those people who had watched him as he walked, all the kind Herries relations who had despised and pitied him. To-day he would revenge himself upon all his family—the crowd of them, so pleased with themselves and their strong bodies and the children they had begotten, so scornful of anyone unlike themselves . . . and the fellow had dared—had dared—to marry his sister!

All morning he limped about the house thinking of a thousand absurd things—how his grandfather Will, now, Heaven be praised, dust and ashes, had looked at him across the dining-table in Hill Street as though he said: 'This poor misshapen creature—how can he be *my* grandson?' How Amery had invited him to ride with him, adding: 'You *can* ride, can't you?' How he had slipped on the stair at the Fortress, and Archdeacon Rodney's young son had muttered (but Uhland had heard him): 'Poor devil!' How Sylvia had looked at his leg and then blushed when he caught her—all, all, all pitying him, despising him, scorning him! Leonardo had filled his room with newts and toads and lizards and from them had constructed a figure so horrible . . . There was power! Ah! there was power indeed! And to-day he would be revenged on them all. He would make that figure, seen all his days as the type of all that he himself despised and hated, cringe and shake and fall—a strange fire ran in his veins so that he felt almost as though his limp were gone and he as strong as any of them.

With the exception of his own place and the servants' quarters, his father's room was the only one in all the Fortress now that was cared for. The rest was tumbling to ruin. The walls were strong, but dust lay everywhere, and all the other rooms were damp-smelling and foetid. But he went everywhere as though he were saying good-bye to it all, a happy, glad good-bye. They called it the Fortress first in admiration, now in jest and mockery. So with this damned country: they thought that they were building a Fortress, eaten up with conceit they were, but one day it would be like this house, rotten and a jest to all the world. Pity he couldn't live to see that day . . .

Later, with his gun over his shoulder, he went in to say farewell to his father.

Sir Walter Herries, Bart., was playing backgammon with his housekeeper, a thin painted woman called Mrs. Throstle. Mrs. Throstle enjoyed bright colours and was expecting friends from Keswick, so she was dressed in a worsted poplin of bright yellow and wore the most elaborate sleeves in the prevailing fashion, ruffed muslin with coloured ribbons at the wrist. She had coral bracelets. Over all this her sharp face peered anxiously at the board, for she was a mean woman, and they were playing for high stakes. Or so they seemed to her. But she always came out right in the end, because if she won she won, and if she lost she went through Herries' pockets at night after he slept and took what there was. But there was not much these days because everything was going to rack and ruin.

She was discontented, too, because Herries would not drink at present. He was sober and cross and peevish. He had struck her last night for saying that Uhland was a lame duck. She hated Uhland, as indeed did all the servants.

Walter, very soberly dressed, gave only half his attention to the game. He had been worried for weeks about Uhland, and his visit to Judith yesterday had done little to relieve him. Indeed, it had added to his discontent, for the Uldale house had looked so bright and shining. He had liked Judith too, that neat, capable, strong old woman, and all the silly enmity over which he had spent so much of his energy seemed to have blown into thin air. But enmity, hatred and all uncharitableness are never wasted, as he was to find out before many days were over.

He looked up at the door opening and hungered with love for his son. He saw that he was dressed for going out and had a gun over his shoulder; at once he was alarmed with a strange interior fear, the room seemed to fill with smoke before his eyes; his hand trembled, and he knocked the backgammon board off the table.

'There now!' said Mrs. Throstle. 'And I was winning too!'

'Clear out!' said Uhland sharply. 'I want to speak to my father.'

Mrs. Throstle rose, trembling. She was terrified of Uhland; one look at his contemptuous face and she shook all over. She gathered herself together, touched her coral bracelets indignantly, tossed her head and went. The round backgammon counters lay on the dirty carpet, but Walter stared at his son.

'Going out?' he asked.

'Yes, Father.'

'Shooting?'

'Maybe.'

Walter rose heavily, stretched his arms and yawned.

'I think I'll come too. Fresh air will do me good.'

'No, Father. I'm going alone to-day.'

Uhland looked at his father and felt, to his own surprise, a certain tenderness. He could remember—he did at this moment vividly remember—old, old days at Westaways when everything had been so rich, many people about, the house shining with colour, and his father bursting with health and self-satisfaction. But his father had wasted himself on emptiness, had let everything dribble through his hands like grain falling idly through the air. Grain falling—it lay now, in layers of dust, thick upon the floor. They had done nothing with their lives, either of them, and he saw for perhaps the first time that if he had returned some of his father's love things might have been otherwise. His father had had no return for either his love or his hate. A dry, wasted man ...

He did what of his own free will he had never done before—limped up and put his hand on his father's shoulder.

'Better I go alone,' he said. 'I'm in a sulky temper.'

Walter was so deeply moved by his son's gesture that he said angrily: 'You are always in a sulky temper.' He leaned his big heavy body towards his son's. He touched the gun.

'Going shooting?' he asked again.

'Maybe,' answered Uhland. 'Good-bye then.' He moved towards the door.

'When are you returning?'

'Oh, any time. Don't count on it,' and he went out, his backward glance from the door showing him his father bending his great stern towards the floor that he might pick up the backgammon counters.

* * * * *

He rode down the hill and then slowly along the ridge of the Fell towards Peter's House. He had plenty of time to be at Skiddaw House by four. It was a day in which everything seemed restrained, as though the sun were longing to break out but was held back by a strong hand. He passed an orchard where the pear trees were a bright yellow, and then in the distance he saw how the yellow hills were already autumnal, the heather resting on them in a rosy shadow from place to place. He had always been alive to beauty, although he resented it often because he felt that it, like the rest of the world, mocked at any cripple; now to-day the shadowed sun, the bright yellow of the leaves, the distant hills, were all part of his own purpose. They knew what would happen, and it was strange to him that they should all be able to see ahead of him, certain of the event before it had occurred.

'Everything is arranged then,' he thought. 'It is quite settled what I shall do. Every past incident contributes to this. I am what I have been made. And yet I could turn back if I wished. I would cheat God if God there be. I am greater than God, because now if I wished I could ride up Ireby Hill again and go in quietly and play backgammon with my father.' He stayed his horse for a moment, and had the fantastic thought that 'just to show them' he would ride back. But he could not; of course, he could not. Old 'Rogue' Herries; his father's words when he was very little: 'Don't you hate that conceited young cousin of yours, Uhland?'; Rodney's young son muttering 'Poor devil!' . . . no, fragment after fragment had with infinite patience been brought together, all that he might ride to Skiddaw House to meet John Herries. And once again at the thought of that meeting his blood was hot.

* * * * *

Jane Bellairs was the only one in the house to see John go. She had two great devotions in her life—one for her great-great-aunt Judith, the other for her uncle John. She eliminated, as did her brothers and sisters, the degrees of greatness from Judith, and called her quite simply (and very proudly) 'my aunt.'

'But, dear, she cannot be your aunt,' tiresome Mrs. Munberry in Keswick had years ago said to her. 'She is far too elderly. You mean great-aunt.'

But Jane had simply thought Mrs. Munberry a foolish old witch, with her grey hair and sharp eyebrows. For all the children Judith was ageless. She had lived, of course, for ever, and would live for ever. She was like God, only more easily loved. But Uncle John was Jane's especial property. When he was absent in London, Jane not only prayed for him night and morning but also talked to him when she was alone, asked him whether she could fetch him anything, and thought about him before she slept, because she was certain that he was lonely. This idea that he must be lonely had come to her at a very early age when, rocking her doll by the fire in the parlour, she had looked up and seen him staring out of window.

She had given him her doll to care for, and also, although he did not perhaps know it, herself at the same time. The others laughed at her for her devotion, especially Veronica, who was a good hearty girl with no nonsense about her. But Jane did not mind when they laughed. She had long grown accustomed to having her own private life, a life that no one understood but Aunt Judith. Her mother least of all, for Dorothy would perpetually be saying: 'Dreaming again, Jane. Where's your work, child?' and Jane would pick up her piece of worsted on which she was embroidering a red rose or a ship with sails and, with a small sigh that nobody heard, pricking her forefinger and biting her lip, would set about it. She was, however, as Dorothy frequently declared, the easiest of all the children, for when she lost her temper she was quiet, not noisy like the others, and could amuse herself quite happily all the day long. Although she was nearly fourteen years of age now she was very slight and small.

'That child will never grow,' Dorothy exclaimed, and Judith replied: 'My dear, don't be foolish. I'm eighty and have never grown an inch since I was eight.'

And now she was the only one of all the family to see John go. All morning she had been painting a picture. This was her favourite pursuit, and here too the others laughed at her because she did not paint easy things like cottages and cows and the sun, very red with rays like wires, setting on a mountain, but things much too difficult for her, like the Queen in her Palace, the whale swallowing Jonah, and Noah seeing dry land. Yesterday on her walk she had seen some horses drinking from a pond, and this morning she had been drawing a great white horse swimming. Beyond the pond there were mountains, and for some reason (she did not know why) it was winter and the pond was black with ice. She covered the pond with purple paint. This painting was to be for John and, before dinner, she looked for him everywhere to give it to him. She found him coming from the stable, leading his horse Barnabas, and the small dog Mumps was with him. He smiled when he saw the little girl in her pink bonnet. Her dress, with its double skirt and fan-shaped corsage, made her quaint while on the other children it seemed quite natural. It was as though she were in fancy-dress.

'Hullo, Janey!' he said.

'Are you going to ride?'

'Yes.' He put his arm around her and kissed her.

'I've been up to Auntie's room and she's sleeping yet.'

Judith had not been well that morning and when she was not well all the house was quieter. Jane considered him. Should she show him her painting? He was busy because he was going riding.

Yes, she would. She *must* show him.

'I've done a painting and it's for you.'

'Let's see.' He bent down, while Barnabas and Mumps stood patiently waiting. All he saw was that some kind of animal was sitting on a floor of purple paint. But he guessed that the animal was a horse.

'That's a grand horse,' he said, pinching her cheek.

'Yes, and it's swimming in a pond all frozen with ice, and then it will ride up the mountain.'

'What a splendid horse! Is that for me?'

'Yes.'

He kissed her and held her for a moment close to him. Then

he put the painting very carefully in his riding-coat pocket.

'Good-bye, my darling.'

'Where are you riding to?'

'Oh, only a little way.'

'Will you be back before I go to bed?'

'Yes, sweetheart.'

'Will you read *Nicholas Nickleby*?'

'Yes, if there's time enough.'

She stood in the gateway waving to him until he was out of sight. At the corner before the houses of the village hid him he turned on his horse and waved back to her. She ran into the house and wondered what there would be for dinner.

* * * * *

When, beyond the village, he was riding by Langlands he noticed an orchard and how yellow the leaves of the pear trees were. That made his heart beat, and the thick grass under the trees, the spikes of some of the sharper grasses, were already brown at the tips. There had been frost every morning of late. Then, as he turned towards Over Water, he realised that Mumps was running most confidently at his side, his little black eyes sparkling, his mouth open, stopping for quick snatched moments to sniff at a smell, his whole person expressing extreme content and happiness.

He must not have Mumps with him on this ride, so he pulled Barnabas up and said sharply:

'Go home, Mumps! Go home!'

Mumps stopped and looked at him as though he had just received the surprise of his life, as though he could not, in fact, believe his ears.

'Go home, Mumps! I mean it.' And he flourished his whip. Barnabas also exchanged a look with Mumps, saying: 'Yes. This is genuine.'

Mumps ran forward, pretending that he had discovered so

rich a smell that John must be pleased, and being pleased, would soften his heart. Then he stood, with one paw raised, intently listening. Then when that was of no avail he sat down and scratched his underparts. Then, that accomplished, he looked up at John pleadingly. All of no value. The stern order was repeated, so, after one more imploring stare, he surrendered and slunk down the road, his tail between his legs. Round the bend, he reconsidered the matter. He saw that his master was slowly riding on, so, slowly, he followed, maintaining a tactful distance.

When John had Over Water on his right and was approaching Orthwaite Hall, he heard a bell ringing, the kind of bell that rings from the belfry of a manor-house calling the servants to a meal. It came beautifully through the honey-misted air. 'It is as though,' he thought, 'some giant were holding back the sun.' Thin patches of sunlight lay on the fields, and on the hills the heather spread in clouds of rosy shadow. All was dim, and the little sheet of water was like a buckler on whose surface someone had been breathing, silver under cobweb, without bounds, raised in air above the soil.

'It's funny,' he thought. 'Aunt Judith has always said that she could see Over Water from the windows of the house. Of course she could not. She must have the neck of a giraffe.' And yet he himself had often thought that he saw Over Water from those windows—a mirage. But how friendly a little piece of water it was! All his life he had loved it—his whole life long.

Then, with a sharp stab of anticipation, he was aware of what he was about. Somewhere already in this misty countryside Uhland Herries was riding. They might meet on the way. He was somewhere near, shadow behind shadow—and the bell, still ringing, echoed in the air: 'This—Time—is—the—Last. This—Time—is—the—Last.' He was conscious of an awful temptation to turn back. Perspiration beaded his forehead. Why should he go on—to his death maybe? This lovely land that all his life he had adored; why should everything have been spoilt for him so long by one person to whom he had never done any harm? No.

He must recognise that Uhland was only a symbol. Life would have been for him always a place of fears and terrors even though Uhland had never been born. What did the ordinary man—men like Garth and Uncle Will and old James—know about such a life, know how it was to wake in the night because you heard a sound, to turn in the street and look back over your shoulder, to watch a picture lest it should drop from the wall, to hear a mouse scratch in the wainscot so that your heart thumped, to expect with every post bad news, to fight, all your life long, shadows, shadows, shadows . . .?

Oh, to be done with it, to throw fear out of your heart like a dirty rag, and then perhaps he would be like Adam, so quiet and sure, a little ironical about life but never afraid of it, with a heart so unalarmed that it could spend itself on love of others. He thought then that he heard a horse's hoofs knocking on the road behind him, and he turned sharply. But there was no one. The bell had ceased to ring. At last, to-day, it would be over. He would settle with Uhland for ever. *That* fear at least should be killed.

He rode on, past Peter's House, up on to the path across the Fell leading to the road that climbed under Dead Crag up steeply past Dash Waterfall. On his right were the Caldbeck Fells humped against the sky and stained now with every colour, the rose and purple of the heather, silver grey where the grass was thin, a bright and burning green of fields between walls, and down the side of one fell splashes of white quartz ran like spilt milk.

He looked about him to see whether anywhere there was another rider. He could see for a great distance now, to the right to the sweep of the Bassenthwaite Woods, to the left where the dark wine-stained sea of heather, grass and bare soil ran in a flood to the feet of the Caldbeck Fells, breaking, as it began to climb, into patches of field, a farm with a white wall, cows and sheep grazing. But no human being moved in all the landscape. Under Dead Crag, before he began to climb, he thought of the ravens for which the Crag was famous. He looked up to where the jagged edge cut the sky, and two birds, as though in answer to a call, floated out like black leaves, circled silently in the still air. The only sound was made by the Dash that tumbled with fierce gestures from the height above. It was full and strong, which was strange when there had been so little rain.

He was sorry that he had not been able to see Aunt Judith before he left, and yet it was perhaps as well. She had sent down word that she would like to see him in her room after her three o'clock dinner, and of course he knew what it was that she wanted—to persuade him at once to return to London. He wondered what reason she would have given: something about Elizabeth, he supposed, and at the thought of Elizabeth his heart seemed to stop its beat. If he did not return from this ride . . . if he did not return . . . Never to see her again . . . He climbed the steep road.

* * * * *

When Uhland reached Orthwaite Hall and looked across Over Water the bell had ceased to ring. Then suddenly it began again, softly, steadily, persistently: 'Going—going—gone . . . '

Uhland looked at the Tarn, and then turning to the hills saw a thick tangle of mist like the ends of a woman's mantilla stray loosely over the tops. If the mists were coming down that would be serious. Many a man had been lost for hours between Calva and Skiddaw when the mist fell. The House would be hard to find, and, as though he had made a bet with some contestant, he was pledged to reach the place by four. The sun that had been shining so warmly when John half an hour before had been there, now was withdrawing. The light still lay in patches on the fields and the moor; down the Caldbeck Fells the shadow slipped, leaving the glow bare behind it as the skirts of a woman might fall.

But Uhland was aware now of a great impatience. Nothing

should cheat him of this meeting. He longed to have John close to him, to see him flinch, above all to put to the final test all that those years and years of shadowing had anticipated. He urged on his horse, hearing the bell follow him as he rode up towards Dead Crag and the shining tumble of the Dash. He looked up at the steep road that ran up under the Crag and saw three birds circling like black leaves above the line of rock.

'Those must be ravens,' he thought, and remembered how, when he was a very small child, he had heard men tell of the ravens that haunted Dead Crag, and how, years ago, after the 'Forty-Five Rebellion,' they had flown above the corpses of men, crying and calling in a vindictive triumph. He looked about him, down to the Bassenthwaite Woods that were now black like iron, then across to the sequence of fell-tops, but he could see no other rider.

'Is he behind me or before me?' he thought, and again that hot excitement as of wine pouring through his body exalted him. He felt a sort of grandeur that he had never known before. His lameness did not handicap him now. He was as good as anyone, and better, for he was on his way to dominate and conquer that supercilious, disdainful fool whom he would have down on his knees before the day was over.

But when he had almost reached the top of the road and the waters of the Dash were loud in his ears, he saw that the mist was beginning to pour like smoke from behind the hills. It came in eddies and whirls of movement although there was no wind. Greedily it ate up the farms, the fields, rose for a moment as though beaten by the sun, then fell again. When he was actually on the height he saw it advancing from every side. He pushed his horse forward and a moment later felt its cold fingers on his cheek. The whole world was blotted out.

* * * * *

130

The first thing that John heard when he started away from the Dash was the eager, excited breathing of a dog. He looked back and saw Mumps, his tongue out, happily racing towards him. The dog knew that now there was nothing to be done. Too late now to order him to go back. He felt a strange comfort as though this were a sign from Fell House.

He was soon lost in the spaces of Skiddaw Forest. There was no forest here; there had never perhaps been trees; the name was used in the old Scottish hunting sense of a place for game. John knew slightly General Sir Henry Wyndham whose land this was, and his keeper Donald Grant, who lived at the House, his present destination. The House was one of the loneliest dwelling-places in all the British Isles, the only building from Threlkeld to Dash. John knew also that, at this moment, Grant was in Scotland, his family with him. He had heard only the week before that the House was closed.

He could not anywhere in the whole world be more alone than he now was. A chill, in contrast with the warm valley below, was in the air, and the patches of heather, the sharp green of the grass where the bilberries had been, the grey boulders, all had lost the brilliance of their colour. He looked back once before he went on and saw the Solway lit with a shaft of sunlight that glittered and trembled under the line of Criffel and his companions. He was leaving that shining world and with every step of his horse was advancing into danger. On his right the flanks of Skiddaw began to extend and he could see the cairn that marked its peak against the sky. Calva was on his left. A moment later he saw the bounds of his journey's end, on the right Lonskill Crag, and on the left, extraordinarily black and angry, the sharp line of Foul Crag, Blencathra's edge. Between them, far away, in sunlight like the smile of another world, was the ridge of Helvellyn. Sunlight behind him, sunlight before him, but his own country dark, shadowed, without form, guarded by hostile crags. He knew that under Lonskill was the House, and at the thought that he was now so near to it a shudder that he could not control took him.

Soon he would come to the Caldew river, and, crossing that, he would move into his fate, a fate that had been advancing upon him since the day of his birth and before whose menace he had been always helpless.

It was then that he noticed the mist. It came on the right from Skiddaw, on the left from Calva. It tossed and rolled, crept almost to his feet. Was Uhland in front of him or behind? And, even as he asked himself, the whole world was blotted out.

CLIMAX TO
A LONG SEQUENCE

III. IN A DARK HOUSE

When Uhland felt the wet mist close in he was conscious of an almost desperate irritation. He was of so morbid and irritable a temperament that he had always been unusually susceptible to weather, to places, to trees and hills. He did not, as did John and Adam, feel that this country was in any case beloved, that, whatever it chose to do, it was to be accepted and welcomed as an ally. It had seemed to him all his life bent on his frustration, and, like others of his kind, he discounted lovely days but recorded all the disappointments and, as they seemed to him, the malignancies.

The fellow, he now contemptuously thought, would take this mist as an excuse: 'I could not find the House. When the mist came on I turned back'—and it seemed to Uhland that there would never be an opportunity again. If he missed this he missed his power over the man. He would hate him no longer but would henceforth hate himself, and, more than that, be choked till he died with this passion of which he could not rid himself.

He rode a little way and could not tell whether he were going forward or back. He had been often in such mists before, but had never been baffled and blinded as he now was, and, as always when it was damp, his lame leg began to ache, as angry as he was at this frustration.

He stopped to see whether he could hear the Caldew. It must be somewhere near, but he had never in his life known such a silence as had now fastened about him. The absence of any sound or movement closed in upon his ears like the beat of a drum. He moved on again, and as one often does in mist, thought that someone was close behind him. It would be just like that fellow to stab or shoot him in the back, an easy way once and for all to rid himself of his enemy, and, although Uhland was not afraid, it would be the last fitting irony of the injustice that he had all his life suffered under to be stabbed in the dark and dropped into space like carrion. He listened. Behind him something moved, pebbles were displaced, or there was a soft crunching of the grass.

'Herries, are you there?' he cried, and his own voice, the voice that he had always despised and hated, came back clogged with wet mist. 'Herries, are you there?'

The scene was fantastic, for at his feet and just in front of him little fragments of ground were exposed, were closed, and were exposed again. The mist immediately surrounding him was so thick that it was like fog and so wetting that he was already soaked through and through his clothes. It cleared at the top of Calva, and the round shoulder of the hill sprang out like a live thing on his left. It was so clear that he could see the patches of bright green and bare boulders lit with a chill iridescence as though in moonlight. Calva frowned at him, then raced under mist again, leaving only a fragment like a bare arm lying nonchalantly in space.

His horse struck pebbles, and then he heard the slow stealthy murmur of the Caldew. Well, he was moving forward, for not far beyond was the rising hill on which the House stood. Behind the House was a wood, and if Wyndham's keeper should be at home they could finish this affair among the trees. No one would see them on such a day.

There should be a little wooden bridge over the Caldew. He pulled in his horse, jumped off and peered around him. Now, if John Herries was really behind him, would be the time for him to come at him, and perhaps they would struggle there where they stood and end it once and for all.

He spoke again: 'Now, Herries, I'm on foot . . . Are you there?' There was no answer. If Herries *were* there he was sitting motionless on his horse, and Uhland fancied that he could *see* a horse there in the mist, and on it a gigantic figure, motionless, waiting. He stumbled and almost fell over the rocks into the stream. With an oath he pulled himself back and began to find his way along the bank. Now he had lost the horse, for the mist was around him like a wall, but the horse whinnied, and at the same moment he discovered the wooden bridge. He went back and led the horse safely across. Now he knew where he was, for at once the ground began to rise. He came to a gate, opened it, leading the horse through.

It was at this point that it was exactly as though someone stood in his path. For a moment he *could* not move, and he felt as though a great hand were pressed against his chest.

'Let me through, damn you,' he said, and stumbled and fell. His lame leg often failed him, but now it was over a rock that he had fallen. He had cut his hand, and his body pressed into the wet soil, just as though someone were on his back holding him down. The soil was filthy, soaking, deep in mire. His cheeks were muddy and the knees of his breeches heavy with water. He pushed backwards and was suddenly freed, as light as air, the mist thinning so that, as he got on to his feet again, he saw the House only a little way above him, swimming in air like a ship in the sea. He moved forward, leading the horse, unlatched the gate, passed through a small tangled garden of cabbages and currant bushes. His feet grated on a gravel path, and he saw that in one of the windows of the House a candle was shining.

* * * * *

Uhland's thought had not been far out. John, as the mist enfolded him, had felt stir in him that weak boneless animal, so long so hated a companion, who whimpered: 'Here is a way of escape. You can say that you were lost, had to turn back.' He stopped his horse and stayed there, listening and considering. At once an odd memory came to him, odd because he had not thought of it for years, and now it touched him as though there were suddenly a warm, strong hand on his shoulder. He remembered how once, when they were little children, Aunt Judith had told them a story of their grandfather, David Herries; how he had run away with their grandmother, years, years ago when she was a girl, and fleeing with her from Wasdale up Stye Head had been pursued by an uncle or someone of the kind— and then by the Tarn, in swirling mist, Grandfather David and the uncle had fought while Grandmother Herries watched, and Grandfather David had killed the other. It had sounded then a grand story, like a story out of a book, unrelated in any way to the warm fires and old arm-chairs of Uldale. Now it was real. The mist that at this moment swirled about him had swirled about David Herries then, and David Herries had won. It was almost as though someone rode beside him, smiling at him as they went. So then he rode forward, but nevertheless the memory of an old story could not kill the struggle within himself. 'Turn back! Turn back!' the boneless creature said. 'You know that you are afraid. You know that when you are face to face with him that old terror will be too strong for you, and at the first word from that voice you'll run.'

And the other companion at his side seemed to whisper: 'Go on! You have nothing to fear. All your life you have been fighting shadows, and to-day at last you will discover what shadows they have been.'

Yes, that was true. It had begun in his very babyhood when in his cot he had seen how the reflections from the fire had made fearful shapes on the wall. Then his nurse, old Mrs. Ponder, how he had shivered as he heard her heavy step on the stair, and her voice as she said, 'Now, Mr. John. I dare you to move!' and he had stood, his heart thumping, transfixed; then the day when she had thrown his rabbit out of window. The day, too, when he had first seen Uhland, Uhland limping down the Keswick street, and that pale face had turned towards him and something in him had bent down and hidden away. The evening, too, when with Adam he had seen Walter sitting his horse, silently, on the hill. But Walter Herries had never meant much to him; the dread of his whole life had been concentrated in Uhland, and it was of no use for others to say, 'But this is phantasmal. There is no reality here.' For his father, too, had found the real world a prison, and, year after year, had allowed his mother to be mistress . . .

He threw up his head. 'I am revenging my father,' he thought, 'and my son, when he is born, will be fine if I am brave now.' For he felt, as many men with imagination have done, that with the vision they are given they can see that no men are apart, that History has no Time, and that all souls struggle for victory together.

So, greatly strengthened and as though suddenly he were seeing his destiny for the first time, he pushed through the mist as someone in a cellar pushes through wet cobwebs.

He now heard the running of the Caldew, and at the same moment thought that Uhland was just behind him. He stopped Barnabas and was aware of a multitude of noises. There was the murmur of the stream, the thin breathing of the little dog, and, it seemed to him, a multitude of whispering voices. Also dimly there sounded music in the air. Since he was a boy he had known that hereabouts was the place in Cumberland for finding the Musical Stones—certain stones and boulders which, when cut, gave out musical notes when you struck them. At the Museum in Keswick there was a good set of these stones, and Mr. Cunningham at Caldbeck had a set on which he and his sons played many tunes. They beat them with a leather-covered hammer. Often as children Adam and he had come up to these parts and searched for them, and he had once had a stone that gave out a great ringing sound like an organ note. He had heard that in ancient days the Romans here had used them in their houses for gongs. This memory came to him now and pleased him. There was certainly some kind of music in the air. He waited. Maybe Uhland was also there waiting, but it was hard to see in the mist. If so this would be a good place to end it.

At last he said out loud: 'Is anyone there?' and again, 'Who's there?' But there was no answer.

He dismounted from Barnabas to find the wooden bridge across the stream, and at once Mumps found it for him, going in front of him and looking back to see whether he were following. After that, it was easy to mount the rising ground, and soon, leading Barnabas, he passed through the gate, along the little garden, and up to the door of the House. The mist floated about the walls in smoking wreaths. He could see dimly the wood. He found, as he had expected, that the door was locked. There was no one there. He went to the window on the right of the door and to his surprise it was slightly open. Then he tied Barnabas to the garden-wall, pushed up the lower pane and easily vaulted into the room. It was so dark that for a while he stood there accustoming his eyes to it, and the mist poured in through the open window as though all the outer world were on fire. After a time he stumbled about, knocking his knees against a chair and the edge of a table. He found the fireplace, and on the mantel his hand closed on a candle. He struck a match from a box in his inner pocket and lit it. He waited, listening. He opened the door and went into the passage.

'Is anyone in the house?' he called.

There was no answer. He heard some hens running. Then he went back into the room, and almost immediately after there were steps on the pebble path outside.

Standing back against the mantel he heard the steps go to the door, he heard the lock shaken, then back to the window, a pause, and Uhland had climbed into the room.

As they faced one another the room at once became of great importance, and when Uhland closed the window behind him the candle, that had been blowing wildly, steadied itself and seemed to watch thereafter with a piercing eye. There was very little in the room. A deal table, and on it a bright green mat and some pallid wax fruit under a dusty glass cover. On the mantelpiece were two large china dogs with bright red spots like a rash on their bodies, a clock that pointed to five minutes to four although it was not going. In the corner there was a grandfather clock that leaned forward drunkenly, on the walls a large highly-coloured print of the opening of the Great Exhibition and an engraving of the Duke of Wellington covered with yellow damp-spots. There was a wheel-back arm-chair with a patchwork cushion and in the corner a child's rocking-horse. In another corner there was a spinning-wheel. The floor was of brick. In the window there was a dead plant in a pot.

Uhland set his gun against the wall and sat down. His leg hurt him confoundedly. He rested his arms on the table, and stared at John. As he looked he was reassured. He had thought that perhaps now when they met at last he would find that there was nothing to be done, nothing to be said. All this chase and pursuit for so long had been a chimaera. He would not be rid of the mad impatience and restlessness in his heart by any contact with this poor fool. He would just look at him contemptuously and let him go. But it was not so. The very sight of John started his rage. John had taken off his riding-coat. He wore a narrow blue tie over which his shirt collar was folded, and his shirt had an inset-breast of the finest linen. He wore a waistcoat of dark blue patterned with tiny dark red flowers. He was not a dandy, but everything about him was exquisitely clean and well-fitting. His features, pale, keen, sensitive, gave him an air of great aloofness and high breeding without, however, any conceit or arrogance, and he seemed, in some way, in spite of his years, still a boy—for his figure was slim as a boy's and his air as delicate and untouched by life as a boy's of seventeen might be.

Uhland knew that he himself was muddied, wet, and that his hand was stained with blood. There was mud on his cheek. Yes, he would spoil some of that beauty and aloofness before he left that house, and once again the blood began to beat, hot and insistent, in his veins.

He tapped with his fingers on the bare table.

'I'm here,' he said. 'What do you want to say?'

'I want to say this.' John found to his disgust that his hands were trembling. He held them tight against his sides. 'I want to ask you a question. Why for years now have you followed me—in London, here in Cumberland—everywhere? I have never done you any harm that I know.'

'I fancy,' said Uhland, 'that I may go where I please. Who says that I have been following you?'

'You know that you have, and that you have done it because it offends me. It must cease from now on.'

Uhland paused. Then he repeated softly: 'It must cease . . . But why?'

'Because I say that it must.'

'You talk like a schoolboy,' Uhland replied. 'We are grown men. Of course I go where I please and do what I please. You are a coward, you know. You are the son of a coward, you were born a coward, you will be a coward until you die. Otherwise you would have faced up to me years ago.'

'No,' said John. 'I could not because you are a cripple.'

At that word Uhland's fingers ceased to beat on the table. A little shiver ran through his body.

'That makes a good excuse for you,' he said at last quietly. 'Now listen to me for a moment. It is quite true that I have always hated you. Your family is a disgrace. Your father allowed your mother to be a man's mistress for many years. I daresay the fellow paid him to keep quiet. Then your father was challenged to a duel and ran away. Then, because there was nothing else for him to do, he shot himself in London. Well, it has not been nice for the rest of us to have such relations at our very gates. It was very painful for my father. From the very first you gave yourself airs, you mocked at my lameness, you spread scandal about my father's manner of life. You were always—although you did nothing but walk about Keswick in your grand clothes—a vain fool. The very sight of you was an irritation, but an irritation that pleased me because you were, and are, so miserable a coward that a very look from me made you quake. And then you had the damned impertinence to marry my sister.'

'We will leave her out of this,' John said.

'Oh no, we will not. That is a score that I have been waiting a long while to pay . . . Why, look!' he suddenly cried, with a mocking laugh. 'You are shaking now!'

'Yes,' John said, and he drew a little kitchen chair to the table and sat down. 'I will sit down. I am trembling, as you say, but that is because you always affect me so. A sort of disgust that I cannot control.'

But, as he spoke, he knew that it was more than disgust, it was fear from the disgust. Now if ever was the moment to which all his life had led. If he failed now, everything would be lost—his father, Elizabeth, their child. And he did not know that it would not be lost, for something within him—the traitor to himself that had been born with him—was urging him to run. 'Run! Run! Climb out of that window and run for your life.' His limbs were moving with a power that was not his own at all. He had to hold his feet against the brick floor. The fight within himself was so arduous that he could scarcely think of, or even see, Uhland. It was something more than Uhland, and something worse.

'If I move I'm lost,' he thought. He fixed his eyes on the pallid, deathly wax fruit. He fixed his eyes but he could not fix his heart. Ah, if only he could rise and throw himself on Uhland, that would be an escape as well as the other, but the man was a cripple, a damned cripple——

'I see,' said Uhland. 'I fill you with disgust. But it's yourself you're disgusted with. Because I found you out years ago. You've cheated the others, who think you a mighty fine fellow. I've shown you to yourself. Every time that I've been near you you've felt what you are. You have at least the grace to be ashamed . . . '

Then an odd thing occurred. Uhland stretched one of his arms out along the table, and his hand lay there, almost under

John's eyes. It was a lean white hand, the knuckles red, and on the back of it thin hairs faintly yellow. The nails were long and dead. The hand seemed to John to curve and twist on the table, like a thing in a nightmare, and, when it was close to him, he was suddenly strengthened. Was it that hand that he had always been fearing? Was this the ghost? Was this all? His eyes cleared. The room was formed and plain. The spinning-wheel was real, the Duke looked at him with grave, stern eyes. His legs were no longer trembling.

'Well,' he said in a clear strong voice that had no quaver, 'whatever the past has been, I am afraid of you no longer. You should have done more with your life than to spend it over one man, in especial if he's the poor creature you think me. I am afraid of you no more, so you can follow me no more. Nor shall you insult my father and mother again. You may be lame or not lame. After those insults your lameness is of no account, and before we leave this house you are down on your knees—on your knees. When you please. Choose your time. We can be here all night if you wish.'

Would his courage last? Was this a true lasting thing that he felt? For the first time he looked Uhland straight in the face.

Uhland withdrew his hand. He now was trembling, but with anger, the choking wild anger that so constantly came to him from the sense of his own ostracism. It was as though, at John's repeated 'lameness,' all the world laughed, and a little crowd of sympathisers inside himself massed together and begged him to avenge them.

'You coward!' he cried in that odd shrill voice that should have been, if fate had been fair, rich, deep and generous. 'Why, you are afraid of your own shadow! You shall stay there—do you hear?—and you shall not move! Stay there without moving until I bid you, and then it is you who shall be on your knees, and beg and pray, and beg——' He half rose, leaning forward on his arms, his thin muddied face staring into John's.

And John could not move. He would have risen and he

could not. Something within him was melting, loosening . . . in another moment it would be too late for ever.

It seemed that an hour passed. It was only a moment. Then, his head bent as though he were putting forth all his strength, at the instant when his power seemed gone, he pushed over the table.

It fell with a crash, the wax fruit with it, and the glass shattering on the brick floor.

His eyes shining, he stood back to the wall. He would not touch the man! He would not touch the man! But all fear was gone. He was strong with his whole strength——

'Come on, Uhland. Down!' he cried, laughing. 'I won't touch you. On your knees and then off with you. Back home——'

He saw Uhland stand. He marked every part of him, his hair thin on the top, the mud on his cheek, his damp stock, the round buttons of his coat. He saw Uhland take his gun from the wall. He thought,'Elizabeth!' Uhland fired.

* * * * *

At the noise the little dog on the path outside began to bark. He barked running up and down outside the closed door. Then he began to whimper, again and again scratching at the door. The room was filled with smoke and mist. Slowly it cleared. Uhland stood for a long while with the gun in his hand, but at last he leant it carefully against the wall and went over to the empty fireplace. He bent down and looked at the body. John lay there, his face hidden in his arm. Very gently Uhland turned him over, unfastened his waistcoat, felt for his heart. John was dead.

'Well, that is the end,' he thought.

He felt no relief; only an increased grudge of injustice. He felt sick, too, with that accustomed nausea that had so often attacked him. He sat in the wheel-back chair, licking his dry lips with his tongue. The whole aim of his life was gone, and what it had been he had now no idea. He was sorry for no one but himself, and even about himself he felt now a bitter, savage irony. All those days and years for nothing. He had had a right to be in a rage, but how purposeless rage was! He was the victim of the grossest injustice, but what a poor, muddy, shabby victim! He felt an especial rage with his nausea. To be sick now would be the last indignity. But he would not be sick. At least he could prevent that. And this was all the long pursuit had come to . . . nothing . . . sickness . . . and his hand was bleeding again. He looked about the room. He knew what he wanted. A piece of paper. He got up and limped here and there, almost stumbling once over John's body. There was no paper anywhere, and why to God was that dog outside whimpering? He blundered against the clock, and it lurched as though it tapped him on the shoulder. No paper anywhere. He knelt down, with difficulty, because his knees were stiff. Then he got up again. No, he would try first the riding-coat. In the inside pocket he found a paper and drew it out. It was once folded. What the devil was this? a crude painting, a sea of purple and some animal, a horse, a cow. But the reverse side was blank.

He sat down at the table and, taking a pencil from his pocket, wrote:

To all whom it may concern.

This is to say that John Herries of Fell House, Uldale, and I, Uhland Herries of High Ireby, met here at Skiddaw House by appointment. After a discussion we quarrelled, and I shot John Herries, he being undefended. After, I shot myself.

Uhland Herries.
September 23, 1854.

He laid the paper on the table, then unfastened his stock and laid that beside it.

He went to his gun, loaded it, placed the muzzle inside his mouth and fired.

PART IV

MOTHER AND SON

BIRTH OF VANESSA

'Eighty-five! Is she, by God!' said Captain O'Brien, putting up his eye-glass.

'Yes,' said Veronica, smiling. 'But you mustn't swear. You swear dreadfully, Captain O'Brien, and I don't think it's at all nice.'

'Do I, by God?' said the Captain. 'I mean to say, Miss Veronica, I'd no idea . . . 'pon my soul, I must get a hold on myself. Is it our turn? Damn the game! Always getting in the way . . . What I mean to say——'

'Yes, I suppose it is our turn. What do you think, Captain O'Brien? Shall we have war with France? Louis Napoleon is *very* dangerous, isn't he? But of course we've got the Volunteers.'

'Ho! the Volunteers!' shouted the Captain in derision. 'The Volunteers! That's good. Damned useful they'll be. But I tell you what, Miss Veronica.' But it *was* his turn. Amabel, who was playing (most reluctantly) with the Reverend Mr. Hall, a bony, black-bearded clergyman from Penrith, had missed her hoop.

The occasion was a garden-party given by 'Madame' to her friends and neighbours on an afternoon of the summer of '59. Most fortunately it was a lovely day—fortunate because in August you never could be sure, the most treacherous month of the year in these districts. But to-day was lovely indeed, as Mrs. O'Brien said over and over to anyone who would listen to her. 'Most lovely! Most fortunate! Who would have supposed? And such a lovely garden!'

The old house was gentle and benign under the small ivory clouds that floated in shreds and patches on the summer sky. The lawn was a smooth stainless green. The part of it that spread under the cherry-coloured wall had been laid out for croquet.

Near the Gothic temple a tent had been set up for tea; the servants were coming backwards and forwards from the house.

Chairs were arranged under the wing of the house near the croquet-lawn, and in the shade of the trees by the Temple there were more chairs, two or three, placed beside Madame's. To these, people were led up in turns to talk to her—'Not for too long, you understand,' Dorothy explained. 'So as not to tire her, you know. But she enjoys everything. She was never better in her life. Yes, eighty-four last Christmas. Most extraordinary! But she has always enjoyed the best of health! She does delight in a talk! Everything interests her!'

'A very pretty scene!' Judith thought happily. Although she was in the shade, the sun warmed her through the trees. She was wearing the black dress with the white lace at her throat and wrists that had been for so many years now her costume, but around her shoulders was the beautiful Cashmere shawl that Adam had given to her last Christmas, a shawl light, soft and bright, embroidered in silk with a heavy knotted silk fringe at its edge. On her head she wore a cap of white lace and, every once and again, she held over her head a black parasol. Against her chair rested her famous cane. Her face now had the pallor of ivory, but the cheeks were stouter than they used to be. Her eyes shone with a startling brilliance. She missed nothing. On her breast she wore a locket that contained Adam's picture. 'A very pretty scene!' but nevertheless she thought the crinolines ridiculous. They were not, perhaps, quite so absurd for young girls like Veronica and Jane, but Dorothy now! Yes, Dorothy was monstrous. She was a woman of fifty-one and had grown very stout. Her crinoline was vast and very heavy. It was of Chinese gauze and had twelve flounces. Her sleeves also had many flounces, and they looked as though a number of horns had been stuck one within another. Her bertha had ruches, embroideries in profusion, and she wore on her shoulders a Scottish plaid which the Empress Eugénie had made the fashion after her visit to her maternal home. A graceful woman might do something with all this—but a woman of Dorothy's figure! And when she moved in the house all the furniture was in constant peril!

The girls were pretty; at any rate Veronica in white, with her bonnet far back on her head, showing her really beautiful dark hair almost to the crown; and darling Jane, so fair, so slender, although no one thought her pretty in comparison with Veronica, was, in Judith's eyes, bewitching.

As the figures moved across the lawn, in their wide swinging dresses, white, rose and blue, the sun shining down so benevolently, no sounds save the click of the mallets and the balls, the murmur of voices, the clink of the china as the servants (Lucy and Emily—*such* good girls) arranged the tea, Judith felt a deep, satisfying content. The only thing was that Margaret was not so well. Her child was due very soon now, but Doctor Bettany said not for a week, he thought. But she had not been well this morning. Adam was anxious. Strange to have, after all these years of marriage, their first child! And Margaret was not so young any longer.

Ah, here was that tiresome, silly Mrs. Osmaston. Mrs. Osmaston was thin, withered and weary. She had had so many children that nothing remained of her but a bone or two, a nervous cough and an interest in gossip. She was neither kind nor unkind, discreet nor indiscreet. The only two facts certain about her were—one, that she had been a mother many many times, and two, that she was exceedingly stupid. She was afraid of Judith, who, she was sure, mocked at her when her back was turned. No one in the world ought to be both so old and so vigorous. There she was, a magazine on her lap, and she had been reading without glasses.

'Oh, what is it you have been reading, dear Madame Paris?' Mrs. Osmaston asked, seating herself with care in the garden chair. Her crinoline was of the latest fashion, that is, its steel hoops were lowered so that they did not begin immediately below the bodice but only at the knees, and in this way the dress fitted round the hips and only began to grow wider below the knees. This scarcely suited Mrs. Osmaston's thin figure, but she was very proud of it and thought herself smarter than any other woman present. And *what* she thought of Dorothy Bellairs! Oh, but she would entertain the family circle when she arrived home this evening! (She could not see, fortunately, the Shade of her great-grandmother-in-law, who, a swearing, horsy, good-natured Ghost, looked out from the Gothic Temple, remembering how she once had drunk tea on this very lawn, and wondered, in her hearty indecent fashion, at this ridiculous Ghost of a descendant-in-law.)

'Yes, what is it you have been reading, dear Madame Paris?'

'Interesting,' said Judith, picking up the *Quarterly Review.* 'There are some comments on Mr. Tennyson's *Idylls of the King.*' She read: '*The chastity and moral elevation of this volume, its essential and profound though not didactic Christianity, are such as perhaps cannot be matched throughout the circle of English literature in conjunction with an equal power.*' She paused and gave Mrs. Osmaston a sharp look. Then she continued, a little lower down:

'*He has had to tread upon ground which must have been slippery for any foot but his. We are far from knowing that either Lancelot or Guinevere would have been safe even for mature readers, were it not for the instinctive purity of his mind and the high skill of his management . . .*'

Judith looked Mrs. Osmaston full in the face and casting the *Quarterly* upon the grass, repeated: 'Chastity and moral elevation! Stuff! Did you ever hear such humbug and hypocritical nonsense, Mrs. Osmaston?'

Mrs. Osmaston, who had just been preparing to say that she thought it one of the most beautiful critical utterances she had ever listened to, sent her Adam's apple up and down in so swift a necessity for reversal of judgment. She gasped like a fish suddenly raised from the water.

'Oh yes . . . indeed, yes . . . very absurd. I have not yet read Mr. Tennyson's *Idylls.*'

Judith wished that she had not been so impulsive. The last thing that she wished was to make Mrs. Osmaston unhappy. The older she grew the greater need she saw in the world for general kindness and charity, and the harder she found it to suffer fools gladly. That was why life was always difficult, amusing and exciting.

She knew that now, simply because of this little incident, Mrs. Osmaston would go away and talk, like a hen scratching in a back-yard. Judith could hear her. 'Not softened in the least by that awful tragedy of five years ago. You would have thought that such a *terrible* thing . . . '

Not softened! Judith's heart and gaze left the garden and the figures moving across the lawn, and she was caught up again, as she so constantly was, into that dreadful afternoon and evening . . . Yes, five years ago . . . when, lying in bed, she had heard first that John had ridden out, no one knew whither, and how then, with a frightened pathetic foreboding, she had lain there listening to every sound, and at last she could bear it no longer but had got up and come downstairs. And she and Dorothy had sat there, waiting, listening. Then the opening of the gate, the rap on the door, the news that his body was outside . . .

And after that, old though she was, she had held everything together. There had been a wild, mad, hysterical letter from Walter; Elizabeth had come, a lovely fragile ghost, and in February of the next year had borne a boy, here at Fell House, whom she had named Benjamin. There had been Jane, too, who for a while had seemed to be mentally unsettled. The poor child had fancied that there was something that she might have done, might have held him there, prevented him from riding . . .

The excitement in the neighbourhood had gone on and on and on . . . It was only, they all said, what they might have expected. There had always been a strain of madness in the Herries. Didn't old Herries in the eighteenth century sell his mistress at a Fair, kill his first wife with unkindness, and marry a gipsy for his second? Hadn't Madame always been crazy, clever though she was? And all the sorry, stale business of Francis and Jennifer came up again, over and over, and then all the drunkenness and evil living at the Fortress, and Uhland of course was mad—everyone knew—but to shoot his cousin who was defenceless, there on Skiddaw, miles from anywhere—and the little dog had been whimpering like a human being when they found the bodies.

But somehow, by sheer strength of personality, Judith had dominated it all and beaten it down. Now at last the full value and force of her character was seen. For one thing so many of them liked her. She had done so many kindnesses, she was no respecter of persons, the same to one as to another, and yet she was dignified and commanding. She was the more commanding in that she no longer went about, and only visitors to the house saw her, and not many of *them*. But when they had visited her they always returned home with wonderful stories. Everyone obeyed her as though she were a General in an army, and yet everyone loved her. She thought of everyone and everything, and yet could rap you over the knuckles with a sharp word. She didn't care who it was that she rapped. The whole County was proud of her, admired her, talked of her without end, told every sort of tale about her. She was a legend.

And here was Adam coming towards them! She knew everything that was passing through his mind. She saw his quick glance at Mrs. Osmaston, his loving look at herself. She smiled back, saying at the same time: 'Well, to my mind there's far too much nowadays of making small children feel that they're born in sin. Do not you think so, Mrs. Osmaston?' She liked the beard that he had grown in the last year. It suited him; he looked well, solid and muscular, not stout as she had once feared that he would be. How dearly she loved the half-humorous half-cynical brightness of his eyes. He suffered fools no more gladly than she—in fact, she thought comfortably, they grew more like one another every day. But she could not persuade him to wear his party clothes. He would wear his sack coat and round hard hat, and the checks of his trousers were so *very* pronounced. All his clothes hung about him loosely, and there was Captain O'Brien with his great moustaches and tightly fitting fawn trousers so *extremely* elegant. She did hope that Veronica would not fall in love with him nor with young Mr. Eustace, the curate, who with his fluffy hair and surprised gaze resembled a chicken just out of the egg!

'How do you do, Mr. Paris?' said Mrs. Osmaston a little stiffly; she was no more comfortable with the son than she was with the mother. And why did he wear such very ill-fitting clothes? He also wrote for the London magazines, which made him very dangerous, for you never knew that he might not put you into something!

Adam sat very close to his mother, his big square body protecting her tiny one. He exchanged, in a whisper, one quick word with her.

'I have just been in to see Margaret, Mother. She really is not so well. Do you think that I should send James for Bettany? He is over at Greystoke, you know.'

She nodded her head.

'Yes, dear, I should. Just as well.'

Adam bowed to Mrs. Osmaston (sarcastically, she felt) and strode towards the house.

Ah, now, Judith thought, they are moving to the tent for tea. She had an impulse of impatience to run across the lawn that she might see that everything was right. But of course she could run no longer. But Lucy was a *good* girl and Dorothy had sense. And one good thing—she could now rid herself of Mrs. Osmaston.

'Tea, Mrs. Osmaston,' she said. 'I see they are going to the tent for tea. Mr. Hattick,' she cried, her voice wonderfully sweet and clear, 'will you take Mrs. Osmaston to tea?'

Mr. Hattick was a stout red-faced manufacturer from Birmingham who had bought a place on Bassenthwaite Lake, a very common man. The County was still undecided whether to cut him or no, but he had been kind to Judith and presented

Timothy with a fine bay, and if he was kind that was enough. And now it would be good for Mrs. Osmaston that she should be taken into tea by Mr. Hattick.

She was watching them moving across the lawn with much amusement when an awful thing occurred. Amabel suddenly appeared, and in her voice were the notes of excited surprise and exceeding pleasure.

'Oh, Aunt Judith—what do you think? Miss Martineau has come!'

Harriet Martineau! Of all appalling things! And now, when she was already a little tired and was thinking that she would go in presently and see how Margaret was . . .

Alas, Judith did not care for Miss Martineau, and had often congratulated herself that Ambleside was far distant from Uldale. She recognised that she was exceedingly wise, immensely learned, and possibly the greatest woman now alive in England, but Judith did not care for so much learning. She had never herself had much education, she was not a Positivist, she detested the thought of mesmerism, and she envied the way in which Miss Martineau milked her own cows and ploughed her own fields. Moreover, Miss Martineau never ceased to talk— about Comte, about America, about her marvellous Cure, about her weak heart, about her pigs and cows, about her novels (Judith thought *Deerbrook* a very silly book), about Mr. Atkinson, about her *Guide to the Lakes*. Miss Martineau spoke always of the Lakes as though they were her own creation and would not have existed had it not been for her. She *patronised* the Lakes. In addition Harriet was all for women taking man's place; Judith did not see how they could possibly do so. They were very nice as they were: pretty Veronica twining Captain O'Brien around her little finger, and Margaret indoors about to present the world with a dear little baby. Harriet wanted women 'to rise up and take their proper place in the world.' As though, Judith thought indignantly, they had not their proper place already. And this was all very bad for Amabel, who said that she did not care for men and would like to be in Parliament. In Parliament! Women in Parliament! You might as well make doctors of them. Amabel adored Harriet Martineau, and was always hoping that she would be invited to stay at the Knoll.

But worst of all was Harriet's trumpet. Judith had, in spite of herself, a little scorn for deaf people because her own hearing was so extremely good. But a trumpet . . .! And Miss Martineau was so proud of it. Moreover, in a most irritating fashion, she would remove it in the middle of one of Judith's sentences. Malicious people said that she always did that if she thought that something was coming that she did not wish to hear. However, here she was—in no time at all she was striding towards them. 'Is it a woman or a man,' an old lady once said of her to William Howitt, 'or what sort of animal is it? said I to myself; there she came—stride, stride, stride—great heavy shoes, stout leather leggings on, and a knapsack on her back—they say she mows her own grass, and digs her own cabbages and taturs!'

She was decently enough dressed to-day, with no ridiculous crinoline (that is in her favour, thought Judith), large boots certainly, and a thing like a Scotsman's bonnet on her head, and one of the fashionable Scottish plaids over her shoulders. In her right hand she held her trumpet; Amabel, listening to her every word, was beside her, and Adam, coming from the house, was not far behind.

'Well, well, well, Madame Paris, and how are you? I have been for the night in Caldbeck and am to be this evening in Keswick. I am giving an address on Domestic Economy as you have doubtless seen by the papers. And I have brought you my *Letters on the Laws of Man's Nature and Development*. It was published as far back as '51, you know, but Mrs. Leeds told me that she was sure that you had not read it, and I thought that I would have your opinion. And here are some peaches straight from my garden. I said to myself, "Madame Paris shall have those peaches because she is a woman I admire. She should have been a man and represented us in Parliament."'

'Indeed I should not,' Judith answered indignantly, and then discovering that she was speaking into the air when she should have spoken into the trumpet, seized that instrument and shouted down into it: 'Indeed I would not have been a man for any money!'

'Would you not?' said Miss Martineau complacently and with a look of kindness at the old lady (for she liked those bright eyes and that independence, for she was as good-hearted and free of meanness as she was egoistic and free of sensitiveness). 'Well, I had no notion that you had a party.'

'Yes,' said Judith, catching the trumpet again. 'They are in the tent having tea. You had better go and have some.'

'Indeed I will not,' said Harriet, laughing. 'I have come to see *you* and I cannot stop more than a moment. My enlargement of the heart, you know, forbids me to stay long on a visit. Old Colonel Albany in Keswick insists on a talk. He says that he has several criticisms to make on my *Suggestions for the Future Government of India.* Criticism indeed! I shall like to hear what he has to say. All these old Colonels are the same. It has needed a woman to tell them the truth about their own affairs.' She kicked one leg in front of her and thrust her trumpet almost into Judith's eye.

'Now tell me what *you* think about India.'

'I, my dear?' Judith shook her head. 'Why, I have no thoughts about anything. I live in the past and not the sort of past that interests *you*, Miss Martineau. My past is all pincushions, lavender-water and parasols. I assure you there was never anyone with less opinions.'

'Don't you believe her, Miss Martineau,' said Adam, laughing. 'She is a mountain of opinions. There never was anyone with so many.'

But Miss Martineau had caught only the word 'mountain.'

'Mountain! That's what I said to Coleridge once——'

'Ah, you knew Coleridge,' Adam said eagerly. She caught that and it pleased her.

'Yes. I talked to him only once. Not that I can say that his career is anything but a warning. All that transcendental conversation, you know, was all nonsense. Nothing but nonsense——'

'Yes, but,' Adam shouted down the trumpet, 'what was he like? Tell us what he was like.'

'Oh, very fine—a perfect picture of an old poet. Neatly dressed in black as I remember, with perfectly white hair. And what I especially recollect was his underlip that quivered with a very touching expression of weakness—very touching indeed. The face was neither thin nor pale as I remember it, but the eyes! No, I must declare, although in my opinion his poetry will not be remembered and as to his philosophy—I cannot express the scorn I have for his philosophy—but I never *saw* such eyes. The *glitter*! The amazing *glitter*, and shining so that one was really afraid to look at them! All the same, the glitter was only opium, you know, nothing but opium.'

'The father of my little Hartley,' Judith thought, smiling to herself—and in some strange way now, at this moment, while the late afternoon sun threw long purple shadows over the grass, and, behind the temple, the trees, whose leaves were tenderly touched with orange, massed like a solid cloud against the line of faint and silver hills, the thick dreaming figure of the poet seemed to wander towards them across the lawn.

The girls, moving like dancers, came smiling from the tent. In the clear still air the rich unctuous voice of the Reverend Mr. Hall could be heard saying: 'Ah, but, Miss Bellairs, you misunderstand me. It is against the rule of my cloth to have a bet with you, but nevertheless . . . '

'Mr. Coleridge! Mr. Coleridge!' Adam could have cried. 'Come and sit with us and we will assure you that your poetry will never die!'

But Miss Martineau must be moving on. She was pleased that that sensible-looking child (Amabel) gazed at her with such evident devotion. Maybe she would invite her to stay at the Knoll. Her heart was warm and kind, and it was not *her* fault that she knew such a terrible deal about so many very different things. But, as she wished good-bye to Judith, she thought: 'I should like to become an old lady like that.' Then she stamped away to her carriage.

She was hardly gone when Will Leathwaite appeared and, standing solidly and quietly beside Adam, said: 'The doctor is come, Mr. Adam.'

'I'll be with you,' said Judith.

He gave her his arm. Veronica came running towards them.

'Aunt Judith, can I help you?'

'No, my dear, thank you. It is growing chilly for me. You must be hostess, Veronica, my dear.'

They went into the house together, she leaning on Adam's arm, Will Leathwaite following them like a bodyguard. It was splendid to have Leathwaite: he was as obstinate as he was devoted, as scornful of what he did not understand as he was faithful to all that he loved. He loved Adam and all that Adam comprehended, but only *because* Adam comprehended.

'Will tolerates me,' Judith said to Adam, laughing.

'Will loves you.'

'Only because I'm your mother.'

'And what better reason could he have, pray?'

Stopping for a moment in the hall she said: 'Ah, there are Harriet's peaches and her book. I shall eat the peaches and not read the book. She's a kind soul, but I never wish to listen to what *she* wishes to tell me. Adam, I'm weary and shall go to bed.'

It was then that, looking up, they saw the doctor coming down the stairs towards them, and in that one glance the world was changed for both of them. Gone were Miss Martineau's book and peaches, crinolines swaying in the sunshine, pleasant lawns and rose-coloured garden walls. Adam jumped to the stairs and caught the doctor's arm.

'Bettany, what is it?'

'Labour has begun,' Bettany said gravely.

'Well, well?'

'It will be difficult. You can do nothing, Paris. Best stay down here.'

But Judith at once took charge.

'Yes, Adam. Wait in the parlour. All will be perfectly well. I am sure of it. Remember Margaret is a strong woman. There, there, Adam.' She leaned up to him and kissed his cheek. 'Don't be nervous. There is nothing that you can do. Women understand these things. Come with me, Doctor. Is there anything further you require?'

Then there came to all of them a sound from above, half-moan, half-cry. It seemed to break the silence, the indifference of the house as a rough hand tears tissue paper.

'Oh, my God!' Adam whispered.

But they were gone. He was alone. He summoned all his fortitude and turned with firm step to the parlour. Will Leathwaite was standing by the hall door.

'Is the mistress bad, sir?' he asked.

'Yes—no—I don't know, Will. But the labour pains have begun. Would you go into the garden and tell Mrs. Bellairs quietly? Don't draw attention to it, you know. Ask her to come in to my mother.'

Leathwaite went. In the parlour Adam sat down on the old familiar sofa with the rosy apples. Nothing was changed, for Judith had forbidden any change. There was the spinet, there was the Chinese wallpaper, the silhouettes above the fireplace of David and Sarah Herries. Only Dorothy's needlework-box spoke something alien. Without knowing what he was doing he had it in his hands, and all his life after he was to remember it— with its polished walnut wood and satin-wood edge, the painted flowers on the top and sides, and inside it a tray painted pink, the wooden bobbins wound with coloured silks, the pincushion, the miniature hand mirror, the folding memorandum tablet in a morocco case, the needle-cushion of red and green wool with yellow beads, and a star-shaped piece of boxwood. The red and green needle-cushion he took between his hands and turned about and about a thousand times.

He had known nothing like this since Caesar Kraft had, on the day of the Chartist meeting, fallen dead at his feet. That had been one of the great crises of his life, because at that moment when Kraft had died in his arms he had resigned for ever all his life's hopes of Men's Brotherhood, of some movement that would catch the whole world up into some heavenly universal understanding and sympathy. Resigning those hopes, he had turned to his mother and to Margaret, the two persons in the world whom he supremely loved. His nature had developed a certain cynicism about the world in general. Men were not destined to understand one another and therefore, not understanding, also would not love. Love was to be found rather in the relationship with one or two individuals and in service to them. So he had lived for his mother and Margaret, and in a lesser degree for John and Elizabeth. John's death had once again set him back, for if so fearful a thing could happen so causelessly what was God about? He understood then that there was real evil in the world, that a battle was always in progress, and that one selfish, cruel act led to many more. One bad thought even had incalculable results. He understood from watching so small an entity as his own family that a battle between good and evil was even there always in progress. His was an age that believed quite definitely in good and evil, in God and the Devil, and in so far as Adam shared that belief, Adam was a man of his period.

With Margaret, after that scene in the bedroom here at Uldale one Christmas, his relation had grown ever richer and richer. He discovered that true love between two persons means a mutual interaction of beautiful, gay and noble discoveries. Both must be fine persons if love is to be full and progressive, and unless it is progressive it is not alive. He learnt that Margaret was far nobler than he, richer in unselfishness, in uncalculating generosity, in ever-growing charity, but as she rose higher she carried him with her. Love was this and only this: a companionship that was grander in trust, in humour, in understanding with every day.

He sat there, his broad legs widely spread, fingering the furniture of the needlework-box, the little wooden bobbins, the boxwood, the needle-cushion of red and green. He was maddened by his inaction. He walked about the room, sat down again. Once Dorothy looked in.

'How is she?' he said eagerly. 'Can I not go up?'

'Oh, well enough. The doctor is doing everything possible. No, better not go up just now, Adam. Margaret is wonderful. Her courage . . . '

Yes, Margaret was wonderful. But if she were to go now . . . A hundred scenes rushed in front of him—Margaret lying in bed, her hair spread about the pillow, waiting for him; Margaret singing some German song as she went about her work; Margaret sitting opposite him, sewing; Margaret listening as he read her some article or criticism or one of his fairy-stories that he loved to write and was so shy of showing to anybody. All quarrels and disputes were forgotten, or if remembered had an added colour and glow because of their intimacy. He crushed the needle-cushion out of shape, he jumped up and shook his fist at the ceiling, then creeping on tiptoe to the door like a child, he opened it and listened. There was not a sound in the house. Where were they all? Were all the guests gone? The hall was in a half-light, but Leathwaite stepped out of the dusk.

'It's warmer in the library,' said Will confidentially, and then relapsed for a moment into Cumberland. 'The spumkey fire's burning fine—and I've told Jeames to give the mare watter and a teate o' hay for he was driving her fast to t'doctor. But t'doctor was on t'road anyway. Lucky thing that!'

He drew near to Adam as though to protect him, and Adam put his hand on his shoulder. They whispered in the hall like two conspirators.

'Will—how is she, do you think? It's been a terrible long time.'

'It's a' reet, Mr. Adam. It's a' reet. Dinna fash yersel' now.'

They stood close together, shoulder to shoulder.

'I don't know what I'd do without you, Will,' Adam said. 'If I were to lose her——'

The two men exchanged a handshake.

'It's not that she's pampered,' Will explained. 'Now some ither lass, delicate, but t'Mistress—she's strong as a horse.'

Adam went into the parlour again and it comforted him that Will was outside, as it were on guard. Will always fell into broad Cumberland when he was deeply agitated, but showed his agitation in no other fashion.

The minutes passed; the clock struck the half-hour. Adam's forehead now was damp with perspiration. It was like him to do as he was told. They would come for him when they wanted him, but his agony gripped his stomach as though he were taking part in *her* agony, as though he were inside her and she inside him. The room was dark now. He did not think to light the candles. He stood in the darkness, his hands pressed the one into the other, the nails digging into the flesh.

In the hall Lucy had lit the gas and saw Leathwaite drawn up stiffly outside the parlour door.

'Eh!' she cried and started. 'I didna see ye.' Then hummed, looking at him:

> The lasses lap up 'hint their lads,
> Some stridin' an' some sydeways;
> An' some there were that wished their lot
> Had been what Ann's, the bryde was,
>   Ay, oft that day.

'Hist!' he whispered indignantly. 'Can't you be still?'

But she tossed her head, smiled back at him and walked slowly up the stairs, the taper in her hand.

Doctor Bettany almost knocked her over, hurrying his little fat body—all fobs and cravat—down to the hall.

As he passed Leathwaite he cried: 'It's a girl! A fine girl!'

'The Lord be praised!' said Leathwaite piously.

Bettany strode up to Adam and wrung his hand. 'A girl, Paris.

A grand girl!'

'Yes—but my wife?'

'All's well. You may see her for a moment—only a moment, mind.'

As Adam tore up the staircase a slow smile lit up Leathwaite's eyes and mouth. Then, feeling in his pocket for his tobacco, he turned towards the kitchen, sharing with Adam the position of the happiest man in Cumberland.

SAYERS VERSUS HEENAN

One of the most remarkable scenes that the London Bridge terminus ever witnessed occurred in the very early morning of Tuesday, April 17, 1860. The darkness of the early April day was illuminated only by some pallid and evil-smelling gas-lamps. The platform, the offices behind the platform, and the street outside the station were thronged with a pushing, swearing, laughing, spitting, drinking, smoking throng, all men, all happy, all strung to a key of an intense excitement. They had assembled that they might be carried by the special monster train to Farnborough to behold in the fields near by the great fight between Tom Sayers, Champion of Great Britain, and John Heenan the American. Impossible to say who were there and who not in that thick semi-darkness smelling of damp hay and train-smoke and escaping gas, unwashen bodies and morning air. At any rate there were fish-porters from Billingsgate, butchers from Newgate Market, pugilists of course, poets and journalists of course, dandies as well, celebrated statesmen, and even, so it was afterwards said, some eminent divines.

Most striking at the first showing was the amazing variety of smell—decaying vegetables, mildewed umbrellas, fumes of vile tobacco and stale corduroy suits—but nobody minded, nobody cared, everyone was happy. Clothes are of an amazing variety; there are the friends of sport, quite naturally in the majority; there may be a white neckcloth and black broadcloth, but the cut is unmistakable; hard-featured men, spare-limbed, fond of burying their hands deep in their coat-pockets and never in their trousers. Some are in fine plush galligaskins, top-boots, fur caps, and have sticks with crutches and a thong at the end. There is the 'swell,' with his long surtout, double-breasted waistcoat, accurately folded scarf, peg-top trousers, eye-glass, umbrella and drooping moustache. And there is the dandy with lofty heels to his varnished boots, great moustache and whiskers, ponderous watch-chain bearing coins and trinkets, starched choking all-round collar and wonderful breezy necktie, and, lastly, there is a certain number of quiet, severe, retiring gentlemen in tremendous top-hats, dignified black with one pearl or diamond in the black necktie, sucking as likely as not the heads of their heavy canes.

The small group of Herries gentlemen going down to enjoy together the great event had members, it appeared, in all these different classes, for Garth, now purple-faced and corpulent (although he was but fifty years of age), might because of his horsy appearance be making straight for Tattersall's. His brother Amery was something of a dandy and wore an eye-glass. Barnabas Newmark (Phyllis' youngest boy, now about thirty, and known to all his friends as Barney) was altogether the 'swell,' with his double-breasted waistcoat of crimson and his trousers of the loudest checks (but, as was characteristic of the Newmark strain, he was, in spite of himself, a little behind the time, coloured waistcoats having just gone out). Lord Rockage (Roger, who had succeeded his father two years earlier) was stout, very fair in colour, with light blue eyes. He was dressed gravely as became his position and sucked reflectively the marble head of his cane. (But he was not reflecting. He was thinking of nothing at all.) The remaining Herries was young Ellis, Will's son. He was now a boy of seventeen and strikingly resembled his father, thin of body with the high Herries cheek-bones and prominent nose, serious, reserved and fully conscious of his duty to the world.

Garth, Amery and young Barney were taking sips of brandy from a silver flask and were as merry as merry could be. Garth was for ever recognising friends and acquaintances.

'Hullo, Sawyer!' he cried to a stout red-faced gentleman in tremendous checks. 'What did I tell you? Didn't I say you'd have a bid for Satan before you'd been on him half an hour? I told you what to do. Just to keep jogging on him to qualify and you'd get all you wanted.'

'We tried him, Mr. Herries,' Mr. Sawyer said in a deep melancholy voice, 'yesterday morning against Polly-Anne and beat her by more than a length.'

'There! What did I tell you? . . . Well, how'll the fight be?'

'I've known Tom,' said Mr. Sawyer, more gloomy than ever, 'since he was a lad high as my boot. Why, I knew him when he was a brick-layer at Brighton. Why, God Almighty can't beat him!'

'Heenan is five inch taller than Sayers,' said Garth, 'and three stone heavier.'

'Why, blast my soul,' said Mr. Sawyer, 'he won't bloody well get near him. There's no one on this bleeding firmament as quick as Tom is.'

It was not more than a shed under whose shelter they were all crowding, and the noise was now terrific, the back-slapping tremendous, the drinking ferocious and the oaths Rabelaisian.

''Pon my soul,' said Rockage vacantly, 'there's a lot of fellers crowdin' about. And there'll not be a Fight perhaps after all. Wish I was in bed, 'pon my soul I do.'

Ellis looked at him with exactly that look of cold superiority that had been his father's in *his* youth. But he was not feeling superior. He was conscious of a deep and burning excitement and of pleasure in the scene. But he would not show it. He was by temperament intensely cautious and by training suspicious, and, mingled with these two strains, there was an odd element of personless, rather noble philanthropy. He was already persuading his guardians, his mother, Stephen Newmark and Amery Herries, that he would like to assist the Institute for Necessitous Orphans in Wigmore Street, and the Home for Irish Immigrants in Penelope Place. He liked to do good with his money on condition that he need not encounter those whom he benefited.

'Odd fish!' Amery had said to his sister-in-law Sylvia. 'Damn' generous so long as he doesn't have to be personal. He'd give anything to a charity and quite a bit to an Italian organ-grinder, but he seems to me to have no heart at all—no feeling for individuals, you know.'

'Wish I were an Italian organ-grinder,' Sylvia had said with a sigh, for although they lived now in two poky little rooms near Victoria Station, they were always quite hopelessly in debt.

So Ellis now felt a cold distaste for all the humanity surging about him, but had someone on the platform begged from him he would have plunged his hand into his pocket and given him a handful of silver on condition that he did not speak to him after. He had come down from Eton last Christmas, although only seventeen, and, after the summer, was to go into the City, in his father's firm of Herries & Herries. He had all his father's genius for turning one penny into two, but he was more deeply concerned than Will had been with the magnificent power of his family. He was, indeed, even at this early age, family mad. The Herries were the greatest family in England; even at Eton, where he had encountered heirs of all the ages and heirs with quite as genuine a belief in their inheritances as his own, he had never wavered. Howards, Buckinghams, Beaminsters, Warwicks, Cecils—they had all, in his own mind, bowed before the Herries. His closest friend at Eton had been young Beaminster, whose mother, then a woman of thirty-eight or so, was afterwards the famous and hideous old Duchess of Wrexe. Beaminster said to him once:

'Someone, Ellis, told me the other day that your great-grandfather was a sort of highwayman fellow who married a gipsy.'

'Quite,' said Ellis, stretching his long thin neck, 'and now see what we are!'

So to-day he felt that this fight was arranged principally for the benefit of the Herries: it was America *versus* Herries. He looked upon the crowd: they were all off to Farnborough to see Herries whack America. It was high time America learnt a lesson; it was not the last time that a Herries would be conscious of such a need.

The bell sounded and they all crowded into the railway carriage. There was no ceremony about places, and Rockage discovered to his disgust that a great 'labouring-man' as he termed him, in galligaskins and a fur cap, already far away in liquor, with a black bottle in one hand and a vast ham sandwich in the other, was spreading all over him, and even before the train had started had planted a large red hand on his own elegant stout knee.

'Here, my good fellow,' Rockage said, trying to move his leg away. But he was wedged remorselessly and, as was his fate constantly in life, no one heard what he said.

Garth Herries and Barney Newmark had secured places together by the window. Just before the train started Garth touched Barney's hand: 'By God, young Barney, look there!'

On the platform a great scramble for places was going on. Everyone was good-natured as, in England, everyone is unless it is felt that injustice is being done. There were shouts and cries, bodies were pushed forward through crowded doors by other bodies, there was laughter and singing. A tall broad-shouldered man with a high top-hat, a rather shabby stock, white hair longer than the fashion and straggling white moustaches, waited quietly apart from the struggle. He had a body that must once have been full and strong. It seemed now to have shrunken, under the black clothes. His shoulders were bowed. At the last moment he walked forward and, without any effort, entered a carriage.

'By heaven!' said Garth. 'I thought he was coming in here.'

'Why?' said Barney. 'Who was it?'

'Walter Herries!'

'What?' whispered Barney in a voice of awed interest. 'You don't say!' He peered out of window, but the train was already moving. He looked across to Ellis who was at the opposite end of the carriage. 'Imagine if he had come in here!' he excitedly whispered. 'What a family scene!'

'Yes, poor devil.'

'What did he look like? They say he was all cut up by his son's death. A pretty little murder that was. What do you think, Garth? Was Uhland Herries mad?'

'Mad as a hatter. Young Harry Trent was up North last year and he thought he'd call on Walter—out of curiosity, you know. Besides he was some sort of relation of Jennifer Herries—John's mother. His father was her cousin or something. Well, he *did* call, and he says he never had such an hour. Gloomy house on the top of a hill. I've stayed there in the old days. They call it the Fortress. But it's all gone to ruin, and there was Walter Herries in a dirty dressing-gown drinking with an old woman. Harry says he was very courteous, walked about and tried to do the honours. And then he took him up to Uhland's room. He'd kept it just as it was when Uhland was alive—cold windy place at the top of the tower they have there. And Harry says he began a long wandering thing about Uhland, said it was all his own fault because it was he taught Uhland to hate John Herries or some such nonsense. Harry says he suggested Walter should get out a bit, do some shooting or hunting or something, but Walter just said that he hadn't the heart . . . Poor devil! Hope we don't stumble on him at Farnborough. Wonder what he's doing down here!'

But the train was now in the country. It was yet dark, the land shadowy about them, but with the running into air and space the hissing spluttering gas in its grimy glass covering seemed at once incongruous and even itself ashamed. They had not gone far when Garth called out: 'Why, Collins! What are you doing here?'

A large handsome fellow with a high, broad head, plenty of brown hair, very gay in a brown velvet coat, white waistcoat and brown pantaloons, was sitting next to Ellis. He jumped up, regardless of Herries, showing himself a man of great size and strength, and wrung Garth's hand.

'Herries, by God! So it is.'

Garth introduced him to the other members of the family. 'Mr. Mortimer Collins, a friend of mine. One of the most promising poets in England; one of the most important editors in England too.'

'Now stop your codding, Herries. How are you, sir? How do you do, sir? Fine day we're going to have. I've come all the way from Plymouth, gentlemen, to see this fight, and by God if the "Blues" interfere I'll know the reason why.'

'He's a friend of Adam Paris,' Garth explained, 'and editor of the *Plymouth Mail*. Christopher North said he was the best young poet in England—did he not, Collins? All *I* know is that he's wiser about dogs than anyone I've ever met and he can tell a pretty girl when he sees one—can't you, Collins?'

All the carriage looked at Collins with great interest, but Collins was not at all abashed, laughed and ran his hand through his brown hair and began to talk at a tremendous rate.

How was Paris? Clever fellow although lazy. Always had his mind elsewhere, and he'd been running off when he ought to be working. Always talking of Cumberland, but Collins could understand that. Collins thought Cumberland a grand place. He'd paid a visit to the poet Wordsworth once—in '48, it was—and Wordsworth had looked like 'an old Roman Senator dressed as an English farmer.' First-rate the Lake Country! Everyone lived to be a hundred there. But who cared about Cumberland this morning? He'd have walked from John o' Groats to Land's End to see this fight. Why, he'd known Tom Sayers since he was a lad. He saw his first fight with Abe Crouch in '49, and although Crouch was two stone the heavier, Sayers smashed his face to pulp. And he'd seen him fight Jack Grant of Southwark for two hours and a half and just beat him. That had been a *grand* fight!

He was so jolly in his general enthusiasm and the way in which he took the whole carriage into his confidence that they all felt very friendly even though he was a poet. Barney

Newmark was especially taken with him because he had always had a notion that he himself might be a bit of a writer. In fact those books *Miss Rich of Manchester* and *Fox and Grapes* (which were declared at the time to be quite as good as Whyte-Melville) and, of more importance still, the *Chapters from the Life of an English Family* might never have been written had it not been for his friendship, begun at this meeting, with Collins. Nor, in all probability, would some of the best passages in *Sweet Anne Page* have been quite what they were had Collins never known Barney.

But now they were approaching Farnborough, and excitement ran mountains high. Two gentlemen were so thoroughly drunk that it was little of the fight that they would see. (In fact they never got further that day than the Farnborough pub.) The train drew up and everyone swarmed out. Once outside, a frenzy seemed to seize the world. Light was in the sky, the grass was fresh to the feet, the trees in their first spring green, overhead (Collins noticed it because he was a poet) larks were soaring and singing. And he was the only one, maybe, in all those thousands who did notice it, for, from every side, multitudes were pouring (the crowd was afterwards estimated at three thousand persons), men climbing the hedges, leaping the walls, running over the grass, racing, laughing, shouting. The meadow that was to witness the great scene had been cunningly chosen, surrounded by ditches and double hedges that it might be difficult for the authorities to take anyone by surprise. Already there had appeared in *The Times* a little notice:

THE FORTHCOMING PRIZE FIGHT

Hertford, *Saturday.*

This afternoon Colonel Archibald Robertson, Chief Constable of the Hertfordshire Police Force, made application to the justices assembled in petty session at Hertford for a warrant to apprehend Thomas Sayers, the

'Champion of England,' and John Heenan, the American pugilist, in order that they might be bound over to keep the peace . . .

It happened that Amery and Ellis were separated, as they approached the meadow, from the rest of their party. They could see just in front of them the broad gesticulating figure of Collins, Garth laughing and Rockage picking his way as carefully as a hen in a hothouse. Amery felt his arm tapped and turned to see Walter Herries at his side. He said afterwards it was one of the most awful moments of his life. It was not only that he had Ellis with him, that, so far as he knew, the two step-brothers had never met in their lives before, but something in Walter Herries' appearance caught at his heart. He was not an emotional fellow, Amery. He had all the caution of his kind of Herries, and then some more, but he had not set eyes on Walter for many years. When he had seen him last he had been stout, jolly, blustering, self-confident, ready to shout any man down, but now he stood beside him as though he were bewildered, lost, and as even Amery, with all his fear of exaggeration, put it, 'he had aged a century.'

'Why, Walter!' he said.

'How are you, Amery?' Walter said gravely. 'I trust you are well.'

'Very, thanks. I thought you were in Cumberland!'

'Cumberland? No. Business has brought me South, and I thought that by coming here I might recover something— might recover something——' He looked at Ellis without any recognition, and Ellis looked at him. There was nothing else for it.

'This is Ellis, Walter. I don't know whether——'

Walter held out his gloved hand to his brother.

'Indeed?' They shook hands. A strange emotion seized them all. For an instant they were so isolated that they alone might have inhabited the globe. Then Walter walked forward by himself as though he had already forgotten that the others existed. It was from that moment of meeting, Amery said afterwards, that young Ellis, he thought, got all his peculiar notions about the family—his sense above all that the family must not be 'queer.' No one knew, no one ever was to know, what Ellis had thought about the terrible Uhland-John scandal. He must have heard about it again and again, child though he was at the time, for all the Herries in London were for ever discussing it. The papers had had, of course, plenty about it, and every decent normal Herries had felt it a dreadful slur on the family. Young Ellis had been undoubtedly conscious of this, had, in all probability, brooded on it. For he was simply the most normal Herries who ever lived; all the Herries' dislike of queerness, poetry, public immorality, all the Herries' distrust of the Arts, of anything un-English, of odd clothes and eccentric talk, met its climax in Ellis. The wandering ghost of the old Rogue and all his family found at last their match in Will's younger son. If indeed there had been for years growing in him a hatred of the unusual, of the 'sport,' the 'misfit,' how he must have hated the Uhland scandal! But perhaps he did not realise this disgust of his fully until the moment when he saw this figure of his own brother, dishevelled, unhappy, alone, at a gathering so particularly normal, British and Herries as this one. In any case this is certain—that after this day he never mentioned poor John or Uhland or Walter if he could help it. You could not offend him more than by any allusion to them.

All his later troubles and the troubles of Vanessa and Benjamin, and of the other Herries connected with them, dated perhaps from this meeting at Farnborough with his brother. It is not fanciful to imagine so. And that meeting, it is also not altogether fanciful to imagine, became inevitable when, nearly a hundred and fifty years before, Francis Herries rode, with his children, for the first time up Borrowdale.

* * * * *

Amery and Ellis soon joined Rockage, Garth, Barney and Collins at the ringside. Garth, of course, had friends who were in the inner circles of Pugilism, so he had seen to it that his little company had fine places, and Mortimer Collins was with them by the right of the Press. The arena was a twenty-four-foot one. Behind the ropes a great multitude was pressed, body against body, and on every face was that mingled gaze of joy, expectation, anxiety and a sort of childish innocence as though no one present were more than eight years old.

For Barney Newmark, compounded as he was of escape from all the repressions of his early youth (his father, it may be said, was deeply disappointed in his youngest son, who seemed to him to have neither reverence for the things that mattered nor any discipline of character), of imagination and sheer joy of living, this scene with the early morning sun overhead, the turf at his feet, the ardent eager crowd, the brilliant green of the prepared Ring, the excitement of the event, and above all his personal adoration of Tom Sayers, made up the supreme morning of his life. (And, perhaps, never again would he know anything so good.) He had never seen Sayers, but had read every scrap about him since he could remember. And he had never heard anything but good, because Sayers was a grand fellow—serious of mind, modest and unassuming, utterly fearless, generous and good-living. To do the Herries justice—men like Garth and Ormerod and Rodney—he was the kind of Englishman they *wanted* to create. They felt indeed that they had created him, and would not have been at all surprised had it been discovered that he had a drop of Herries in him somewhere. It might be that every man in that crowd felt that he had created him just as he had created this England that was beginning once again, after years of uncertainty, to dominate the whole world. Nelson, the Duke, Tom Sayers—they were all Herries men.

So Barney waited, his heart beating in his ears, his mouth a little open, and his hand resting on Collins' broad shoulder.

'That's the great Tom Oliver,' said Collins.

'Oh, where?' gasped Barney, and was pointed out an aged and grizzled gentleman superintending the last details, testing the ropes, looking up at the sky, consulting with other important gentlemen, inspecting anxiously his watch. For there was not a man in the crowd who was not aware that at any moment the authorities might arrive and the Fight be 'off.' And if that occurred this multitude of amiable citizens would be changed in one brief moment into a howling mob of savages!

It was seven-twenty by Barney's watch. A great sigh of excitement went into the air. Sayers had thrown his hat into the ring and a moment later followed it. So this was his hero! For a second of time Barney was disappointed. Sayers was no classical beauty. His face at first sight was ordinary, that of a quiet commonplace stable-man or agricultural labourer. He seemed slight in figure although he had great shoulders, but nothing, it seemed, of a chest. Nothing extraordinary, for a moment thought Barney. Heenan's hat followed, and a second later Heenan was inside. Then when he stripped a murmur of admiration followed, for this was surely the most magnificent human being God had ever made. Heenan was six feet two inches in height, Sayers but five feet eight, so that the American towered over his opponent. Moreover, Heenan was a beauty. The sun, growing ever more powerful, shone on his shoulders; his chest was superb, his face handsome and distinguished. Sayers looked an ordinary hard little middle-weight, which was what by weight he really was. Moreover, he was eight years older than Heenan.

So that when Sayers stripped Barney drew a deep breath of alarm. How could this stocky grave little fellow hope to approach that giant? The thing was absurd, and he heard comment all around him expressing the same fear. 'The match is a horse to a hen,' said a wrinkled dark man beside him. A big stout gentleman in a very high hat swore with many oaths that 'Heenan would knock Sayers into a cocked hat in ten minutes,' and someone else cried out: 'Tom may beat him, but may I be fried in hell if he can eat him.'

Collins seemed to understand Barney's alarm, for he turned to him and said: 'All right. Don't you worry. It's not that Tom's so quick—Charlie Buller was quicker and so were Langham and Ned Donally—but you wait till you see the force he uses—and his timing! There's never been such timing since the world began! It's the way he moves that saves him. You watch!'

And Barney did watch. He saw Sayers look at his man, then nod as much as to say 'I can manage that.' Then they tossed and a groan went round: 'Tom's lost the toss,' and a large crowd of Americans in Heenan's corner shouted with glee. Sayers now must take the lower ground, but Barney's hope rose again when he saw him stand in so perfect an attitude, tapping the ground with his left foot, his arms down, his head well back, and a smile on his face.

'Oh, God, make him win!' Barney whispered to himself. 'He must win! He *must* win!'

They shook hands and then, as they moved round, each man to his right in order to avoid the other's right hand, they laughed at each other, as cheery and friendly a laugh as you could see anywhere on a lovely spring morning.

They sparred, closed, and Sayers got down easily. Their seconds sponged them down, gave them water to rinse their mouths with, and they came up again. It was plain that Sayers was absolutely confident. He had beaten big men before—size was nothing to him. Heenan led and led again, but always missed; then he got one on his opponent's mouth, and Sayers reeled. Sayers returned but was banged on the forehead and went down in his own corner, whereupon the Americans whooped their delight.

And it was now that the great crowd became part of the fight. Wives, mistresses, children were forgotten. All the trades and all the labours, the small shop, the wide curve of the field as the horses ploughed it, the window at the Club, with the last private scandal, the hiss of the white wave at the boat's keel as it swept from the shore, the call on the bare windy 'top' as the sheep-dog ran to his master's bidding, the gossip under lamplight at the village wall, the last climb into the dark wood before the lovers found their longed-for security, all aches and pains and ills, triumph and failure, all bitterness and jealousy, all were lost and forgotten as though they had never been. Every man was drawn into that Ring and fought for a victory that seemed just then to be a whole life's aim. Garth forgot his last quarrel with Sylvia when for the thousandth time she had wept and he had sworn, Amery thought nothing of that 'pretty good thing' in Railway Shares that Ormerod had told him of, Rockage forgot his cows down in Wiltshire, Ellis forgot his dignity, and Collins thought nothing of his ambitions that he hoped would bring him from Plymouth and establish him in London as the finest writer of his time. Barney? Barney was part of Sayers' very soul. He had always *been* Sayers. Every blow that Sayers dealt was Barney's— every knock that Sayers got he felt on his own heart.

Only Walter—standing not far from his relations— remained in a world that would not set him free. He watched because something was going to happen. His loneliness would be terminated and he would return to a moving, breathing life from which, since that moment when they had told him that Uhland was dead, he had been always excluded. He bent forward, watching intently, but it was neither Sayers nor Heenan that he was seeing.

Four times Sayers was down, and every time that he fell all England fell with him. Once Heenan got in a severe right, once trying to avoid the sun he slipped, and once Heenan with a terrible left altogether floored him. Nevertheless, Tom's footwork was marvellous, in and out, in and out, avoiding that long arm and always on the retreat when a blow threatened him, so that the force of it was lessened.

Collins was in an ecstasy. 'Oh, look at his feet!' he cried. 'Look at his feet! Oh, the darling! There's beauty! There's movement!' He was beside himself with excitement, gripping Barney's arm, rolling his head to the rhythm of the fighting, stamping with his feet on the ground. Nevertheless, the sun was bothering Sayers (he tried continually to get Heenan to change his ground but always failed), he was now severely marked and had an awful cut over his eyebrow.

Would he last? Many voices, shaking with excitement, the words coming anyhow, could be heard saying that Tom was a beaten man. 'The American's too big for him.' 'He's taken a size too large for him!'

Barney caught Mortimer Collins' arm and in a piteous whisper said: 'He isn't beat, is he? Oh, he can't be! He can't be!'

'You must wait,' said Collins between his teeth. 'He hasn't begun.'

It was then that Walter Herries suddenly began to feel deep down in his loneliness that everything would be different for him henceforth if only Sayers won. Uhland could not return, but life would begin again. That strange cessation of time that for five years now he had endured would lapse. It was as though he waited for a door to open, and, even as, years before, Georges Paris had staked his future on the result of a wrestle on a hill-top in Cumberland, so now Walter Herries held his breath and waited.

'Now!' suddenly cried Collins. 'Do you see that?'

Heenan had sent out a smashing blow which Sayers had avoided, and then, jumping right back, Sayers had landed a terrific hit on the American's eye. It was one of those sliding upward hits, almost splitting Heenan's cheek.

And now Sayers was growing happy. You could see it in his quiet confident gaze, the hint of a smile that played about his bruised lips.

'I've got him now! I've got him now!' Barney whispered, his nails digging into the palms of his hands in his excitement. Indeed, it seemed that Sayers had. Stopping a hard lead with his forearm he dealt a harder one, then suddenly, as though inspired by the kindly heavens, launched out with such a thunderbolt that it seemed as though Heenan's nose must be crushed in. The tremendous fellow was all but lifted off his legs; the Americans in his corner gave a kind of 'Oh!' of wonder, and how the rest of the world shouted, Herries and all! Even Ellis cried: 'Bravo, Sayers! Bravo, my man!' just as though he had been an honest hard-working gardener in the Herries employ.

But for five foot eight to raise six foot two from the ground was no minor feat. Yes, Tom Sayers for all his quiet peace-loving friendly countenance could hit.

Again in the seventh round Sayers struck Heenan another fearful blow which sent the blood gushing from Heenan's nose; so weak and tottering was the American that he grabbed at Sayers' body and they hugged, although Sayers got in some nice body blows before they fell together.

And Barney, in his innocence, thought it all over. The American couldn't stand any more of that; another little tap and he'd be gone, put to sleep for the rest of his natural.

'Oh, he's got him! he's got him!' he cried, enchanted, dancing up and down on his two feet like a little boy, and even Walter, not far away, began to feel as though a great weight were lifting from him.

'I think Sayers is winning,' he said very gravely to a man with a broken nose, standing beside him.

'I wouldn't be so sure,' said the man with the broken nose. 'Why isn't Tom hitting more with his right?'

Barney, in fact, was increasingly aware now from the atmosphere around him that something was going wrong. What it was he couldn't tell. Everything *seemed* to be all right. To look at Sayers you wouldn't suppose that he had an anxiety in the world. His face, that would have been solemn as a churchwarden's had it not been for the twinkling crow's-feet about his eyes, was expressionless and innocent. He had the earnest and serious gaze of a student of Mr. Darwin or Mr. Huxley. But something was wrong.

'What is it?' Barney whispered to Collins.

'It's his arm, his right arm,' Collins whispered back. 'I think he's broken it.'

Barney always said afterwards that, of the three or four most dramatic crises in his life, that moment when Sayers broke his arm in his fight with Heenan (or a tendon as it turned out after —a happening quite as disastrous in the circumstances as a broken arm could be) was the most thrilling. Life seemed to stop: the world was held in a frozen mask, the air like ice, and no sound in the universe. Exaggerated it sounded later, but that's how it was just then.

And now it was that Barney Newmark loved Sayers, loved Sayers as he loved himself plus the love that he had just then for Miss Nellie Blossom of the Adelphi plus the love that he had for his mother, brother, and sisters, and his French bulldog Louis. All the different loves of his life were concentrated in that little stocky man when he saw him holding his right arm across his chest in the orthodox position as though nothing were the matter, relying now altogether on his feet for his defence and his left for attack, although it had always been his right that had won him his victories.

And then the beautiful thing happened, for Sayers grinned, grinned as though he were greeting an old crony, and Heenan, although his face was marked as though it had been slashed with sabre-cuts (for knuckles could cut into the flesh as gloves cannot do), grinned back. Indeed so completely was Sayers master of himself that, sending Heenan down with a horrible smasher, he used the twenty-five seconds that he might have had for resting in going over and peering into Heenan's face to see what it was like when they had wiped the blood off it. He might get some useful information that way.

Next there was a terrific round: one of the historic rounds in the history of British boxing, when they fought for a quarter of a hour and were, both of them, so badly exhausted at the end of it that they had to be carried to their corners by their respective seconds.

It was after this round that a new element entered into the fight. Heenan was now a fearful sight, for his face looked as though it were gashed with deep wounds. He was bleeding dreadfully, and one of his eyes was completely closed. The gathering of men, who felt as though they, too, had been fighting all this while, began, spiritually, to move in a new world, or rather in a very old primitive one. The tenseness was frightful. Men drew deep breaths and groaned in agony of spirit, stranger held stranger by the shoulder as though he would never let him go. Sweat was beaded thickly on Garth's forehead. Amery could not stand still but kept beating with his fist on another man's shoulder. The betting was now frantic. The Americans kept up a continual roar from their corner, and a strange rhythmical stir seemed to beat through all that multitude, the mass of human beings rising and falling with every movement of the two fighters.

They, indeed, seemed less seriously concerned than anyone else, for once Heenan picked Sayers off his legs and threw him, and then there they were both laughing at one another, and it was a strange sight to see that great American with one eye closed and his cheek in strips laughing as though this were good fun—although a trifle rough perhaps!

Indeed only once in all this time did Sayers show a sign of anger, and that was when he spat some blood and the American laughed. He was stung with that and rushed at Heenan, sent him reeling with a left, and then another and then another! When he hit him a fourth blow Heenan staggered; had Sayers had his right arm he might, indeed, have finished the whole thing with a knock-out. Of one blow on Heenan's ribs the *Times* correspondent afterwards said: "It sounded all over the meadow as if a box had been smashed in." On the other hand, had Heenan been clever with his right the match might ere this have ended the American way!

It was now that a sort of madness seemed to swing down upon that meadow. Not an ignoble madness either, for here were these two men, heroes if ever heroes were, laughing like boys at play, and one of them with his face a pulp, blinded, so that he struck his second in mistake for his opponent, and the other had been fighting for an hour with one arm useless, a mass of bruises and fearfully swollen. Nor was their Cause ignoble, for they were showing to all the world that their countries had strength and courage, restraint and control, fairness of mind and an honest cheerfulness, manifesting these qualities indeed a great deal more plainly than their countries often did!

And now all the Herries (save Walter only) were shouting like mad: even Ellis was crying 'Go on, sir! Well done, sir! Very fine indeed!' and with him were shouting many other Herries, the old Rogue with his saturnine humour, and stout David, his son—the best wrestler in Cumberland—and old Pomfret waving a bottle, and young Reuben in defence of the bear, young Francis rising slowly to face his invisible enemy, and poor John winning a victory in the loneliness of Skiddaw. They were fighting to be free, as every man in that crowd was fighting to be free—with every blow that Sayers struck, with every reply of the mighty blinded Heenan, three thousand men drove with them to freedom.

But the spirit of madness grew more powerful. Sayers was weakening, Heenan blinded. They had been fighting for over two hours, and in the rear of the crowd policemen—the hated 'Blues'—were trying to break their way. Once Heenan caught Sayers, closed, and hit him when on the ground. What a yell of 'Foul!' went up then, and the Americans roared back 'No foul!' and the umpire said that all was well because 'the blow was struck in the heat of fighting.' Would Sayers last? *Would* Sayers last? Barney himself now was weak at the knees, his mouth was dry, his eyes burning. He had been fighting, it seemed to him, week upon week. As for a moment he leaned forward, his head rested on Collins' shirt. It was soaked with the sweat of his body. And Walter, in his place, was shaking. He did not know it. He knew neither where he was nor how he had got there—

only it seemed to him that Uhland was fighting there in the Ring, and that the moment would come when he would turn to him, crying out:

'Father, you must come and help me. I'm nearly beaten'—a cry that Walter had all his life waited for in vain.

Then, suddenly, came the climax. Heenan had Sayers' head under his left arm when in a corner. He was too weak to do anything but lean on the stake and hold on to Sayers as though trying to strangle him. He said after—and it was likely enough it was true—that he was too blind to know what he did.

Sayers did all he could to free his head, but could not; with his left he got in a blow or two. But Heenan twisted round so that Tom's neck was hard against the upper rope and then he leaned on it. Poor Tom was black in the face and it was plain that he could not breathe.

Then came pandemonium; men were fighting and yelling. 'Foul!' 'Foul!' 'Foul!' The umpire called out 'Cut the rope!' The ringside was broken and the crowd poured in, hemming the fighters round so that they could only stand up against one another. Each hit the other and they both fell down—there, prone, at the feet of their admirers.

The police stopped the fight.

They had fought for two hours and twenty minutes. The result was a draw. The last great contest of fisticuffs on English soil.

* * * * *

Walter moved in a dream. On a wall in front of him that seemed always to be receding, a great cock with a crimson crest was crowing. It crowed and crowed.

A little common man in a fur cap kept pace beside him.

'Well, Guv'nor, that wor' grand. I call that grand!'

'Thank you,' said Walter. 'I enjoyed it greatly'—and went back to the Fortress.

SHE VISITS THE
FORTRESS FOR THE LAST TIME

———————————————

Elizabeth, forty-seven but looking oddly like a young girl in distress, confused in fact by her inexperience, stood one very wet morning beside Judith's bed and stared at the old lady with, if the truth is known, a good deal of irritation. At her side, the cause of her worry, stood her son Benjamin, now aged seven.

'It isn't,' said Elizabeth, in a clear sweet voice, 'as though he didn't know he'd done wrong, Aunt Judith. He knows perfectly well. Besides, Timothy beat him when he found out the truth. But he doesn't care in the least.'

Judith in her lace cap, mittens on her little hands, her face smiling and serene, the article in *The Times* about Mr. Lincoln and the North and what the Americans had better do next open on her lap, knew two things—one, that Elizabeth wished her to be very serious in order that Benjamin should be impressed, and the other, that she thought it high time that Elizabeth gave up her widow's cap and black silk dress. Poor John had been gone nearly eight years now, and gentle colours, silver grey, dove colour, rose, suited Elizabeth so very well. Moreover, Elizabeth would be all the happier if she married. Mr. Morant of Brough was eager to marry her. She was wasted as a widow, and Benjamin was altogether too much for her. Judith was smiling because she was thinking of the other children who had been too much for their relations. She had been too much for David Herries. Adam had at one time been too much for herself. Barney Newmark had been too much for Phyllis and Stephen. But Benjamin was a little different, for in this present time children, whatever they thought in secret, had outwardly to conform. All over England children were conforming, saying 'Yes, Papa' and 'No, Mama,' looking up to their parents as to God, believing (apparently) all that they were told about both the creation of the world and the creation of themselves (the first in six days exactly, the second in a gooseberry bush), above all observing Sunday with the ritual and solemnity of a Sacred Order.

All this was correct, Judith supposed, although it had not been so when she was young, but she was now a very old woman and must not expect the world to stand still. (The only question was: was it perhaps going back? But how could one ask that when Britain was triumphant among the nations?)

It was Sunday that had been young Benjamin's trouble. He was quite unlike Adam as a child, for although Adam had been independent and gone his own way he had given no one any trouble except when he had disappeared for a whole day without warning. Moreover, he always listened to reason. But Benjamin would never listen to anyone, and this was the stranger when you considered that he was the son of John, who had always listened to everyone too much. It was perhaps because of John's tragedy that everyone had been over-indulgent to Benjamin in his babyhood. Poor little infant, born only a few months after his father had been brutally murdered, murdered by the child's own uncle! Could anyone have a more pitiful start in life? Had Benjamin been a delicate, sensitive soul everyone would have approved and everyone would have been satisfied. But, so odd are the workings of nature, that that was the very last thing that Benjamin turned out to be! He was plump, healthy and merry. No one had ever known him to cry. He laughed all day. He did not of course know as yet of his father's tragedy, but it was feared that when he did know it would not affect him very greatly. It was not that he was cruel, nor that he was heartless, but he had none of the right and proper feelings. At Uldale, Veronica and Jane made much of him. Dorothy petted him, even Tim paid him attentions. They all thought him a sweet little child, for he was round and rosy and had large yellow curls on the top of his head. But he yielded to none of their blandishments. Jane was the only one who could do anything with him, and she not very much. It was not that he was hard or selfish. He was everybody's friend, would give everything that he possessed away to anybody (they had to stop him giving his toys, marbles, sweets to the village children); no, the awful thing was that he had no morals!

That seems a hard thing to say about a child who was only just seven, but what they meant by it was that he had no idea at all of the difference between right and wrong. The first occasion had been when he had stolen the piece of sandalwood out of Dorothy's needlework-box. She had missed it; they had searched everywhere for it. Benjamin had been challenged, had denied that he had it, and then it had been found on his person. Timothy had whipped him, Elizabeth had explained to him what a dreadful thing a lie was, but he had remained cheerful and unrepentant through it all. But unrepentant was the wrong word. He was simply unaware that he should not tell a lie if to tell a lie was of benefit to him. He laughed like anything when Dorothy, in her vast crinoline, tried to instruct him.

Of course he was very young at the time, and Dorothy elaborately expounded to Elizabeth that very small children never knew the difference between right and wrong. They were born in sin and only later became the children of Grace. But whether Benjamin would ever be a child of Grace seemed to Elizabeth, who knew him better than the others, a sadly uncertain question.

He was for ever in hot water, and at last he committed his worst crime: he dropped a handsome silver riding-whip of Timothy's into a deep empty well at the back of the stables. On this occasion he at once confessed. He said that he wanted to see how far it would fall. He was whipped, sent to bed without supper, lectured. He minded nothing, would not say that he was sorry, and at last was brought up to Judith to see whether she could do anything with him. He looked at the old lady in the big bed and thought how small she was. His round and chubby figure smiled all over at the old lady, and the old lady smiled back at him. This, thought Elizabeth in despair, was not at all what she had wanted.

'It makes it so much worse, Aunt Judith,' she said, 'that it should be Sunday.'

'I don't know, my dear. Do you think that it does?' She drew off her mittens and then with her slender white fingers used a silver knife to peel a large rosy apple. She had always for breakfast a cup of coffee and an apple, a meal that everyone thought eccentric.

Benjamin watched the peeling of the apple with wide-eyed excitement. Would she be able to strip the whole apple without breaking the skin?

'You see, Elizabeth dear,' Judith went on in her very small voice that had a touch of tartness in it like a good preserve. 'I'm nearly ninety years of age, you know, and though I've got all my faculties, thank God, still I do live a great deal in the past. It's very hard for me to tell very often which *is* the past and which the present. You see, for one thing I've lived in this bedroom much of my life—always coming back to it. It was very much the same when I was a little girl as it is now. Of course the wallpaper's changed. It used to have blue Chinese pagodas on it. Very pretty it was. But that tallboy is the same, and this blue tester over my bed, and these charming acanthus leaves carved on the wood . . . What was I saying? Oh yes, about Sunday. Well, you see, living so much in the past I don't understand this not allowing children to amuse themselves of a Sunday. Of course they get into mischief. There is nothing else for them to do.'

This was not at all what Elizabeth wanted. And the old lady was becoming very garrulous now. Moreover, Benjamin, fascinated by the apple, had drawn ever closer and closer to the bed and had completely forgotten that he had come there to be scolded. He was grinning with all his might and, unconsciously, his small chubby *and* grubby fist was stretched towards Judith.

'There! would you like a piece?' She cut off a section with the silver knife. 'Now what do you say?'

'Thank you, Aunt Judith.'

'They all call me Aunt Judith. Isn't it charming? And I'm ninety years old. Well, well . . . ' She put on her silver-rimmed spectacles. 'That's the only thing, Elizabeth, that's beginning to fail me. I can't see to read newspaper print as I did. Ah! there's another poem about the poor Prince Consort, although he's been dead six months. And as to Mr. Lincoln—the *Times* man says that if he would only——' She was aware that Elizabeth wanted something of her. She stared at Benjamin severely over her spectacles.

'Your mother is very unhappy about you, Benjamin, because you will not say you are sorry to Timothy. You are seven now and quite old enough to know that you mustn't throw other people's things down wells.'

He smiled at her.

'I'll say I'm sorry,' he said.

'But are you sorry?'

'No.'

'But are you not sorry to make others unhappy? And do you not see that the whip belonged to Timothy? What would you say if Timothy took your soldiers and threw them in the road?'

'He can have all my soldiers,' said Benjamin.

'You see, Aunt Judith,' Elizabeth said in despair, 'it is quite impossible to make him realise.'

A new tone came into Judith's voice, that same tone with which once she had spoken to Will at Stone Ends, once to Mrs. Ponder, and more than once to Walter.

'Benjamin,' and he was suddenly grave, looking up into her face. 'Will you please go at once to Timothy and make your apologies? Without waiting another minute, please.'

'Yes, Aunt Judith,' he said, and instantly left the room.

'There, you see,' Judith said, greatly pleased. 'All that is needed is a little firmness.'

Elizabeth shook her head, smiled, shook her head again.

'I don't know. He's such a funny boy. He'll be going to school presently—that's, I suppose, what he needs. But I am so frightened for him. He seems to have no idea at all as to what is wrong. He plays with the servants just as though they were not servants at all. He is so restless. Jane tries to teach him, but he will never settle to his books.'

'There, my dear,' said Judith comfortably. 'Come and sit down for a little. Benjamin has his own idea of right and wrong just as I had when I was a little girl. He is generous and loving, is he not? And he is happy too.'

Elizabeth sat down beside the bed.

'Aunt Judith, I'm not tiring you?'

'Tiring me! Oh dear, no. Why, it is only the beginning of the day. I can do with so very little sleep now, or perhaps it is that I sleep most of the time——'

'There is another thing,' Elizabeth began.

'Yes, dear, tell me.'

'I am most unhappy about father. Oh, I know that it would be of no use to go and see him. He would not see me, I suppose, if I did go. We have talked of it before and decided that it would be of no use. But now I hear that he has a really dreadful woman there, a Mrs. Pangloss—a terrible creature who bullies him and of whom he is afraid. Father afraid! Why, when I lived with him you would say that he would never be afraid . . . But it is terrible to sit here and know that he is shut up in that horrible house with that woman. I don't know what I should do, but it makes me so unhappy—thinking of it—being sorry for him.'

Judith stared in front of her. Then suddenly she clapped her hands.

'I know!' she cried. 'I'll go myself and see him!'

'Oh no, Aunt Judith! No, no! Why, it's a dreadful day! It's a deluge—and you haven't been farther than the garden for months.'

'That doesn't say that I couldn't if I wanted to. I'm lazy, that's all. It's an excellent idea. I have wanted to speak to Walter—

poor Walter. Yes, it is all over, our quarrel—quite finished, and it has brought misery enough on everybody. Yes, I'll go and see Walter. An excellent idea!'

There was a knock on the door. Dorothy, Margaret, Adam and the three-year-old Vanessa all entered. Every member of the family paid a visit of a few minutes every morning. This had become a ceremony as almost everything to do with Judith had now something of the ceremonial about it. Not that she wanted it to be so. All that she wanted was that she should feel that she was in touch with everybody. She loved them all, man, woman and child—and she also wished to know exactly what they were all about.

Dorothy was dressed for going out. She was in the very newest fashion—a brown 'pork-pie' hat with a dark red feather, a chignon, and her crinoline raised several inches from the ground, revealing that her stout feet were encased in miniature Hessian boots. This was the first time that Judith had seen these and at once she burst out laughing.

'Oh, Dorothy, my dear. What *have* you got on?'

She sat up in bed, leaning forward, settling her spectacles exactly on her nose that she might see the better.

Dorothy blushed, but she was as phlegmatic and good-natured as she was stout.

'Very handsome *I* call it. And I am wearing an American Cage for the first time. You've always complained that my crinolines are too large.'

'I don't know, I'm sure,' said Judith, 'why with your figure you should run such risks.' Then, to Vanessa: 'Come here, my darling, and see what I've got for you. Give me that little silver box from the table, Adam.'

Vanessa promised to be a very beautiful child. She had hair as dark as Jennifer's had once been, and large dark serious eyes. She had Margaret's broad calm forehead and something of Adam's humorous, almost sarcastic twinkle. When she had been a baby sitting quietly on her mother's lap she would unexpectedly look at you inviting you to agree that the world, although pleasant, was quite absurd. She already adored her father, and he worshipped her. She had a lovely little body, slim and straight. Baby though she was, she carried herself with a beautiful easy natural gesture, bearing her head high and looking all the world in the face.

As a child she was no trouble at all. Adam had insisted that she should be called Vanessa.

'There was once a Vanessa, a lovely lady. And there was an Irish Dean—and there were some letters . . . '

'Oh, you mean Swift!' said Dorothy, who was as literal as any Herries. 'All the same it's a very odd name.'

'My grandmother,' said Adam, 'was called Mirabell, and that was a man's name out of a play by Congreve.'

'Yes,' said Dorothy. 'But I don't see why because your grandmother was odd you should be.'

'Don't you?' said Adam gravely. 'I do.'

'I do wish, Adam,' said Judith as he brought her the little silver box, 'that you wouldn't wear that hideous sack coat. You are too stout for it.'

'Yes, Mother,' he said, smiling. 'But it's comfortable.'

(And oh! how she loved him! When he approached the bed, bent down and kissed her, her whole body thrilled and it was all she could do not to put her arms around him and hold him tight to her. But not with all those women in the room. Oh dear, no!)

'There, darling.' She took two sugared almonds out of the box. This was a daily ritual.

'Thank you, Grandmother.' Adam lifted the little girl up, and for a moment the three of them, grandmother, son and grandchild, were caught together into a loving relationship that no one else in the whole world shared.

'And now,' said Judith comfortably, 'I am going to get up. Send Lucy to me, somebody, and tell James to bring the carriage round. You can go in the barouche to Keswick, Dorothy. I am going up to Ireby to see how poor Cousin Walter is doing.'

She knew that this would be a bombshell and she enjoyed greatly the effect of it.

'What!' Dorothy cried as though she had just heard that the end of the world had come. 'Going out! On a day like this! When you haven't been out for months! To the Fortress! Why, you're crazy, Aunt Judith!'

And even Margaret, who thought now that everything that Adam's mother did was wise, said: 'Oh, but, Mother—surely that is incautious! Listen to the rain!'

'Thank you, my dear. My mind is quite made up.'

Adam, who knew that the more his mother was opposed the more determined she was, said, 'Well, then, Mother, if you go up there, I go with you.'

'Certainly not. What should I want you for? It is quite time I had a little air. Now it is settled. Go along, all of you.'

'But, Aunt Judith——' Dorothy, who was in truth deeply distressed, broke in. 'You can't——'

'Nobody says can't to me!' Judith answered. 'No one ever has, and no one ever will.'

'But Doctor Bettany——'

'Doctor Bettany doesn't know everything. It will do me a great deal of good. And there is something I must say to Walter Herries.'

'But you know what that house is. And there is some horrible woman there now. She will be rude to you and——'

'No one is ever rude to me. At any rate after the first minute. My mind is quite made up, so it's of no use your talking, Dorothy. Now I want one word alone with Adam, if you don't mind.'

Elizabeth, who had been listening in great distress, stayed behind the other two.

'Aunt Judith, *please*. If it is for my sake, I beg you not to go. I would never have said anything if I had thought you would have such an idea——'

'That is quite all right, my dear,' Judith said, smiling at her. 'Your father cannot eat me. I am too old an old lady for anyone to be rude to me. The drive will do me good. Now, go and see that Benjamin isn't getting into mischief. Jane will be teaching him his lesson.'

She was left alone with Adam.

'Mother, is it wise? Walter is very odd, they say, and the house in terrible disorder. At least let me go with you. I can remain outside in the carriage.'

He sat on the edge of the bed. She laid her hand in his large brown one.

'Is it not strange?' she said. 'Do you remember, Adam? In this very room I undressed you and bathed you and you asked all kinds of ridiculous questions. And now see what you are! You are still untidy as you were then, and you have that same brown gipsy colour. And you are not as stout as I feared you would be——'

He sighed. Then he looked at her whimsically. 'Aye, I'm brown and heavy but not fat, and I'm not a dandy—and what I am as well is a failure!'

'Oh no, Adam! Oh no!'

'Now come, Mother. You had great hopes of me, hadn't you? And I've disappointed all of them.'

'Of course not,' she said fiercely. 'All that I hoped for you when you were a baby was that you would be a farmer and live in Watendlath. That, I suppose, was the mistake of my life—that I did not go to Watendlath. But it doesn't matter now. That is the best of being old—nothing matters very much. It is very pleasant to sit outside and watch.'

He laughed. '*You* watch! Why, you are in the middle of everything! No one does a thing in this house but you know it——' He paused, then added slowly: 'We are rather a multitude here. Let me see, not mentioning the servants there are—you, Dorothy, Veronica, Tim, Amabel, Jane, Elizabeth, Benjamin, Margaret, Vanessa and myself. Eleven of us.'

'And not one too many!' she said sharply. 'Now, Adam, I know what you are going to say. You are not to mention buying that land you were speaking of. We have plenty of money. The house is large. There is room for everybody.'

He looked at her with that deprecating shy glance that he had always used with her, since he was a baby, when he had something to confess.

'I have bought it, Mother. The thing was settled yesterday.'

She took her hand from his. All that old anger that rose in her when she was circumvented, all that old distress and alarm that she always felt whenever he was going away, seized her. She began to tremble all over. She glared at him through her spectacles. She pushed *The Times* away from her so violently that it fell on to the floor.

'Now listen, Mother,' he began, speaking quickly. 'I am forty-seven years of age. I have tried everything and failed at everything. Once I tried to do something for my fellow-men and *that* failed. Then I tried to write, and although that did not exactly fail it has never come to anything at all. Mortimer Collins was right when he abused me one night and said that I failed at everything because I could not *stick* at anything. As soon as I was settled anywhere I wanted to run away. I have *that* from you, Mother. You know that I have. Only I haven't the character that you have, nor am I so unselfish. You would have been a wanderer all your days had you not thought so much of others. But I—except for you and Margaret, Kraft and John— I've loved no one but myself! But John's death shocked me. Kraft's death shocked me once and John's completed it. I must settle. If I do not now, I never shall—and there is only one place where I *can* settle. On my own piece of ground in this country. Then I fancy that I still can do something. They all say that I can write—Dickens said so, and Yates and Collins. I shall never write anything that matters *much*, but it will be something. It is not that I shall be far away. The piece of ground above Manesty that I have bought is no distance. I shall come here constantly. But I must have my own place, and Vanessa must have *her* home to grow up in. There are too many women in this house, nor is it fair for Margaret.'

'I am sure dear Margaret is very happy,' Judith broke in.

'Yes, she is happy, but not so happy as she would be in her own home. You *must* see it, Mother. You who are so wise and so sensible . . . '

She saw it. She had always had the capacity to see other people's point of view. But this was the end—the *End*.

She had only a few more years to live. Adam was all that she had in the world. If Adam left her . . . All that she said was:

'Pick up *The Times* for me, will you, dear? I think that it is *most* ridiculous that Germany should wish to have a Navy. I saw a very funny picture in *Punch* last week——'

He bent down and kissed her and, when he felt her body tremble, he put his arms round her. But he said no more. He knew that she would realise this was best for himself and Margaret, and that when she had realised that she would never say another word on the matter.

Nor did she. All the while that Lucy was dressing her she scarcely spoke. When the dressing was finished she sat down in a chair.

'Lucy, did I not hear that you are engaged to be married?'

'Yes, Madame.'

'I hope he is a good man.'

'Very good, Madame. He helps Mr. Boulter, the butcher, in Keswick.'

'Oh yes . . . I hope he is sober.'

'He never touches a drop, Madame.'

'Well, I trust that you will be very happy. We shall be sorry to lose you.'

'Thank you, Madame.'

Veronica came in and helped her downstairs.

'Thank you, my dear. How pretty you are looking to-day!'

'It's terrible weather. Do you think you ought to go out, Aunt Judith?'

'I don't think—I know,' she answered. 'Now you can tell

James that I am ready.'

James Bennett, son of Bennett Senior (now with God), a stout sturdy fellow and practically speechless, arrived with a very large umbrella to shelter her over the garden-path. She was settled in the carriage with rugs and a foot-warmer. She waved out of the window to Veronica and Jane in the doorway, and Margaret, Benjamin and Vanessa in an upper window.

But, so soon as the carriage had started, she fell into a fit of melancholy—indeed saw herself, a poor little aged worn-out not-wanted creature, lying at the very bottom of the sort of damp dark insect-ridden well into which Benjamin had thrown Timothy's whip. Such a mood was very rare with her. Now for a quarter of an hour she thoroughly indulged herself.

In the first place the weather helped, for it was one of the worst days of rain and storm that the year had yet seen. From the eastern sky the rain swung in a solid sheet—you could see it, slanting, as though in the folds of some thin grey stuff blown by the wind against the horses' heads. It hissed through the air and all the ground was running with water; you could see through the window rivulets of rain bubbling on the grass, and the rain leaping on the roadway; the wind drove it across the land from Solway in gusts of lines and spirals and curves.

'Dear, dear,' Judith thought. 'What a day to choose to come out in after months indoors.' She wondered what impulse had decided her on this visit; she was so very comfortable indoors, and this announcement of Adam's had swallowed Walter completely as though he never had been.

It was as though her whole life through she had been trying to catch Adam and he had always eluded her. Of course he loved her, but not as she loved him, for she must share him with Margaret and Vanessa. Margaret was an excellent woman and Vanessa a sweet baby, but after all they were not his mother. Here to her own surprise and disgust she felt a tear trickle down her cheek. She took her handkerchief and wiped it indignantly away. It was years since she had shed tears; not indeed since

John's death, and then only when she was alone. But when you were old your body was feeble, boast as you might to others. You could not be sure of commanding it.

This decision of Adam's was dreadful. He said that he would see her often, but he would not. Once he was away there on the hills above Derwentwater his visits to her would be fewer and fewer. She cared of course for the others—for dear Jane especially—but they were not inside her heart as Adam was. And she was not—although she would not admit it—at home in this new world that was growing up around her, a world of material riches and prosperity, a world in which the men seemed to be divided from the women so that an elaborate sort of hypocrisy sprang up between them when they met. Dorothy was shocked—or thought it proper to be shocked—if you talked of cows calving or sheep lambing. Jane and Amabel were quite resigned to being old maids, it seemed. The countryside was covered with old maids, and yet, on the other hand, all the girls in the County thought of nothing but marriage, only they must not say so and indeed must pretend that they had no notion of the barbarous practices that marriage involved. It had been very different in Judith's youth, and she had a sudden picture of herself and Georges and Emma Furze in London and the things that they would discuss and that other people would do!

'If it goes on much longer like this,' Judith had said to Dorothy the other day, 'there will be no more babies, for parents will be ashamed of creating them!'

She disliked too a kind of religion that was beginning to be prevalent, a religion that Dorothy took an interest in and that even the beautiful Veronica pretended to admire. It came, she believed, from Oxford, and Mr. Hall and Mr. Eustace were its local prophets. It consisted, so far as Judith could discover, in talking in a high affected voice, bowing and scraping in church and professing the saintly life. She believed that Mr. Hall *was* perhaps a Saint—she knew that he gave everything away and lived entirely on potatoes—but Mr. Eustace with his shrill voice and ogling eyes revolted her. She had been given to read a novel that, so she was told, portrayed the ideal saintly character of this religious movement—*The Heir of Redclyffe* by Miss Charlotte Mary Yonge—but she had found it mawkish and unreal and had wanted to throw it into the fire. In all this she was of course very ignorant; she knew nothing at all about the Oxford Movement, but it all helped to make her feel, when she was depressed, that she had lived far too long and had wandered into a world that was not hers.

However, she was not often depressed and she did not intend to be long depressed now. She dried her eyes, blew her nose and tried to pretend that she was as independent of Adam as she was of everyone else in the world. If he *wished* to go and live on a patch of ground above Derwentwater, why, let him go! How absurd of her, when she should be thinking of her approaching End, to be disturbed by what *anyone* wished to do! Nevertheless the pretence was not very successful. The very thought of Adam, smiling, untidy in his sack coat, so ludicrously absent-minded, so clever (as she thought him), so well-read and wise and learned but so exceedingly modest about it . . . she had only to think of him to bring him right into the carriage beside her! And so, after all, it might be when he was living on Cat Bells! He could not *really* be very far away from her!

The carriage was now driving through the storm up the hill to Ireby. She must prepare herself for the encounter with Walter. This meeting with him was in fact no new idea. She had had it in mind ever since the awful catastrophe of John's death. She must tell him, before she died, that their quarrel was ended, that she forgave him everything—yes, even the deaths of Francis and Reuben—and she must try to console him a little and try if he would not perhaps see Elizabeth and his grandson.

As Bennett, down whose cape the water was now pouring in a vicious stream, whipped the poor horses up the hill, the carriage met the full force of the storm. The wind tugged at the windows, the rain lashed them, and she rose to the vigour of it. 'This is the way I like it,' she thought. Something in her bones, that had crept into them when old Squire Tom carried her the first day of her life through the snowstorm, excited her now. She pushed her nose against the window to see whether she had arrived, but could realise nothing because the wet blur of the rain was so thick. Then the carriage stopped; Bennett got down from his seat. With difficulty he opened the carriage door and then had to push his chest right inside to avoid the wind. His rough red cheek, fresh with rain, was close against Judith.

'Well, are we there, James?'

'Yes, Madame.'

'What do we do now?'

'Well, Madame . . . best for me t'pull t'bell while you stay inside t'carriage.'

'Pull it then.'

She could see dimly through the window now and thought how desolate the Fortress had become. The building was dark, naked and repellent. The stone seemed to have blackened under rain as though it had been smoked. The wood behind the house moaned and wailed. A pile of earth stood near the flagged path in the garden as though in preparation for a grave, and all the plants were beaten down with the wind. A tree somewhere rocked and screamed. She could see so dimly that she could not be sure what she saw. She could fancy that figures moved in and out through the rain, and especially her fancy, the growing faintness of the sight of her old age, made her imagine that the shape of a woman in a black cloak or shawl moved out from the trees and stood motionless, staring at the carriage.

Suddenly she disliked so greatly staying in the carriage alone that she picked herself up, found her cane, adjusted her bonnet and climbed down into the rain, then walked with great assurance up the flagged path and joined Bennett.

She heard the bell pealing through the house as though the place were empty and deserted. She could smell the wet stale smell of laurels and elder bushes. Then the door opened and a slatternly girl poked her head through. Just then there was a gust of wind so violent that Judith, slight as she was, was blown into the house.

She stood in the hall and the girl gaped at her.

'You'd better close the door,' Judith said gently. 'It is terrible weather, isn't it?'

The girl's hair had been blown across her cheek, and she stared at Judith as though she were an apparition.

'I think I'll sit down,' Judith said, and so she did on a hard straight-backed oak chair with arms that she remembered well from the old Westaways house. A cat came into the hall, mewing . . .

'Who might you be wanting?' asked the girl.

'Would you tell Sir Walter Herries that Madame Paris from Uldale would like to see him for a moment?'

The cat came over to her and rubbed against her leg. She bent down and stroked it, then with her two gloved hands resting on her cane leaned forward and waited.

She did not have to wait long, for a door swung back and there stood before her a great fat woman in a mob cap. 'This,' she thought, 'must be the Mrs. Pangloss of whom I have heard,' and noticed with great dislike her face red as a ham, her thick bare neck, her big uncontrolled bosom, her long peering nose and other more unagreeable features. Her personal, almost passionate, love of cleanliness made a woman such as this very unpleasing to her.

The hall was dark and the woman stared about her.

'Well?' she said, glaring at the girl. 'What are you standing there for? Haven't I told you——?'

'There's someone——' said the girl.

The woman turned to Judith.

'Yes?' she said. 'What can I do for you?'

'I was wondering,' said Judith, 'whether I might see Sir Walter Herries for a moment. Pray forgive my sitting down, but I am not so young as I once was.' She smiled.

The woman at once recognised her. She said: 'Oh yes? Indeed! Well, I fear that Sir Walter is not very well to-day and is unable to see anyone.'

'I am sorry to hear that. Perhaps if I were to see him for a moment only——'

'Impossible, I'm afraid.'

The woman stood staring as the maid had done. Judith was so famous a figure that this visit was astonishing. The woman's slow brain doubtless was moving through a maze of questions. What did old 'Madame' want? Did this threaten her own power here? Was there some plot hostile to herself?

'Would you at least,' said Judith patiently, 'tell Sir Walter that I am here?'

'Mustn't disturb him.'

'It is of importance that I should see him—great importance.'

'Excuse me,' said the woman more insolently, as though she had made up her mind that Judith was not to be feared. 'Another day perhaps, but to-day Sir Walter is not to be disturbed. I'm in charge here. I'll tell him that you inquired.'

The door to the left of the staircase opened and Walter appeared. He was in slippers and a faded snuff-coloured dressing-gown. At first he could not see who was there. Then, almost knocking against the chair, he stumbled back.

'Why, Judith!' he cried.

She held out her hand.

'I am delighted to see you, Walter. Your housekeeper said that you were indisposed, but I shall not keep you long. Can you give me five minutes with you alone?'

He plainly did not know what to do, and she was so sorry for him and felt so strong an impulse to carry him off there and then from under the sharp nose of Mrs. Pangloss that any old enmity there might ever have been fell, dead, once and for all.

The woman did not move.

'Why, certainly,' Walter said. 'I have not been well. Mrs. Pangloss was correct. This is Mrs. Pangloss, my housekeeper.'

Judith gave a little bow.

The woman said angrily: 'Now you know what the doctor said—that you wasn't to see anyone, no matter who it was, and you'll catch your death away from the fire, you know you will. Sorry, ma'am, it's the doctor's orders, and another day when he's more himself it won't matter, I'm sure—but I have to see to his health. If I don't, nobody does.'

Here, however, Walter plucked up courage; it must have shamed him that Judith of all people should have seen him thus.

'Very well, Mrs. Pangloss. You are acting for the best, I am sure, but now that Madame Paris has come all this way on such a day . . . Pray ask Alice to light a fire in the library. That will save you the stairs, Judith. Allow me to give you an arm.'

Mrs. Pangloss stood there, looking at them. She never moved and, after they had gone, stood staring at the spot where they had been.

The room into which Walter led Judith had already a fire burning in the grate and a rich brooding odour of spirits about it. A decanter and two tumblers, one half filled with something that was, Judith thought, gin and water, stood on a table. This, she realised at once, had been Mrs. Pangloss' sanctum that morning. Otherwise it was desolate enough. A picture of a hunting scene hung crooked on a nail and there was a screen with pictures of boxing scenes pasted on to it. Very little else. Walter settled Judith in an arm-chair whose grey and disordered stuffing protruded from the seat. A window looked out on to the soaked and neglected garden. The wind whistled behind the wallpaper. Walter sat down on a hard chair near Judith. She was greatly distressed at the change in him. She had last seen him three years before, riding in Keswick, and on horseback, wrapped in a high riding-coat, he had had something of his old carriage and even, she thought, arrogance. Now he had a rugged grey beard, his cheeks had fallen, and as he sat with his old dressing-gown huddled about him he looked more than his seventy years.

'If that woman was rude to you,' he said abruptly, 'I shall dismiss her.'

'Not at all,' said Judith cheerfully. 'She said you were not well and should see nobody.'

'She's a good creature in her way,' he went on. 'She means well by me—the only one who does.'

'Now, Walter, that's nonsense. We all mean well by you if you will let us.'

'Fine words, Judith, fine words.' He drew the dressing-gown closer about him. 'I'm always cold now. This house is damp. You wouldn't think so when I built it, but the damp's come in just as everything else has gone out. What have you come for?' he asked bluntly. 'We've been meeting like this all our lives, but our meetings never come to anything.' Then as though he had said nothing: 'How old are you now?'

'I? I'm nearly eighty-eight.'

'Eighty-eight! Wonderful! And still able to get about.'

'Well, I don't get about much now, you know. There is plenty to do in the house.'

'Yes; got your fingers on everything, I suppose, just as you used to. What have you come to see *me* for?' he asked again.

'I have come for two reasons, Walter. First, I want you to know that our old feud is over. At least on my side. You must not think that I am angry or feel any enmity. The past is dead. At any rate our quarrel is dead.'

He rubbed his finger against his stubbly cheek. 'The past is never dead,' he said. 'You know that as well as I do. When you come to our age we live in the past. It is all I do live in. Back—back—to when my son was alive, when he could walk into this room just as anyone did and say 'Good morning.' Not that he cared for me, of course—he never did that—but he was there. He was in this house. I could hear him moving over stairs. You could tell his walk, you know, because he limped. Uhland was lame from birth, you know, Judith, and that is what made him bitter—that and my telling him when he was a baby that he had an injustice, being lame. And so he had an injustice, poor boy, and cleverer than anyone in the County. That is why he thought poorly of me. He could see I had no brains, never had any. But it's too late now. The harm's been done, done years and years ago, before we were born.'

He would have continued to talk for ever. Indeed he had forgotten her, but she was so deeply touched that she rose a little in her chair, leaned over and took his hand. Even as she did so, she thought: 'Twenty years ago! If you had told me that I would ever feel so tenderly! But what does it matter now? We are both so old!'

He let her hand hold his, which was hot and dry to the touch.

'Listen, Walter!' she said. 'That is what I have come to say. You must not think that you are alone in regretting the past. That old quarrel has done us all much harm, but I feel that—that—that catastrophe eight years ago—it was terrible, tragic—but John and Uhland by dying rid us all of an enmity, something bad in the blood, that must not come back again. John left a son, you know—a grandson whom you have never seen—and it would be wicked, *wicked*, if his life was spoilt by it. It seems to me now when I am old that we cannot do anything without affecting someone else, and one bad, selfish cruel thing can spread and spread into the lives of people we never see . . . I want you now to be friends with us all, to see Elizabeth and your grandchild . . . to help us all so that his life at least shall suffer no effects from all that past trouble. Let Elizabeth come . . . '

She had not been sure that he had heard anything that she had said, but at the repetition of Elizabeth's name his body trembled and shook, he caught his hand from hers and sprang to his feet.

'No, no!' he cried, swaying on his feet and gesticulating with his hands as though he were beating someone away from him. 'She's no daughter of mine and you shan't come round me with all your talk. She left me, and good riddance. She married my boy's murderer. Oh yes, she did! Don't you tell me now! Do you suppose that he didn't taunt him with his lameness, and she too?

Uhland knew. Uhland heard what they said, the two of them. Now you can go, and pretty quick too, and don't let me catch you here again . . . And put some coal on the fire before you go,' he said, his voice suddenly dropping. 'This room's as cold as hell. Hell's cold—not warm as they say. This is *my* house, and no enemy of my boy is going to sit in it.'

He stood looking at her, shaking, his legs wavering.

'Well, you are an old woman,' he said, sitting down again. 'You can stay if you like, but don't you talk such nonsense. You ought to know better at your age.'

'Very well,' she said quietly. 'I'll stay, Walter, but not if you're rude and violent. We do no good by shouting at one another.'

'No, I suppose we do not,' he said, nodding his head. 'I tell you what it is, Judith. I'm not used to company. A while ago I went to London. You didn't know that, did you? And I saw a Fight—a fine Fight it was too, but the man I wanted to win didn't win, and so I came home to be by myself. I said, "Now if you win, everything will be all right. Uhland will come back." But he didn't win, and so what was the use in seeing anybody any more? So I came home, and I'm not very good company. You must forgive me.'

She saw that there was nothing more to be said just then about Elizabeth. Nevertheless something had been achieved by her visit. They sat close together now like two old cronies.

'You see, Walter, I'm very old—very old indeed. I may die at any time. Not that I mind dying, but I wouldn't wish to leave any bad feeling behind me when I go. When you are as old as I am, bad feeling seems so very stupid—and I hope it won't continue into another generation. Your grandfather, David, used to tell me many stories about my father. Fancy! He has been dead now almost a hundred years! But David Herries used to say that he thought all the trouble in our branch of the family started when my father as a young man sold his mistress at a Fair in a temper. You've heard the old story. It's a legend, they say now, but it was all true enough, I believe. My father was a good man but he had

205

a hot temper. That is perhaps what Uhland had too—but now those stories are all so old and so long ago and there is a new generation growing up. Dear little Vanessa, my grand-daughter, such a pretty child. And Benjamin, your grandson—a very lively high-spirited boy. I don't want them to be in any family quarrel when they grow up. The world is more sensible now than when I was a girl—too sensible, I sometimes think, with people like Mr. Gladstone and so much church on Sundays. Of course I think young people ought to go to church, but not as a duty. I'm rambling on, but what I really mean is that I want Vanessa and Benjamin to grow up without any hatred. Hatred is silly—waste of time and temper.'

She had talked on, but it seemed that he had listened to none of it. He only sat there staring in front of him, scratching his cheek. She was trying to reconcile him with the stout, cheerful, bullying man she had once known. How could Jennifer and the others have feared him as they did? He had never had any brains, only some instincts, and so he had collapsed under the pressure of events. You must have either intelligence or spiritual faith to stand up against life. When you had both you could be a conqueror. Jennifer had never had any brains, so she had gone the same way.

'Well, I must go now. Will you help me to my carriage?'

She rose a little unsteadily. When she stood beside him her little body was at his height, he sitting.

She kissed him.

Then, to her distress, she saw slow unmeaning tears trickle down his cheek. He did not try to stop them. He did not perhaps know that he was crying. Gently she stroked his rough unbrushed hair, speaking to him as though he were a child.

'There, there, Walter . . . Things are not so bad, my dear. I will come again and see you. I am glad that we are friends at last. If you want anything, you have only to send to Uldale. There, there, Walter. Remember that we are all your friends. You are not alone any more. Uldale is no distance, you know.'

He rose slowly, looked about him in a bewildered fashion, then very courteously offered her his arm and conducted her to her carriage.

ON CAT BELLS:
ESCAPE FROM ECSTASY

Adam, turning on his side, caught the light from the window. The morning clouds, fiery with gold, were piling up above Walla Crag. *His* field—the field of all his life with its five little trees and its arch of sloping green—rolled into the glow; then, as though with a sigh of satisfaction, held the light; the little trees stood up and stretched their morning limbs. He looked at the field, thought that it was late (but they had not returned from Ambleside until one this morning), looked over his shoulder and saw that Margaret was yet deeply sleeping, then stretched out his brown hand to the bedside table and found Barney Newmark's letter.

There was light enough now to read by. Barney described Thackeray's funeral:

'. . . You would have been moved, Adam, although you thought the man proud and sensitive. So perhaps he was, but he had reason to be. Maybe he was the loneliest man I have ever met. One of the kindliest too. I could not but remember the first time I ever went to his house—his table covered, not with books and papers as you might think, but with compasses and pencils, bits of chalk and India ink, and little square blocks of boxwood. He was drawing, not writing. There were no signs of the author in the room, only the appliances of the draughtsman, and when we chatted he would rather talk about drawings than about books. And in what a kind, generous way, putting his hand on my arm, he said: "Well: and how can I be of any service to you?"

'And then there I was at Harlesden and a labourer going to his work said, quite casually: "You must make haste if you want to see him buried." It was a bright December day, everything shining and glittering, a dense black crowd waiting by the grave, and then the hearse—quite a common one, one of those plain, dull, black-painted boxes upon wheels without feathers or any ornament, drawn by only two horses: two or three carriages following, and then the straggling mourners—Dickens looking defiant as though he would like to knock someone down, Cruikshank, Millais, Louis Blanc, and the *Punch* people—you know, Mark Lemon, Leech and Tenniel—a lot more. The eight men could scarcely carry the coffin—he was a giant, wasn't he? Then the short ceremony—thank heaven it is so short!—and the mourners elbowing their way through the crowd to take a last look. And wasn't this an irony? There was a heavy prosaic policeman by the grave and as we filed past he said to the man in front of me: "Now don't be in a hurry; follow each other to the right, and you will all see comfortably." Would not Thackeray himself have liked that? The younger men of course are saying that he is already old-fashioned, but I myself think . . . '

Adam did not just then discover what it was that Barney thought. He put down the letter and lay for a while looking out across the Lake to Walla Crag. Thackeray was dead and he himself was forty-eight, and his mother, amazing woman, was eighty-nine; the Americans were fighting one another, and Bismarck was bullying the Danes; he must widen the vegetable-patch beyond the trees to the right of the house, and to-day he would start his fairy-story—the one that had been in his head for more than a year now—and young Benjamin was riding over for the day and night from Uldale. It was the last week of his holiday before he returned to school—and here he was, he, Adam Paris, who had done nothing with his life as yet at all, but was happy, happy, happy . . . here in this January of 1864, in his own cottage that he had helped to build with his own hands under the brow of the hill, and Margaret his wife lying beside him, and their child cradled in her arm (for in the night, when they had returned, she had wakened, climbed out of her cot and demanded to come to them). Well, well . . . and Thackeray was dead, dead and buried.

He stretched out his hand again, this time for a volume of a novel. The novel was called *The Ordeal of Richard Feverel*; it was written by a young man, George Meredith. Although it had been published some four years or so, he had only now heard of it. An unusual book! Fantastically written but new—new in thought, in style and in audacity. And Thackeray was old-fashioned. Thackeray was dead. He rolled over and laid his arm very lightly but protectively over Margaret. They had sailed all the perilous seas now and were in harbour, through passion (but Margaret had never been very passionate), through that strange period of isolation the one from the other, when they knew one another too well and yet not nearly well enough. (That had been ended by the scene at Uldale that Christmas-time.) Then through the wonderful stage of renewed passion and a heightened glorious intimacy. (This stage had included Caesar Kraft's death and the end of Adam's 'Brotherhood' ambitions.) Then, back in Cumberland, out of passion and into this, the real glory of every marriage that can attain it, a confidence, a trust, an intimacy so great and deep and calm that it was like Derwentwater there beyond the window.

She would never *quite* understand him. There was a vein of cynicism running through his nature that was quite foreign to her. Nor would she ever understand his restlessness. Once she had his love and the love of their child, and *knew* that she had them, nothing could ever disturb her again—except, of course, losing either himself or Vanessa. Always when he left her, even for an hour or two, a little wrinkle lined her calm brow. She was not *really* happy again until he had returned. But she was no longer possessive as she had once been. That was because she was sure of him now.

At that thought he moved a little restlessly. Did he want her to be sure of him? Did any man want his wife to be sure of him, and was not every wife unhappy unless she *was* sure? That was perhaps one of the eternal misunderstandings in marriage. And in this his mother completely understood him. In every way his mother understood him, shared his restlessness, his longings, his disappointments in himself, knew him as no one else did. He and she were wanderers constrained by the circumstances of life to be stay-at-homes. Had he not married Margaret what a useless, worthless wanderer he would have been! Like his old legendary grandfather! Yes, he had been lucky to marry a woman like Margaret, so good and loyal, faithful and true. Once he would have been wearied and irritated by too much goodness and fidelity.

He got out of bed very quietly and went down to the yard behind the house for Will to sluice him down. Although it was early January and mortal cold, he did not shrink from the sluicing. The yard was hidden from the world save for the little wood on the rise of the ground. No windows looked on it, and it was sheltered from the wind. Will was already there, cleaning the boots and hissing away at them like a hostler. He straightened himself when he saw Adam and stood up, grinning, his yellow forelock straggling over his forehead, his eyes as blue, direct and unflinching as those of an honest and fearless child, his body balanced easily on its strong legs.

'I'm late this morning, Will.'

'Aye. You was late last night.'

'Lovely day.'

Will looked up. The sky was blue and laced everywhere with little clouds that still had tints of amber and rose.

'Cold this morning,' Adam said.

He looked at Will with great affection. The whole day started wrongly if he did not have a brief talk alone with Will at the beginning of it, for his relation with Will was that of man to man, rid of all the uncertainties, sudden crises, sudden darknesses that haunt like ghosts the relations of the sexes. In a way Will understood him better than did either his mother or Margaret. In a way Will loved him better than did either of the women, for it was a love completely unselfish, that asked nothing in return, that was disturbed by no moods or reticences. When Adam was in a temper or caught into some creative distance far from all human agency or had a cold or a headache or felt his liver, Margaret was disturbed as though she were in danger of losing something (although she had learnt to conceal this disturbance, Adam knew that it was there and it irritated him), but Will was unchanged. Let Adam have what mood he wished, Will loved him just the same. He could be jealous, and was often confoundedly obstinate and pig-headed, but his loyalty, devotion, trustworthiness never varied a hair's breadth.

Two wooden buckets filled with cold water stood side by side. Adam threw off his shirt and breeches, then shivered as the cold air struck his bare flesh.

'Quick, Will. Quick, you devil!'

Will took up one bucket in his two arms and with a heave threw the water over Adam. Then the other. Then quickly he caught a rough towel that was hanging on the back of the kitchen door, seized Adam and rubbed him with great violence, hissing furiously.

Adam ran into the kitchen and stood naked in front of the roaring fire. Now he was glorious. He was in fine condition. Drops of water clung to his beard and his hairy chest. His flesh was firm and strong. His heart beat like a good steady hammer. He took deep breaths. Will watched the operation with high satisfaction.

'You know, Will,' Adam said, stretching out his bare arms, 'my mother has told me that her father used to have his man swill him down at Rosthwaite where he lived, in just this way. He was a queer character, he was. My mother has a heap of tales about him from his son, her step-brother. He was years older than she was—David Herries, I mean. And now she's nearing ninety. Takes you back a long time, doesn't it?'

'Aye,' said Will. 'It does that. We're born and we're wed and we're dead before we know. 'Tis odd when you think of it, Mr.

Adam, that folk make the fuss they do when they're dead so quick. About little things, I mean. Now there was that man from Seathwaite last evening. Was in here with a long tale about a cow he'd lost. I told him not to fret and he was furious, as though I'd stolen the damned cow myself. Mary will be in likely. I can hear her coming.' This was the old woman from the farm half-way to Grange. She came every day as help.

Adam pulled on his shirt and breeches and went upstairs.

* * * * *

Later he was sitting in his room waiting to begin his fairy-story. This room—not very large—was square, papered a dull rather shabby red, and the two windows looked full on to the Lake and Walla Crag. The wall opposite the windows was lined with shelves, and there were his books, not a great collection, some four or five hundred in all.

They were, moreover, a mixed lot, in no sort of order. A faded row of little blue volumes of the *Iliad* and *Odyssey* had for companions *Pickwick* in its shilling parts (the covers of some of the numbers disgracefully torn), Rogers' *Italy* with the handsome illustrations, Arthur Young's *Travels in France* and Leigh Hunt's *Story of Rimini*. There were thirty volumes of the 'English Poets,' ten of Chaucer, *Sir Charles Grandison* and *Tristram Shandy*. On the table at his side were two volumes of *Richard Feverel*, Huxley's *Man's Place in Nature*, and *The Woman in White*. By itself on the other side of him was a fresh brilliant copy in green and gold of Barney Newmark's first novel[1]—*Dandy Grimmett*—in three volumes.

'They have bound young Barney very handsomely,' he thought. (He still looked on Barney as an infant although he was now nearly thirty-four years of age.) He felt a pang of envy, regret, sadness. There was young Barney, of whom no one had thought very much, publishing his first novel and some of it not bad either, especially the racing scenes, the fight (plainly taken from Sayers and Heenan), and the last chapter when old Dandy, dying, is brought back to his rooms in London and hears the carriages rolling to the theatres, the cries of the newsboys, and the thick heavy ticking of the clock on the marble mantelpiece. 'He's been influenced by Thackeray, of course—not doing anything new like this young man Meredith. But is it important to be new? Nothing is new but superficials. He can paint a scene that is real. He knows his world . . . Damned clever sketch of his father, old Stephen. He'd deny it, of course . . .'

His mind went floating away to the Lake that lay in the morning sun like a snake's skin, grey and rippled, convulsed, it seemed, with little shudders. The sunlight hung above it on the flanks of the hill as though afraid to descend. He pushed open the window and looked out, heard the stream running at the back of the house, smelt the dead bracken, the gritty flakiness of the dead earth, and saw a snowdrop, solitary and beautiful, bend its stem in the breeze.

He heard Vanessa calling. His heart warmed. It was all he could do not to go out to her, but he knew that once he had left that room incident after incident would occur to prevent his return to it, as though a malicious Fate were determined for ever to hold him back from doing anything. With a sigh he closed the window and went back to the table. He picked up a number of *London Society* that had just arrived and read from the serial story:

'"Nor need you wish to do so, Miss Fleming," said Jane quickly. "Nor, if you were thrown on the world, would you ever be what Milly and I are now. We have had unusual advantages from our cradles, and with great natural aptitude, have improved them to the uttermost."'

He sighed again. 'Great natural aptitude . . .' 'Improved them to the uttermost.' No, people did not talk like that. Why were novels so silly?

But this seemed to encourage him. *He* was going to write a fairy-story. He sat down resolutely, drew the paper in front of him and wrote in his firm strong hand:

THE DWARF WITH THE PURPLE COMB[2]

He sat, looking out of window, biting the feather of his quill. Then he was off and away!

Once upon a time there was a King who had five lovely daughters. The names of the five Princesses were Hazel, Rosamond, Amaryllis, Mellicent and Mary. Mary was the youngest and she was not given so grand a name as the others because the King, her father, had wanted to have a son and was so grievously disappointed when the Doctor told him that the baby was a girl that he shut himself into his bedroom for four and a half days and refused to see anybody, even the Queen. He lived all that time on bread and water. So at least it was said. But Fortunatus, the son of the Woodcutter in the Forest near by, saw the Palace gardener climb on a ladder and hand through the King's bedroom window a gold tray that had on it a gingerbread cake, a roast goose, a Christmas pudding and a dish with oranges, plums and apricots.

Fortunatus told his father, the Woodcutter, what he had observed, and his father said that he must never mention it to anyone or he would lose his head. Mary, who was the loveliest child ever seen—she had hair as dark as the ravens and a smile so sweet that everyone at the Court loved her—was always punished when her sisters did anything wrong. For example, one fine morning Princess Rosamond was given a beautiful dress by her Fairy Godmother (it was her birthday). The dress was made of tissue of silver and it had buttons of green jade, a collar of emeralds, and the sleeves were decorated with the feathers of the Bird of Paradise. When Princess Mellicent saw this beautiful dress she was so angry because *her* Fairy Godmother had given her on *her* birthday only a needlework-case. So she took the gold scissors from her needlework-case and when Princess Rosamond was practising the piano in the Green Drawing-room she went into her sister's bedroom and cut the beautiful dress into shreds.

Now when this was discovered and Mellicent had confessed to what she had done, Mary was put to stand in the corner of the Audience Chamber with her face to the wall so that everyone who passed by could see her.

It happened then one fine morning that Fortunatus, the Woodcutter's son, was sent by his father to the Palace with a wheelbarrow full of logs for the Royal fireplaces, and, peeping in (for he was a very inquisitive boy) at the door of the Audience Chamber, he saw the lovely little Princess standing with her face to the wall . . .

Little Vanessa ran down the path and up the road. It was time for Benjamin to be coming, and from the corner where the stream ran from the tops straight like a silver arrow into the Lake you could watch the higher bend of the road. She danced about, clapping her hands because it was cold.

She was wearing a dress of green and black checked taffeta, which was the new material. She was immensely proud of it and had begged to be allowed to wear it because Benjamin was coming. She was already tall for her age, carried herself to her full height, and now, when she was dancing, every movement was natural in its grace as the silver pattern of the stream, the dull amber of the dead bracken and the bare wood whose trees were flushed in the distance like an evening sky against the grey Lake filmed with ice. Skiddaw and Blencathra were powdered with snow, and hard round clouds like snowballs hung above their lines. Vanessa's mind was intently fixed on Benjamin. Although he was over four years older she thought that he was a perfect companion. She was even then an excellent listener; her curiosity was acute, and she could never be told enough about anything if someone wanted to tell her. Benjamin told her the most extraordinary things. Everything that happened at Uldale was of absorbing interest to her, and she spent so much of her time with grown-up people—her mother and father, Will, and Mary from the farm—that although she was entirely a child and in many things still a baby, she understood the *lives* of grown-up people, knew why they did things and could *imagine* their world. Her grandmother—the old lady who was as smart as a pin, all white and black (and the very *whitest* of white!) with her cap, her ivory cane, her shoes with the silver buckles, who was so kind, amusing, understanding, but could, all in a moment, be so sharp and commanding (very like the Queen of England)— was to Vanessa simply the most miraculous person in the world, composed of magic, fire, ice, diamonds. There she was in her room, older than anyone had ever been, but more acquainted with all that Vanessa was thinking than anyone save her mother. Then there was Aunt Jane, the nicest of all the Aunts. Aunt Veronica who was beautiful, Aunt Amabel who could throw a ball like a boy, Uncle Timothy who was so big that he could take the whole of you in his hand if he wished, Aunt Dorothy who was always busy, James the coachman, Daniel the stable-man, Martha the cook—and so on, so on—a whole *world* was in Uldale. One could never have enough of it.

And Benjamin was her Uldale story-teller. She would like him to go on for hours telling her things, but he could never be still, never stay in one place more than five minutes. And Vanessa thought this unusual, because his mother, Aunt Elizabeth, was so quiet. She would sit all evening in the same corner of the sofa reading a book—only often, as Vanessa had noticed, she was not reading, but would put down her book and sit staring in front of her. Benjamin had no father, which, Vanessa thought, was terribly sad for him.

Ah! there Benjamin was! He came trotting round the corner on Albert, his pony (named after the Prince Consort, who had died the very month that Uncle Timothy gave it him). Mumps the dog was running at the side. Mumps loved Benjamin, and even now, when he was ten years old or more, would never leave Benjamin's side could he help it. The boy saw Vanessa and waved his riding-whip. When he came up to her he burst out laughing. His round, plump face was crimson with the cold air and the exercise, and his funny small nose needed wiping.

'You're wearing a new dress!' he shouted.

'Yes,' she said, still dancing. 'And there's ice on the Lake. It will be frozen perhaps to-morrow—enough to skate on.'

They went up the path to the cottage, and as soon as Benjamin was off the pony he felt in his coat-pocket and produced a large, very sticky chunk of toffee.

'Have some!' he said, trying to break it.

'Did Uncle Timothy give it you?'

'No. I stole it from the kitchen. Mother said I wasn't to have any because I was sick last time from eating so much, so I had to get it from the kitchen, and Martha nearly caught me.'

Benjamin always puzzled Vanessa in this way, because he was for ever doing things that he was told not to do. When he was caught he never lied nor did he seem in the least to mind punishment, but it appeared that you had only to make a rule for him to want to break it.

However, she took some of the toffee and, with their mouths full, they went round to the back to put the pony up and see Will. When they were in the back-yard Benjamin turned a somersault. He had just learned to do it. 'There's a boy at school called Turnip,' he explained. 'And he can do it and he said I couldn't, so now I can.'

'What a funny name to have!' she remarked.

'They call him that because his *real* name is Turner—see?' Benjamin said, turning head over heels again.

* * * * *

In the living-room of the cottage Adam had few books, but he had been given two things out of the parlour at Uldale and these he prized over all his other possessions—one was the old spinet with roses painted on its lid, the other the music-box with the Queen in her green dress and the King in his amber coat. When Judith, growing too old to argue violently with Dorothy, saw that big heavy new furniture was coming into the parlour do what she would, she insisted that Adam should have the spinet for his cottage. She would have given him the sofa with the red apples also had she not felt a superstition. Her hand had rested on that when she had made her great decision . . .

Adam's living-room had not much furniture. There were the wax flowers that he had bought Margaret at the Pantheon. The square carpet had eight groups of flowers on a light pink ground. There were three carved mahogany chairs with needlework seats and backs. There was a chiffonier bookcase, brown and gold with marquetry panels. These things had been presents from various members of the family. Carey Rockage's wife had given him two cornucopias, Will Herries the bookcase. On the walls against some very variegated wallpaper was a water-colour called 'The Lady of the House,' an engraving of Watendlath, and a Baxter print, 'Dippers and Nest.' In one corner of the room was Vanessa's joy, a Peepshow of the Central Hall at the Great Exhibition. Over the mantelpiece was hung a Sand Picture, 'Saddle Horse,' by James Zobel. Barney Newmark had given him this one Christmas. So the room was an odd jumble, and he didn't care for anything in it save the music-box and the spinet. But it was in this room and among these things that he experienced a little scene with young Benjamin. He had reached a point in his fairy-story where the Dwarf had tapped on the Princess Mary's window. The Palace Garden was flooded with moonlight. She came to the window and, standing on the top of the ladder, he whispered to her that, if she would come with him, he would take her to the orchard and there, hidden in the ground at the roots of an old apple tree, he would find for her the Purple Comb . . .

At that point everything had ceased. He could see no more the Princess, the Dwarf, young Fortunatus. All had vanished, the Lake rippled under its silver shading of ice, and Blencathra had the bloom of a plum. Soon it would be time for the meal. He was hungry, so, rubbing his hands, he went into the living-room. A moment later Benjamin came in.

'Uncle Adam,' he asked, 'can you wrestle?'

'No,' he said.

'Try,' said Benjamin, and without a moment's warning he pushed himself on to Adam. He butted his stomach with his round head, tried to bring his arms together around Adam's broad thighs, twisted his small legs round Adam's thick ones. He put a ferocious energy into this, blowing and grunting, straining every muscle in his body. For a moment he made Adam rock. Adam could feel the muscles of the boy's leg strung to their utmost against his calf. The two small hands tore at his waistcoat. A button flew off. The hands groped inside his shirt, pinched his flesh.

'Hi!' he called out. 'That's enough! You're hurting!'

'I'll do it! I'll do it!' Benjamin gasped. 'I'll bring you down!'

Adam, laughing, put out his arms, caught the boy to him with a bear's hug, then swung him into the air and held him there.

'Now what will you do?'

Benjamin kicked. Then he was rolled on to the floor, lay there for a moment panting.

'Things look funny from here,' he observed. He got up. 'I haven't it right yet. There's a trick you do with your left leg. Next time I shall manage it.' His hair was dishevelled, his cheeks crimson, his shirt open. He grinned.

'You have torn one of my buttons off,' Adam said.

'Oh, that's all right. Aunt Margaret will sew it on for you.'

He came close to Adam, leaned against him, looked up at

him, smiling, but with a strange mature glance.

Adam said: 'Are you liking school? I hear that you were in all kinds of trouble the last term. Why was that?'

Benjamin nodded.

'I can't help it, Uncle Adam. If anyone tells me to do anything I don't want to do it.'

'Why's that?'

'I don't know. I expect it's because my uncle killed my father. There isn't another boy in the whole school whose uncle killed his father.'

The words came out quite easily, with no sense of self-consciousness, no unhappiness—a clear statement of simple fact. To Adam those words were like thunder in his ears. The floor seemed to rock. He didn't know that the boy had any notion of the way that his father had died. They had, all of them, for years been in a conspiracy to prevent any allusion to it before the boy, and although at first it had seemed a vain hope that he should not hear, as the years passed they all thought that they had succeeded, for when Benjamin spoke of his father it was quite naturally. He seemed to believe that he had died of some illness just like any other man.

Benjamin nodded.

'You thought I didn't know. I have known for years and years and years. First a farmer at Peter's House told me. I know just what they did. They rode through the mist to Skiddaw House. They had arranged it all, and my uncle shot my father and then shot himself. And my father hadn't a gun. So you see I'm different from all the other boys, and I'll be different all my life.'

Adam did not know what to say. He moved off and looked out of window. Then he turned round.

'Your father,' he said, 'was a very fine man and I loved him. He always did the right thing and so must you.'

Benjamin answered quickly, as though he were speaking in someone's defence.

'I love my father more than anyone, and if I had been there

with him I would have taken the gun from my uncle and shot him, and all my life I'll kill men like my uncle who are beasts and cowards. I don't care. I'm not afraid of anyone, and I'll never do something just because someone tells me . . . ' His voice suddenly was the voice of a small boy. 'I'll be like Robin Hood. He was an outlaw and I'll be an outlaw. I have a band of outlaws under me at school and we're not afraid of anybody.'

To Adam there came a quick picture of a wood, a pool, a man on a white horse and himself dancing in defiance of that rider's whip . . .

He came across the floor to Benjamin and put his arm around him.

'I was like that myself once and now I'm an old gentleman who writes fairy-stories. The great thing,' he went on, holding the boy close to him, 'is not to be bitter against life because of what happened to your father. Don't allow things that have happened in the past, Benjamin, to spoil your life. The past is past. They are ghosts, all those dead men.'

'My father is not a ghost,' Benjamin said. 'I have his picture and a riding-whip he had and his hair-brushes. I took the hair-brushes out of Mama's room and I've hidden them. No one knows where they are but me. And one day I shall meet someone like my uncle and I will shoot him just as he shot my father, except that he shall have a gun, so that it's fair.'

Adam shook his head. 'That's no good,' he said. 'Because a wrong was done once, to do another wrong doesn't make things better.'

'Look here, Uncle,' Benjamin said. 'I can make a somersault. I *think* I can make two now. Here! Look!' and he turned two somersaults, one after the other, in the space between the chairs and the table. He tumbled straight into old Mary who was helping Margaret to bring in the meal.

* * * * *

222

Had Benjamin affected him? When they were sitting after the meal quietly watching the sunlight stain the flowers of the carpet, the gilt of the bookcase, and strike, as though maliciously, the simpering self-importance of 'The Lady of the House,' he felt a curious and abnormal ecstasy of perception. It seemed to him that his senses were all tingling with an extra activity.

Margaret, opposite him, was making a basket-cover in old silk patchwork. On a ground of dark green she was forming a kaleidoscope pattern of glittering scraps—flakes of crimson, sea-green, primrose, hyacinth blue, the rose of apple orchards, the gold of corn. On the grey stuff of the lap of her dress the fragments of silk lay scattered, her look so serenely safe and happy that it caught at his heart. Once and again she would glance up at him and smile. Vanessa and Benjamin were stretched on the floor, their heads together, looking at a book of Japanese drawings. From where he sat he could see the brilliant figures of birds and men in blue and crimson carrying burdens over bridges and the wide expanse of purple seas. Everything was colour and everything was peace. Tiny details seemed to wear a heightened significance, the buttons on Vanessa's dress, freckles on Benjamin's snub nose, the needlework pattern on the chairs.

He was filled with a kind of immortal ecstasy. This he had achieved. Through all the disappointments and failures of his life he had caught this and held it—love, fatherhood, security. The patch of ground upon which his feet were set was his, this hill, the silver birch gleaming in the sun beyond the window, the stream of music he could hear, this Cumberland that all his life long he had worshipped, and beyond it England, the hills running to the sea, the valleys running to the South, all this land that, now that he had his home, flowed to the North, South, East and West, running from his door to all the seas, his for ever and ever, although his realisation of it lasted only for a moment.

His happiness caught him at the throat. His eyes were blinded. He moved in his chair, and Margaret looked across at him and smiled.

Then Benjamin glanced up at them and sprang to his feet.

'I want to go out! Come along, Vanessa! I'll race you!'

They opened the doors and ran out into the garden.

It was as though he had himself spoken. He felt suddenly that his security was dangerous. He did not want it. He was bound, a prisoner. Somewhere, a small child, he was running, running, escaping, shouting, and his mother was with him. Panting, they raced up the hill to see the sun rise. The woods fell below them, the Tarn was dark, and he could hear the sheep rustling past him up the dark path. His mother was a gipsy and he was her gipsy son. He could see the lights from the painted carts—a horse neighed . . . waving his arms and shouting he breasted the hill . . .

* * * * *

He woke as though he had been sleeping, and saw Margaret choosing the colours from the fragments of silk, holding a scrap of rose against the light to see how it would do . . .

'I'll be back, Meg,' he said.

He went to the door and almost ran from the house. He began to climb through the dead bracken above his stone wall. As he mounted he heard the voices of the children from the garden, a cart was creaking down the road that was already a white ribbon. The Lake rose and he saw that the sun had veined it with patterns of light, here there were pools of grey and ashen pallor and there deep shadows of saffron—all confined by the hills, Skiddaw, Saddleback, Walla Crag. As he climbed, the Lake and the hills climbed with him. The air was cold like a whip, but so fresh that it struck his cheeks as the water had done when Will sluiced him that morning.

Then he began to run, he called aloud, he shouted. He stumbled and fell over the stones and thought how old Rackstraw had told him once: 'Clouds and stones! Stones and clouds! That's what this country is!'

His breathing hurt him like a knife, for he was no child now but a stout middle-aged man with a beard and middle-aged habits of comfort and laziness. But he liked the catch at his lungs, the bruise on his knee where the stone had hit him. He climbed, stumbling, waving his arms, turning to catch the Lake and the hills with him and draw them up. He did not know that he was climbing like a madman, climbing as he had never climbed that hill before, because he was part of the hill, the wind, the sun. He hurled himself over the last boulders and flung himself on the strong, resilient turf, lying there at full length, his arms spread out, his chest heaving. Why should he ever return? Something wild and authentic in his blood beat in his brain. Margaret, Vanessa, his mother, they were nothing to him because he was not himself, Adam Paris, but something beyond himself, beyond time, the past, the present and all that was to come.

He lay on the turf, the soil was in his beard, his hands dug into the short sweet grass, the grit of the land, chilled, hardened with a frost that had outlived the midday sun. He stood up. Below him was Derwentwater to the east, Newlands to the west veiled now in the shadow of the lengthening day. He saw Catchedicam to the left of Helvellyn top, and southwards was Langdale Pike o' Stickle. Why should he ever return? He started to run again on a surface so buoyant that it seemed to run with him. Up the easy slope of Maiden Moor, Scafell and Gable coming to meet him between Eel Crag and Dale Head. Why should he ever return? Borrowdale and Grange were below and now the Pillar was in view between Dale Head and Hindscarth. He might race on for ever—Hindscarth and Robinson, then down to Buttermere across to Ennerdale, over to Waswater, to Eskdale and the sea!

He was a wandering man, a lost man, a man at last his own master!

He shouted. 'Oh, hoi! Oh, hoi!' All the hills echoed him as it seemed to him, and the waters of a thousand streams roared about his ears.

He flung out his arms and embraced the world . . .

* * * * *

Folly! He sat down, hugging his knees. He brushed the soil from his beard. He pulled up his trousers to see whether his knee were bleeding. It was not. He could barely see the scratch. Two sheep came wandering towards him and stood a little way off him, watching. Then, reassured, began to graze again. The sun was gone; it fell swiftly behind the hills on these January days. Helvellyn burned in a haze of rosy smoke, and all the air was frosty as though the ice had suddenly thickened on the Lake below and the hills around him. Maiden Moor, Robinson were breathing in gusts of cold thickened air. The sky paled to become the white field of one solitary star that glittered, a spark of frosted fire. Dusk and a great silence enwrapped the world.

He started home. The thought of home was comforting. Margaret sitting by the fire, and he would tell Benjamin and Vanessa a story . . .

He started down the slope, singing as he went.

A DAY IN THE
LIFE OF A VERY OLD LADY

She rose and then sank again, sank and rose, on a great billowy cloud of softest down. The movement was so exquisite, and she was herself so lazy, that she abandoned herself completely, although there were, she knew, a thousand things that she ought to be doing. Everything, far and near, was of a dazzling white save only Adam's nose that was purple and dripping with cold. Had she the energy she would tell him that he must blow it. There was the cloud available and it would irritate her, did she allow herself to be irritated, that he did not make use of so convenient a remedy. But she would not permit herself to be irritated. She was altogether too happy. As she rocked she sang softly to herself a song that Emma Furze had taught her, but she would not sing loudly lest she should wake Georges who was snoring on a cloud near by. How well she knew that snore—it was part of her whole life—and although she did not care for snores in general, Georges' snore was her own property and he must sleep long, here in Watendlath, for yesterday had been the clipping and he would be weary.

Moreover, just round the corner was the whole family— Dorothy, Tim, Veronica, Amabel and dear Jane. They were busy at some game. She could not quite see them, but she knew what they were about. Practising at archery, as indeed they must, for in a week's time there was the contest in Keswick and Veronica had a chance of a prize. It was winter, but in visions such as this all seasons are confused. How lovely she looked, Veronica, her body stretched, her bow held straight from her arms, her beautiful head thrown back! But Jane would be clumsy. If she were not careful they would laugh and then Jane would blush, pretending not to mind, but hurt at her clumsiness . . . and she would call from her cloud, as so often she had done before, 'Jane! Jane! I want you!' simply to save her.

Things began to press in upon her consciousness. A great white bird, the sunlight glittering in silver on its sweeping wings, flew slowly above her head, and the white blossom fell, at a touch of the warm breeze, there across the lawn in the orchard, the petals hovering, wavering . . . hovering, wavering! The sheep, their fleece stained with red, were pressing up the road at Watendlath, and Charlie Watson, motionless on his horse, watched them go. There was something that she must say to Charlie Watson, and so, raising herself from her cloud, she called softly 'Charlie! Charlie!'

The sky was blinded with a white radiance. The great bird, shaking showers of brilliance from its wings, beat upwards towards the sun. The radiance was so bright that she put her hand before her eyes, crying out with joy at so much loveliness, then heard—close beside her—Jane's eager laughing voice.

'Wake up, Aunt Judith! Look at the snow! It has fallen in the night! There never was such a beautiful day!'

She turned her head, rubbed her eyes, then reached for her spectacles. Putting them on she caught, in one sweep, the whole of the real world, for Jane had drawn back the blinds and, from her bed, she could see the flanks of Skiddaw glistening in crystal snow, and snow heaped on the window-sill. Above it all, there was a burning blue sky and the sun blazed over all the room. Jane stood there with the basin of water, the sponge, the soap, the towel, the silver brushes, the ivory comb, and, on a table not far away, breakfast was waiting.

'Well, my dear,' she said with a little sigh of happiness. 'I've had a very good night, thank you. I woke once and heard it strike three and that was the only time. Dear me, what a splendid sunshine! And how are you, Jane dear? I hope you slept well. I dreamt you were practising archery with Veronica.'

'I have had a very good night, thank you,' said Jane, and at once she began, with a dexterity and neatness that Judith adored (she would allow no one but Jane to perform these offices), to hold the basin, to see that the sponge was not too full, and then, when the washing was concluded, to bring the round mirror with the green wood and the gilt doves, so that Judith might see clearly to brush her silver hair.

'Mary will be in shortly to set the fire. There are plenty of logs. I told James yesterday.'

'What is there for breakfast?'

The tray was brought to the bed and carefully arranged.

'I chose those two brown eggs myself. And there is the damson preserve.'

'Dear me, how pleasant!'

'Adam is coming over to-day, you know.'

'As though I could forget, my dear.'

'He is bringing Vanessa.'

'Of course, of course,' Judith said, quite crossly. They would treat her—even dear Jane did this—as though she found it difficult to remember things. She remembered everything—*everything*. It was true that it seemed to her as though Georges and Charlie Watson were still in the room. Past and Present were one and the same. Jane herself would discover that one day. But because she, Judith, was ninety-five years of age (she had had her birthday a week or two ago) was no reason why they should think her helpless. It was true that she could not, any longer, walk very much, but for the rest she was as active and alive as any of them. She took off the top of one of her eggs and said:

'How is everybody? How is Timothy's cold?'

'Bad. But he doesn't mind. He has ridden off to Orpen Farm to see about the Hunt to-morrow. With the snow like this it will be difficult, but it will thaw this afternoon, I dare say. It never lies long here.'

Judith enjoyed her breakfast. Every morning as she drank her tea and ate her toast and preserve, she considered her state. She was no hypochondriac, but from a kind of outside consideration she summoned her forces. Had she a headache? Did her eyes smart? How was her throat which, a day or two ago, had been a little sore? How was that sharp pain in the right elbow? And the soreness just above the left knee? Was her stomach (which Dorothy thought it most indelicate ever to mention) preparing to upset her or was it lazy and good-natured to-day? (She saw her stomach as a kind of cat, sometimes full of warm milk and purring, sometimes in the worst of tempers, always selfish.)

But how was the Captain of her Ragged Army, her Heart? Everything depended on her Heart. While she felt that her stomach was definitely hostile, didn't care a rap about her, her Heart, she considered, was on her side, disliked extremely to distress her, would not miss a beat and then beat twice in a hurry if he could help it. Her Heart was a Gentleman who was making the best of it in very difficult circumstances.

Although she held this review every morning she never spoke to anyone about it. She could indeed carry on a perfect domestic conversation with Jane at the very moment when she was saying inside herself: 'Well, Knee, are you wishing to be tiresome to-day? You are very quiet just now, but I dare say you've got something up your sleeve for later on.'

And, behind all this, was her terrific pride at reaching her present age. Every morning when she woke to find herself alive she made another triumphant notch on the slate of her mind. It soon might be—it might be indeed at any moment—that she would slip into a stage of semi-consciousness when living would be nothing but a dreaming preparation for Death. When that came she would not be able to reckon her triumph, so now she would make the most of it. On November 28 last, her ninety-fifth birthday, she had had messages, letters, gifts, from Herries all over the country—from Ellis and his mother, Janet and Roger at Grosset, Stephen Newmark, Phyllis, Barnabas, Katherine (who had married Colonel Winch of Forrest Hatch, Salisbury), Emily, from Garth and Amery and Sylvia, from the

Ormerods at Harrogate and the Cards at Bournemouth, from all the Witherings near Carlisle—yes, from Herries and Herries all the country over. They had all been kind and generous, but she knew what it was that they had all been thinking. She must reach her Hundredth Birthday! At all costs SHE MUST LIVE TO BE A HUNDRED!

Not for many, many years—not in fact since old Maria Herries who had been born on the day of the Battle of Naseby—had any Herries come so near to a Hundred. Great-Aunt Maria had missed it, and they were all disappointed even now, after all this time, that she had done so.

But Judith was their pride and their hope. True that she had not always been their pride, true that her father had been a disgrace, that she herself had married a rascal of a Frenchman who had died shamefully in a drunken scramble, that she had lived like a farmer's wife in the country, that she had had an illegitimate son, but that was all long ago. She had become a famous person, a legend. All over the country Herries said: 'Oh yes, we are a strong stock, live to a great age. There's old Madame now, ninety something, and commands a houseful of women up in Cumberland as though she were twenty. Wonderful old lady! She'll reach her Century, you may be sure. Nothing can stop her.'

Judith knew that they were saying this and she was proud of it. Of course it was foolish, but then the Herries *were* foolish—foolish and rather charming, in their childishness. When she felt well, as on a morning like this present one, she thought that she could live until two hundred. Why not? What was to stop her? There *were* days when she was infinitely weary and longed for it all to be over. But as soon as the bad days passed she forgot them.

To-day her mind was as clear as a crystal. She remembered everything. Timothy's cold, the calf that had been born two nights before, the new maid Hannah from Seathwaite, the proposal that Captain Forster of Runner Hall, near Penrith, had made to Veronica a week ago (would she accept him? She was thirty-one years of age and had she not been so beautiful would have been long thought an old maid), a chair that Dorothy had bought for her in Carlisle (it was of hand-carved walnut and its seat was covered in maroon plush; Judith had thought it hideous but did not wish to hurt Dorothy's feelings), Adam's visit, a present of a miniature set in Bristol jet ware (tea-pot, sugar-box and cream-jug) that she had for Vanessa. Jane had found it in Keswick and it was exactly what Vanessa loved . . . all these things she had in mind while Jane talked and the snow glittered, the sun flooded the room, and the damson preserve tasted most excellent . . .

* * * * *

Afterwards she had her bath, warm and delicious, while the logs blazed and the large tortoise-shell cat purred on the rug; then Jane helped her to dress and at last she was seated in her arm-chair near the fire ready for the Visits.

'I think, Jane dear, I'll be able to go downstairs a little this afternoon!'

What a picture she made, Jane thought, in her black silk with her snow-white cap, the lace at her throat and wrists, the thin long gold chain that hung almost to her waist, her black shoes with the glittering buckles!

'Yes, dear, I think you can on such a lovely day.'

It was at this moment when she was not so well, just before the Visits, that she had to pull herself together, to drag herself up out of that other world, the Watendlath world where Georges and Charlie laughed and rode, where Christabel and Jennifer quarrelled before a fantasy of masked figures, where an old man with a long white beard stroked his nose . . . On her bad days that past was more real than any present. But not to-day. She was all alert, and when Dorothy, followed by Amabel, entered with their 'Isn't it a beautiful day, Aunt Judith?' and Dorothy began at once, as was her custom, with a cheerful 'tit-tat-tat-tit' of conversation (her manner with very old people) Judith was all alive.

Dorothy was wearing a new dress, the upper skirt caught up almost to the hips and the back of the skirt descending in a straight sloping line from the waist to the ground. The upper skirt was of brown silk and the lower of bright blue taffeta. This suited her stoutness better than the old exaggerated crinoline. Judith knew at once what the new dress meant.

'You are going into Keswick, my dear?'

'Yes. Veronica is coming with me. *What* do you think? Veronica intends to accept Captain Forster!'

Here was news indeed! One less of the great virginal army! And Captain Forster was not so bad. On the stout side and not very clever, but devoted, with a charming place, money enough, a kind heart. Veronica should have been in London. She might then have married *anybody*. But she was lazy. There was something of Jennifer in her blood. She had told Judith once that the only man she had ever really loved had been a farmer from Buttermere way. That had been only her fun. Of course Veronica would never think of such a thing! But why not? Had not Charlie Watson been a farmer?

Never mind. Here was Captain Forster—plump, clean, adoring.

'Are you certain?'

'Well, she hasn't confessed it in so many words. But he is to be at the Osmastons'. I am *sure* that she means to accept him.'

Amabel, who was always dressed severely and thought men contemptible, tossed her head.

'What she can see in that fat man!'

'Well, dear,' said Dorothy complacently, 'it is she that is going to marry him, not you.'

'Yes, thank heaven.'

They talked for a little, then Dorothy said:

'We will leave you now because I think Elizabeth wants a

word. She is unhappy about Benjamin.'

'What has he been doing?'

Dorothy sighed.

'What hasn't he been doing? He had a fight in the village last evening with Marston's boy, and his report from Rugby has come. It is terrible, really terrible. You must speak to him, Aunt Judith. You are the only one who can do anything with him.'

They went and Elizabeth came in.

Elizabeth was fifty-four and as beautiful now as she had been at twenty. She wore a grey dress, her fair hair flat on the top and gathered into a large bun at the back of her head, a golden glory even in that so hideous fashion. She had the air of remoteness that had been hers ever since John's death. She was not priggish nor superior in this. She joined in everything that went on, laughed, sang, played games, hunted (she was still a splendid horsewoman), but nothing could bring her into the real current of life that the others shared. She loved her son, she loved Judith, she loved Jane, but even they, even Benjamin, were shades compared with John. When he was killed she received a blow that was mortal, and Judith, seeing her, knew that the Herries battle was not yet over, and that the consequences of old long-ago histories had still their own history to make.

But because of her own story she understood Elizabeth as did none of the others. Her own Georges had suffered sudden death, as had John, and for ten years after it she, too, had been herself a dead woman. She had had the fears for Adam that Elizabeth now had for Benjamin, but she had been spared because fate had chosen John for its mark instead of Adam. All the more reason that she should help Elizabeth now.

Elizabeth, sitting close beside her, began at once.

'Aunt Judith, we have had Benjamin's report, and it is dreadful.'

'What does it say, my dear?'

'It says that we must take him away if he does not improve. They acknowledge that he is clever but he will not work, he obeys nobody. He is always fighting.'

'Well, my dear, he is a healthy boy and has to let himself go, I suppose.'

Elizabeth shook her head.

'Yes, but he will obey nobody and he does not care. When I speak to him he only smiles. He is not cruel nor selfish. In fact, as you know, there never was a more generous boy. It is not that he is absent-minded. He throws himself altogether into anything that he is doing. But there is something *wild* in him. He says he wants to be a gipsy!'

'A gipsy!'

'Yes. He wants to go away in a caravan and eat roasted hedgehogs. Then . . . there is another thing . . .' She hesitated. 'Two afternoons ago I saw him kissing Hannah; in the passage under the backstairs. Of course it was nothing. He is only a child—he is not yet fourteen and he is tremendously honest. He conceals nothing. He says that he bet her a shilling that he would kiss her . . . I am in despair. He is so merry, always laughing and doing things for others—but he will listen to nobody!'

'He kissed Hannah, did he?' said Judith, thinking how different he was from his father John. And from her own Adam too.

'Yes,' went on Elizabeth. 'I am sure, too, that it is my fault. Aunt Judith, I have been wrong not to *force* my way into Ireby. But I hated it so that time I went . . .'

(Two years before Elizabeth had gone to the Fortress, had asked for her father, had suffered a fearful scene with Mrs. Pangloss who had refused her entry.)

'You know that I have written again and again and he has never answered. But if I had gone and refused to be beaten by that horrible woman and stayed with father whatever she did, I feel that Benjamin would respect me more. He never speaks either of his father or his grandfather. I don't know even now whether he knows . . . whether he knows . . .'

She broke down, hid her head in her hands, then suddenly

knelt at Judith's feet, burying her head in Judith's lap. The old lady gently stroked her hair. Even on her very alert days she had moments of slipping off into a dream. Now with her hand on Elizabeth's hair she saw the room filled with sparkling snow: whorls of dancing crystal filled the air, which was shot with splinters of golden sun. The windows had faded and a great sea of virgin snow, upon whose breast waves of iridescence quietly formed, broke and formed again, spread from the hills' horizon there to her very feet. She was herself as light as a snowflake, and it seemed to her that she had to exert especial power not to float away on the current of that white loveliness and never be seen again . . . Was this Death—and if it was so, why did men fear it? So sweet, so friendly, so just . . .

'. . . You see, Aunt Judith,' Elizabeth's voice came like a soft key closing a door, and the room swam back, the bed with the hangings, the ugly chair that Dorothy had given her (oh, why had she forgotten to thank her just now?), the sparkling buckles on her own shoes. 'I seem to have no will-power any longer. I do things with everyone else, but my real self is not here. It is away with John. It is as though he were always whispering to me things that I ought to do—be more firm with Benjie, live with father and make him more comfortable. I had will-power once, but John's death did something to me. Grief doesn't break your heart as the novels say, but it takes your character away. I don't *grieve* for John. I am sure that he is happier now than he ever was here. But I am not alive. When you lost your husband did you feel at all the same?'

'Yes, dear, I did, just as you describe. For nearly ten years I lived with the Rockages in Wiltshire and I had no real life at all; but it comes back in the end. Nothing can kill you. Nothing.'

Elizabeth rose from her knees and stood before the fire, her long slim body irradiated by the leaping light, her soft grey dress like a cloud against the sparkling logs.

'Aunt Judith,' she said. 'Do you believe in God?'

'I don't know.'

'You are not certain?'

'My dear, I have been a pagan all my life long. I know now that everyone is very religious, and if you don't go to church on Sunday it's very wrong, but in my young days it wasn't so. Going to church is just a fashion, I think. At one time it's the thing and at another it's not. My husband thought it foolish to believe in anything you couldn't see, but a great friend of mine, Reuben Sunwood, was as sure of God as I am of this room. For myself, now I am so very old, there *seems* to be another world— but that may be my old age and my body failing. On some days, you know, my hearing is bad and I cannot see very well. Then I seem to be in another world. But I don't know. When one loves someone very much one seems to go beyond bodily things. When one's in a bad temper or loses one's spectacles or the servants are tiresome it's different.' She rapped her fingers impatiently on her spectacle-case.

'Dear Elizabeth, you must pull yourself together a little more. It is quite right what you say. Benjamin needs more discipline. Send him to me, my dear. This morning. In the afternoon I'm often sleepy.'

Elizabeth bent down and kissed the dry, withered cheek. How *very* old Aunt Judith was! It was wrong to trouble her, but then she liked to be troubled.

'If I can find him I'll send him to you now.'

When she was alone in the room again she gave a little sigh of satisfaction. She liked to be alone, and she liked also to be in the centre of things. She was happy this morning because neither her heart nor her stomach troubled her, because it was a beautiful day and because, old though she was, they still wished to consult her. The world was whirring around her! Veronica would marry Captain Forster, Benjamin was naughty, Adam would soon be here . . . She arranged her spectacles on her nose, picked up from the table at her side a number of the *Spectator* and read its opinion of Mr. Longfellow's *Hiawatha*, an old poem now but still criticized with reverence: '*Mr. Longfellow's*

Hiawatha is one of the really permanent contributions to modern literature, and no other genius known to us would have been in any way equal to the work. It is not the grasp of imagination, so much as the grace and sweep of a peculiarly majestic fancy—a fancy like the impulsive fancy of children . . . How bright and playful is the picture of the lower animals with the little Indian prophet . . . But it is not only in the details, it is in the whole spirit of the poem—the fanciful joy and beauty, the equally fanciful weirdness and gloom—that we enjoy the touch of a master hand.'

Well, that was very nice for Mr. Longfellow. But she was not sure. The writer used the word 'fanciful' a great many times. That was perhaps a warning. In any case she could not read for very long in these days—Jane read to her every afternoon—a lengthy poem, read aloud . . . No, she thought she would not bother with *Hiawatha*.

There was a knock on the door, and Benjamin came in. He was shooting up; he was no longer the small chubby child. He would not be a handsome man, although he had fine clear eyes, a splendid colour, and a strong stocky body. As usual he seemed to be enjoying a joke of some kind. She could see that he knew that he had come to be scolded and was endeavouring to be grave.

'Is that you, Benjie? Come over here where I can see you.'

He came and stood beside the chair in the attitude of straitened attention that children must observe before their elders. His cheeks were flushed with the cold and his hair was in disorder. He tried to arrange it with his hand. He looked her in the face, giving her all his mind, not as Adam had so often done when he was small, thinking of something else.

'Now, Benjie, I have sent for you because they tell me that your report has come from Rugby and it is shocking. They say that you will be sent away if you do not behave better. Your mother is very unhappy. What have you to say?'

What had he to say? How very, *very* old Aunt Judith was! And so small and so tidy. There came from her a pleasant scent of exquisite cleanliness and the smell of some flower, a carnation perhaps. But what must it be like to be as old as that? Why, her father had been born at the very beginning of the eighteenth century! There wasn't a boy at Rugby who had a relation as old as this! Something to be proud of. He pulled himself together and tried to attend. He always attended to the thing in hand, and the thing in hand at the moment was that Aunt Judith was going to scold him about his report. He didn't mind. He liked her. He liked everybody.

'I am very sorry, Aunt Judith.'

She kicked one shoe impatiently.

'Yes, but that is not enough. You must do something about it. You are a big boy now and threaten to be a disgrace to us all.'

She looked at him and her heart melted within her. She worshipped small boys, and although Benjie was very different from her own Adam, he had Adam's independence. She adored independence.

'Why are you so naughty?'

'There are so many rules and they teach you such silly things.'

It was the tradition in England that all children obeyed absolutely their parents, did nothing that their parents didn't wish them to do, were preparing, one and all, to be the heroes and heroines of the future. But Benjie seemed unaware of the tradition.

'You know you belong to a very fine family,' she began, 'and, when you grow up, everyone will expect you to make your family proud of you.'

'I know. They are always talking about the family, but I don't see why I should think about the family. I'm myself, aren't I?'

'Yes, but——'

'When you were a little girl you ran away. Your father was always against the family. My grandfather shot himself in London and my father was killed, when he couldn't defend himself, by my uncle. I'm not like the rest of the family. I'm different and I'll always be different. Mother and Aunt Veronica and Aunt Amabel and Ellis and Cousin Amery—*they* are the family. But I'm different. I'm by myself.'

Her heart began to beat furiously. Her eyes dimmed. She could have caught the boy to her and kissed him. And with that odd exaltation (so bad for her heart) was fear also. Would this battle *never* be ended? She seemed for an instant to behold her father, whom she had never seen, standing, erect, triumphant, against the snow . . .

She beat down her emotion and in a voice that trembled a little said: 'Yes, but, Benjie, you must understand that being different is *not* amusing—not amusing at all. It seems to you, I daresay, very splendid to stand up now and say "I'm different," but I'm a very old woman and have had great experience and I can tell you that the world does not like people to be different, and especially our family does not. You can't know yet how powerful the world is and how *right* the world is too, because if everyone was independent and refused to suit themselves to the world's rules, nothing would ever be done. My father learnt that, I have learnt it, your grandfather learnt it. You *have* to do as you are told unless you want to fight all your life long.'

'I do like to fight,' he broke in eagerly. 'You see, Aunt Judith, I think it's stupid to do things just because other people do them.'

'Yes, but do you never think of others? You must see how selfish it is always to have your own way. You can see how unhappy you make your mother——'

'But I don't *want* to make her unhappy. I don't want to make anyone sorry for what I do. They needn't be, only half the time they are glad they are sorry.'

She had nothing to say. She was on his side, so terribly on his side, and yet it would never do if he were disgraced at Rugby . . .

'Well, then,' she said as though some silent comprehending confidence had passed between them. 'You must promise me to do your best for the sake of those who love you—for your mother's sake and mine. Will you promise?'

He smiled, staring straight into her eyes. She really was a *dear* old lady and he was proud of her because she had lived to so great an age. He nodded.

'All right, Aunt Judith. I'll try.'

'And you won't fight?'

'Well, I don't know . . . I can't promise if another boy goes for me——'

'You won't be the first in any case?'

'It's so hard often to tell who *is* the first. You see——' But this was too technical.

'Kiss me then. And I shall expect a good report next term.'

He kissed her. How dry her cheek was! Towards the door he turned.

'There's one thing,' he said. 'Why do I never see my grandfather?'

'Your grandfather?'

'Yes. Up at the Fortress.'

'He is very ill and sees nobody. He was very unkind to your mother once, you know.'

'Yes, but that was years ago. You can't go on remembering things for ever, can you? I shall go one day and see him.'

Then he came back to her chair and, grinning, said: 'Aunt Judith, would you like to see my ferret?'

'A ferret? Oh, I don't like ferrets.'

'You would this one. It's grand. James gave it me.'

'Very well. You can bring it one day.'

He nodded and went humming out.

The talk had affected her deeply. She took off her spectacles, wiped her eyes, put them on again. Her heart was beating oddly. It was not good for her to be agitated, but what was she to do when all the old questions, so long answered and dismissed, came surging up again?

When Jane brought her her dinner she found her greatly excited. She had her favourite dinner—fried sole, apple-pudding—but now she did not care. The talk with Benjamin had, although it was so short, exhausted her: old terrors and

alarms would surround her and hem her in, did she allow them.
'I don't think I'll come down this afternoon after all, Jane
dear. I'm a trifle tired.'

'You have seen too many people, that's what it is,' Jane said
firmly. She had the air a little, as she arranged the silver dish
containing the apple-pudding in front of Judith, of a witch or a
fairy, someone from another and slightly inhuman world. She
was growing into that especial product of the British Isles, the
queer old maid, someone enterprising, eccentric, kindly, and
very much alone. Jane would be eccentric, she would suddenly
snap her fingers, dress quaintly (she was wearing now a funny
old black velvet jacket), roll her bread at a meal-time into little
pellets, talk to herself, but she had a heart as rich and warm
as any fairy godmother. She loved Judith with a passion that
was almost unholy. Although she was religious, virtuous and
indeed prudish, she would have committed any crime for Judith,
married anyone, killed anyone, stolen from anyone. So now she
realised that Judith was weary and had added in a moment, as
old people do, twenty years to her age. An hour ago she had been
seventy, now she was ninety, soon, if one were not careful, she
would be a hundred and ten.

'Yes, I don't think I'll go down . . . Jane, what do *you* think
of Benjamin?'

'He is a fine boy. I love him!'

'Yes, yes, of course!' She knocked her silver spoon against
the plate. 'We all love him, but I am afraid that he is a very
naughty boy.'

'Oh, he has fights, but so do all proper boys.'

'Jane, why don't you marry someone?'

Jane blushed. She said almost in a whisper: 'I don't like men—
not in that way.'

'Dear, dear!' said Judith. (She was beginning to recover.) 'It
was a very nice way. Everyone is so prudish now that they are
ashamed to talk of going to bed with a man. It's perfectly natural.
Nothing to be ashamed of. But although they won't speak of it

they think of nothing else. It's all the same whoever it is—Mrs. Osmaston, Helen Withering, Mrs. James Anstruther. How shall we marry our daughters? We must put our girls to bed with a man the first possible opportunity, do everything we can, dress them so as to accentuate their figures, throw them at every man we see, everything to marry them—but speak of what happens when they *are* married—oh, dear me, no!'

Jane disliked it when Judith talked like this. She did wish that she wouldn't.

'Now, there's Dorothy! In *such* a flutter this morning because Veronica is going to marry. She'd marry Amabel to *anybody* if only somebody would have her, but a pestle and mortar is the only thing Amabel will ever marry. Yes—well, that pudding was very good. I think I'll have my nap now so as to be ready for Adam.'

When Adam came she was quite ready for him. Her nap had refreshed her. The afternoon sun shone into the room like the reflection from a pale cloud of gold. The eaves were dropping with the heat of the sun and, when her spectacles were on, she could see blue shadows on Skiddaw. There was a strange mountain lightness over everything, and the logs in the fireplace were crimson with heat, and crackled like mad. As soon as Adam came in, sat beside her, took her hand, they were enclosed as though there were no one else in the world.

She wanted to talk about the Trades Unions. She had had a letter from Horace Newmark, who was in business in Manchester. 'He is as proud of all the chimneys as though they were bluebells,' she said. 'He says Manchester is nothing but smoke and dirt and it's grand. It's making England what it is, the mistress of the world. Stuff! Who wants to be mistress of the world? So like a Herries!'

Two years before, a man called Broadhead in Sheffield had, it was proved, paid for men who had rebelled against his Union to be murdered, and had paid out of the funds of the Union of which he was secretary. The tyranny of 'rattening' whereby noxious workers' tools were destroyed, women were blinded, men were shot at, was prevalent, and in Manchester, among the brickmakers, the clay which offending brickmakers were to use was sometimes stuffed with thousands of needles in order to maim the hands of those who worked on it. But the investigations into these crimes had proved, too, that many of the conditions of work were iniquitous and had remained unaltered since the days of Elizabeth.

Judith was greatly interested. 'What do you think, Adam? What about these Trades Unions?'

'I think they are necessary. The more England becomes an industrial country—and she *is* now the first industrial country in the world—the greater the power of the working-man. He will rule England one day, mark my words, and I hope he'll be wise enough to know what to do with the power when he has it. That was the trouble with the Chartists. They weren't wise enough nor clever enough. But in fifty years' time there'll be few big families left. Everything will be shared—and quite right too.'

'I don't know,' Judith said. 'England was very nice once when there were no railways and no chimneys. Isn't it strange? I've been in a sedan-chair and saw a boy hung in the streets of London. Yes, and bears were baited, and I've danced at Vauxhall. I feel sleepy. It's the fire. Where is Vanessa?'

'Vanessa is downstairs with Benjamin.'

'And how is Cat Bells?'

'Cat Bells is covered with snow.'

'And how is dear Margaret?'

'Margaret sent her love and is coming soon to see you. She is baking to-day and Will is helping her.'

'It all sounds very pleasant. And how are you yourself?'

'I am very well.'

'And the book?'

'Nearly finished.'

'It's not a fairy-story this time.'

'No, it's about two boys at the North Pole.'

'What do you know about the North Pole? You've never been there.'

'No. That's why I know so much about it.'

'But how can you write about what you've never seen?'

'There are two sorts of writers, Mother, just as there are two sorts of Herries. One sort believes in facts, the other sort believes in things behind the facts.'

'The books I like best,' she answered, 'are those that have both sorts in them.'

'For instance?'

'Jane is reading me a very amusing story called *Under Two Flags*. It's silly, of course—not like real life at all—but most enjoyable. And then there's *Alice in Wonderland*. And then there's Mr. Huxley's *Man's Place in Nature*.'

Adam laughed. 'Mother, what a ridiculous mixture!'

'They all come to the same thing in the end.'

'What thing?'

'The world is made up both of fancy and reality, I suppose. Oh dear, I don't know . . . Adam, now that I cannot move from this house I can see how *nice* England is.'

He smiled.

'Yes. I know you say "Foolish old woman at her age to love anything with a passion." But I am not senile. The moment I'm senile, Adam, you shall drop a pill into my chicken-broth and finish me off. No, I am very wide awake, and I can see that all my life I've loved England. Why do you not write a book about England?'

'How would *you* do it, Mother?'

'Oh, I would put in everything—men sowing the fields, the horses ploughing, old ladies selling sweets in the village shop, Mr. Disraeli with his oily hair and Mr. Gladstone with his collar, Horace's Manchester chimneys, all the Herries thinking *they've* made England, my father riding up Borrowdale, the snow on Skiddaw, the apple-pudding I had at dinner, sheep on a hill, the man lighting the lamps in Hill Street—and you, Adam, running by Charlie's horse in Watendlath, at Chartist meetings in London, writing stories at Cat Bells . . .' She broke off, her finger to her lip. 'That gives me an idea—I have an idea!'

'What idea?'

'No matter. I shall tell you when it has got further on. Dear me, I've talked such a deal to-day. One day I talk; another day not a word. Sometimes I sleep all day. I'm ninety-five, you know.'

'Yes, I know. You're always telling me.'

She took his arm and, quickly, shyly caught his hand and kissed it.

'My whole life has been you and Georges.'

'You said it was England.'

'You *are* both England to me. We are sunk in the country, you and I, up to our necks. That's why I am so strong. Do you know, Adam, I have never had a day's illness in my life? Even when I was bearing you I was only ill for an hour or two—ugh!—that was horrid. There was an elephant . . . '

He drew his chair closer, bent over her and put his arm around her.

'Are you sure you are not tired?'

'No, indeed . . . I was a little but I had a nap. I can go to sleep whenever I wish. Oh yes, I remember! Benjamin! Adam, what do you think of Benjamin?'

'A grand boy—brave, generous. He will do fine things.'

'I am not so sure. He has had a dreadful report from Rugby.'

'All the best boys have.'

'Yes, but he was in here this morning and I scolded him, and he said that he didn't care because he was different from other boys, different because of his father and his grandfather.'

Adam nodded. 'Yes, he told me that once too. But that's all right. It's only that he feels wild sometimes. Why, I feel wild myself at times, Mother. A year or two ago I went mad and ran up Cat Bells—thought I would never come back.'

She smiled. 'I am delighted that you are wild still sometimes. I thought you were so contented that you'd never be wild again.

If I had the strength I'd climb out of the window now just as I did when I was a child. Is Vanessa wild?' she asked.

He sighed. 'Vanessa is an angel. But I am sometimes troubled. She is so generous, so trusting, and believes in everyone.'

'Well, there is no harm in that as a beginning.'

'No, but she must suffer . . . Oh well, we all suffer. She adores Benjie. He is her God at present.'

'Can I see her?'

'Yes. I will go and fetch her.'

He went quickly from the room. She thought—Benjamin, Vanessa, the new generation, and I shall be gone . . . soon I shall be gone. How strange and how familiar that thought that this room, her old companion, would continue with Skiddaw beyond the window, the snow falling, and she not here to see it, to move the chairs, dust the china, put a log on the fire . . . She looked at the table where was the parcel of the miniature tea-set. She'll like that, she thought. She had always adored giving presents. Adam came in, bringing Vanessa with him. Vanessa was ten and tall for her age. She was wearing a dress of red taffeta, and her little skirt stood out stiffly. She had beautiful legs and arms, and her head with its black hair was carried with a wonderful dignity for so young a child. She came and made a curtsey, then she kissed the old lady, then waited patiently, smiling.

'I have a present for you, my dear.'

Vanessa's whole body was transformed with joy. You could see that her heart was beating with excitement; she compressed her lips so that she should not burst out into indecorous cries.

'Yes . . . Bring me that parcel, darling.'

She brought it very carefully. It was unwrapped. She knelt down on the floor so that she could see the wonder. She picked up each tiny piece, the tea-pot, the cups, the saucers, and held them, one by one, against the light.

'Oh!' she said slowly. 'It is the loveliest . . . Oh, Aunt Judith! I never thought . . . I never expected . . . ' Then she reached out for her father's hand. He pulled her to her feet. Even now, with all her joy, she controlled herself. She remembered how old Aunt Judith was, she kissed her tenderly and with great care. Then she stared at the precious things as though she would never take her eyes away.

'Do you like them?'

'*Like* them!' She curtsied again, then turned to the window as though her feelings were so great that she must hide them. Once again the three of them had the sense that they were enclosed, away from all the world, rapt into a private communion of happiness.

'I must show them to Benjie,' she said.

Judith nodded. 'Yes, show them to Benjie. And come again and say good night before you go.'

'I will be off too,' Adam added. 'I will help her to carry the tea-things.'

'Yes,' said his mother, her sharp eyes staring with some secret excitement. 'And send Jane to me if you can find her. My idea! My idea! I must go on with my idea!'

She tapped impatiently on the silk of her dress.

'Tell Jane I want her at once. *At once*—whatever she may be at!'

Jane arrived, quite breathless. She had been washing Dorothy's bitch Maria, an old and sulky spaniel who was washed every Thursday, come what might: and to-day was Thursday, Dorothy was in Keswick, and there was no one else . . .

'I've left Hannah to finish her!'

'Now sit down and get your breath.'

'What is it, Aunt Judith? Adam says you have an idea.'

'Yes, I have . . . Look in that wardrobe near the window, and among those bundles of letters you will find a manuscript book in a dark-green leather cover. Yes—that fat one . . . Now you have it? There's not a word in it, is there? No, I thought not. Francis gave it me years ago on a birthday. He thought the dark-green leather handsome. Now bring the little writing bureau closer. That's it. Near the fire so that you will be warm and will hear what I say. Excellent. Have you a pen that suits you? Now listen, my dear. I was talking to Adam about England. You know old ladies talk and talk until they are quite exhausted. I have often noticed it—the older you are the more you talk. Dear Pennyfeather at Keswick was like that. Her last years you could *not* stop her . . . a constant flow. Well, now I intend to talk to some purpose. Adam and I said we love England and so we do. Then I had an idea. You know I never saw either my father or my mother, but my half-brother David—he was old enough to be my father, you know—would often, before he died, poor man, tell me stories of them. He liked to take me for a walk, or we would ride to Bassenthwaite or Caldbeck or to the Dash, and all the way there and back he would tell me about the old days and my father.

'Now I think that I should write it down—or rather that *you* should, Jane dear. I may die at any moment. Oh yes, I may—of course I may—and what a pity! All this lost for ever. No one knows it but I. And that was a very odd life my father lived in Borrowdale. David told me that he remembered exactly the night they first arrived in Keswick. No, but wait. You shall write it down. Do not you think it a good idea, Jane?'

The old lady was so eager and excited that it would have been cruelty to prevent her. But Jane did not wish to prevent her. She was herself greatly interested in that world and in that very strange man, her great-great-grandfather. How very curious that the *father* of Aunt Judith sitting there so comfortably before the fire should be her own great-great-grandfather! It was like stepping on to a magic carpet and swinging back into another fairy-world. So she took her pen and began to write in the dark-green leather book.

'Now tell me, dear, if I go too fast. Well, you'd better begin in this way. "I, Judith Paris, was born at Rosthwaite in the valley of Borrowdale, Cumberland, on the 28th of November in the Year of Our Lord 1774 . . . " There! Have you got that? That's a good solid beginning, I think, rather like Macaulay's *History*. Now to continue. "I never knew my dear father and mother because they both died on the day I was born, and had I not been found and rescued from the cold by Squire Gauntry of Stone Ends, who happened to be riding past that day and heard me crying, I should undoubtedly have perished."

'Have you got that, Jane?' She peered over her spectacles on the very edge of her nose. 'Let me see, my dear. Yes, you write very nicely. Am I going too fast for you?'

'Not at all, Aunt Judith. How very interesting this will be!'

'I hope so. I certainly think it may. Well, to continue. "It is not, however, my own history about which I write, but rather about some of the early days that my father spent in the valley of Borrowdale. My father himself lived to a good age, and I myself am now a very old woman, so that I am a link with the long-ago past. I have heard very much of what happened in those long-ago times from my half-brother David Herries. David Herries was my father's son by his first wife, and he was fifty-five when I was born, so that I could have been his grand-daughter. He was very famous as a young man as a boxer and wrestler and runner. He had great strength as a younger man, but when I knew him he had grown stout and was living very happily with his family at Uldale, where I also was living. He would take me for walks and rides, and it was then that he would tell me these stories.

"'He told me that he remembered exactly the night that he first arrived in Keswick. He could remember every detail, and so do I, even at this distance of time. How he was in the inn at Keswick in a big canopied bed with his sisters Mary and Deborah. The canopy that ran round the top of the bed was a faded green and had a gold thread in it. There were fire-dogs by the fire with mouths like grinning dragons. And he remembered that a woman was sitting warming herself in front of the fire, a woman he hated. Then his father came in and thought he was sleeping. He remembered that his father was wearing a beautiful coat of a claret colour and a chestnut wig, and there were red roses on his grey silk waistcoat. He remembered, too, that his father said something to the woman by the fire that made her very angry, and she began to talk in a loud, heated voice."'

Jane went on, and in that clear little voice like a bell Judith refashioned this old world to her, describing the inn and the servants running hither and thither with candles, some relations who had a meal with them, and how David's uncle wanted to make him drink wine and he would not. Then the dark mysterious night-ride to Borrowdale, and how he sat on the horse in front of his father and how proud he was, and his father asked him whether he were frightened, and he answered bravely that he was never frightened where his father was. How then they came to a house on a little hill and David ran forward and was in the house first, and there were two shining suits of armour in the hallway.

'There,' said Judith suddenly. 'I am tired. That will be enough for to-day. I think you shall help me to bed.'

'Oh, Aunt Judith,' said Jane. 'That *is* interesting!'

But Aunt Judith was weary. She had suddenly collapsed, her head nodded, she yawned and yawned and was almost helpless in Jane's hands as she undressed her. It was dark now beyond the window; a faint powdery blue framed the silent masses of snow; some stars, lonely in that cold sky, were like sparks blown up from a fire. Jane drew the cherry-coloured curtains. She saw that Judith was propped up with pillows and two candles lit by her side (how tiny and soft her body had been—like a child's), then she left the room to return with some tea, a small sponge-cake and some raspberry jam in a blue glass saucer. Then, most unfortunately, Aunt Judith lost her temper. It had been a tiring day, there had been something too exciting about that dropping back into the past—the past that was not only the past, but the present and future as well.

So she lost her temper over the sponge-cake. It was a plum-cake that she had wanted. Dorothy only yesterday had promised her a plum-cake.

'But, Aunt Judith, it is not good for you. Doctor Bettany said that plum-cake was too rich——'

'Doctor Bettany never said anything of the kind.'

'But indeed he did!'

'So I am a liar! Thank you, dear Jane. I am glad I know.'

'No, of course not. But you know that last time you were upset——'

'I was not upset!' She was trembling, her eyes were filled with hot tears of anger. She was in a rage, so that for tuppence she would have taken the tea-tray and thrown it and its contents all over the room. How dare Jane say that she was a liar! And she hated this soft soppy sponge-cake! They thought they could do what they liked with her! She was so good to them all, and yet they tried to starve her! After listening all day to their troubles they could so ill-treat her!

She took the sponge-cake and with a shaking hand threw it into the middle of the floor.

At that same moment Adam and Vanessa came in to say good-bye, and with them were Dorothy and Veronica back from their party. But Judith did not care. She was not ashamed. They should see whether they could bully her.

'You promised me plum-cake!' she cried to Dorothy.

'Oh, I am so sorry! . . . Aunt Judith, Veronica is engaged to be married! Captain Forster——'

'I don't care! You think you can do what you like with me, all of you, just because I am an old woman——'

But the sight of Veronica's beautiful happy face was too much for her.

'Oh, well . . . Come here, my dear, and give me a kiss! There! That's right! Don't spill the tea-things! What did he say to you? Did he go down on his knees? Were you very gracious? . . .'

* * * * *

A long while after as it seemed to her, the room dark save for the flicker from the fire, she lay there, very happy, on the edge of sleep. It had been a wonderful day. She had never left that room, but all the world had come into it. The elderly Dorothy, Adam, Elizabeth, with all their personal histories hot about them, and the young, Veronica engaged to be married, dear Jane so sweet and good, and the children, Vanessa and Benjamin. All the generations! They had come to her for advice and help and to tell her what they were doing. They had wanted to know what she thought. They could not get on without her.

She herself had welcomed the sun, eaten delightful food, read a little, given a present, discussed serious matters like God and the Trades Unions with Adam and Elizabeth, sunk back into the past, thought of Georges and Warren and Adam as a baby, and then gone behind that again to her own childhood and dear David, and then back beyond that to a hundred and forty years ago when her father had been a young man and worn a claret-coloured coat—all this without leaving her room, all within a day. And she was ninety-five. All the Herries all over England were waiting to see her grow to a hundred!

Well, she would. Nothing was going to stop her! How could she possibly disappoint such a great number of kind relations?

So, in that happy thought, she slipped away and once again was rocking on that billowing cloud of softest down. She rose and then sank again, sank and rose . . . Georges was sleeping near to her. He was snoring with that snore so familiar to her that it was also hers. All about them the world was of a dazzling white, shining with a million crystals.

She rose and then sank again, sank and rose . . .

AT VICTORINE'S

In London, a boy aged fifteen stood on an October afternoon pressing his nose to the window of a house in Hill Street. This boy was young Benjamin Herries.

This was the day, the evening, the night of his life, for on this day, October 14, 1870, he was to become a man.

It had all happened in the most surprising manner, and the cause of it had been the death, one evening while he was drinking his tea, of old Stephen Newmark. Everyone had been expecting him to die for years, but with that priggish obstinacy characteristic of him he had refused to go, degenerating into a tiresome silent old gentleman with a female nurse of whom, in the opinion of the family, he was much too fond.

Poor Phyllis had predeceased him by some years; as he was not a Herries no one had very much interest in his attaining a great age. He died in the act of pronouncing one of his almost hourly anathemas on Mr. Disraeli.

Most unexpectedly it was decided that young Benjamin must be present at his funeral. It seemed that Stephen had a great regard for Elizabeth and had declared that 'he would do something for her boy one day.' So Benjamin had been sent for from Rugby (where he still survived, much to his own astonishment); Lady Herries had invited him to stay in Hill Street for the funeral, and here he was.

The funeral, two days before, had been great fun. Everything was great fun for Benjamin, and he could not be expected to feel much grief for Stephen Newmark, whom he had rarely seen. Moreover, he noticed that Stephen's children were not greatly downcast, and his own close friend Barney made no pretence of sorrow.

'The Governor never liked me,' he confided to Benjamin on the way to the funeral. 'He disapproved of me altogether and never even looked at my novels. I don't blame him for that, but I'm not going to be a crocodile about it. I leave that to sister Emily.'

Lady Herries, who was now a rather ancient and (in Benjamin's opinion) a very silly lady, did the honours with much satisfaction, and Ellis Herries, already a man of importance in the world of affairs, was dignified and solemn. Benjamin had got considerable pleasure out of his days in town. He had never really stayed in London before.

He had had a number of projects. Why should he return to Rugby? He thought of being a stowaway in some vessel chartered for the West Indies or (his old cherished dream) joining some gipsies somewhere. He took a liking to an Italian organ-grinder, with whom he talked in Berkeley Square, and fancied that he might buy a barrel-organ. But his principal notion was that, if he could get money enough, he would escape to France and, in some way, slip into Paris and enjoy a bit of the Siege. He had followed, with eager excitement, the Franco-Prussian War from its commencement. He had cut out from the illustrated papers pictures of the Emperor, Bismarck, MacMahon, Palikao, Bazaine, Frossard, the young Prince Imperial, and many of the Empress. He was in love with the Empress; he would be delighted to die for her. He wanted nothing but to run on some mission for her, be shot in the discharge of it and fall dying at her feet. He could not understand why his companions at Rugby were on the whole so indifferent.

Then, with the catastrophe at Sedan, his whole soul was on fire. He learnt every detail of the battle by heart. He knew the exact positions of Bazeilles and Balan, of the Donchery bridge, where were the Villa Beurmann, Illy, and the fatal spot where the Prussian Guards crossed the Givonne. He was sure that, had he been in command, he would not have fallen into so complete a trap, and the moment when the Emperor, old and sick, cried out 'The firing must be stopped at all costs!' was, for him, a real agonising piece of personal experience.

He hated and detested the Prussians; he adored the French, and Barney, listening to him, was amazed that so young and jolly a boy could feel so intensely. When he read how the Empress, escaping from Paris, hailed a cab and was recognised by a street urchin, he drew a deep breath as though he himself had only just missed a great peril.

And now that Paris was invested it was for him as though he himself shared the siege. When he heard how, on October 7, Gambetta escaped from Paris in a balloon he shouted 'Hurray!' and gave all his pocket-money towards a dormitory feast in its celebration. However, here he was now in London, and his own immediate affairs demanded a lot of attention. To-morrow he was to return to Rugby, and he had a sad feeling that he *would* return instead of making use of this magnificent opportunity of adventure. Indeed, had it not been for his mother and Aunt Judith, he would have certainly tried the stowaway adventure. But they would grieve, although why they should he could not understand. But women were queer and these two women he did not wish to hurt. Moreover, Aunt Judith was so *very* old. He had better wait until she was gone.

Then, this very morning, after breakfast, Barney had arrived at Hill Street and, pulling Benjamin aside, had whispered to him that he intended that evening to take Ellis and himself out to dinner. 'Not a word to a soul,' he confided. 'Emily and the others would make a terrible row if they knew. But we must do something. These last days have been too gloomy for anything.'

So Benjamin stood at the window, all ready dressed, waiting for Barney to arrive.

It was the bewitching hour when the lamp-lighter has gone his way and the lamps star the streets like nectarines. A faint wisp of fog—having in it to Benjie's excited nostrils a slight sniff of gunpowder (he was thinking possibly of Paris); from beyond the window came magical sounds of London, the clop-clop of a horse, the rattle of wheels, feet mysteriously echoing, the distant plaintive murmur of a barrel-organ. On the top of area steps belonging to the house opposite a housemaid was entertaining, for a moment, a policeman. A brougham was waiting a few doors away and down the steps came a stout, pompous, old gentleman, pilloried in starch, a red shaven face and a white waistcoat and white gloves that seemed to Benjie too big for him. The fog increased a little, the lamps spread into a hazy iridescence, some old man in a large and battered high hat came slowly down, ringing a bell and calling out something in a melancholy voice, a carriage rolled by with two footmen in cocked hats standing up at the back of it—and always that soft rumble of sound as of a fat, comfortable nurse singing lullaby to her children.

His excitement was intense; it was all that he could do not to jump about the room, turn his favourite somersault. But Lady Herries or Emily Newmark might come in at any moment. He thought them safe and secure in the great cold draughty drawing-room upstairs. But you never could be sure. Grown-up people were always creeping about and opening doors unexpectedly, like that old beast 'Turker' Evans, head of his House at Rugby. His thoughts were oddly jumbled. It was a pity that Ellis was coming; it would be very much pleasanter without him. Not that he disliked Ellis, or he would not did he not patronise him. Of course Ellis was *years* older, a grown-up man who did business every day in the City. And he was very kind. He had given Benjie ten shillings only yesterday, but, for some dim obscure reason, Benjie would rather not have taken it. Ellis did not really like him—not *really*, as Barney and Adam Paris and Thornton Minor and James at Uldale liked him. And then again, looking out at the lamps and the misty street, suppose there was no God as Barney said. Barney had sprung this astonishing piece of news upon him at the funeral.

'Of course there's no God,' he had said, as though he were sure of it.

'Well, what is there then?' Benjamin asked.

'Nothing at all,' Barney had answered gaily. 'We're nothing but monkeys, old boy. You are old enough now to read Darwin. He'll tell you.'

What an astonishing idea! Then all this going to church and saying your prayers, that had been going on for hundreds of years, meant nothing at all. There was no gigantic old man with a white beard sitting on a cloud and listening! His mother and Aunt Jane and the others were all taken in! A stupendous thought! But he had only Barney's word for it, and you could never be sure whether Barney meant what he said!

Oh! there was the organ-grinder coming round the corner! He could just see him in the dim light, and there, joy of joys, from the opposite side was the muffin-man approaching! There *must* be a God, or why should there be muffin-men and organ-grinders? Would the organ-grinder have a monkey? The door opened and Lady Herries entered. She was a little, faded, old woman now, and Benjamin was certain that she painted her cheeks. He thought she looked ridiculous, her dress bunched up behind and her rather scanty hair dressed in a cascade of curls at the back of her head. She was, of course, in the deepest black and she walked with small mincing steps.

'Why, Benjamin! Dear me! Why has William not lit the gas! All alone! Emily was asking for you! Come and tell me what you have been doing. Ellis tells me that you and he are going to have dinner at some quiet place with Barnabas.'

'Yes,' said Benjamin. 'Won't it be fun?'

'I don't think this is quite the time to talk of fun, Benjamin dear. It has all been very distressing. However, you are too young yet to realise what death means.'

The front door banged. That must be Barney. They went into the hall, and there, praise be, Barney was, looking very smart in his evening dress and high black hat. He was growing stout, and looked like a very amiable clown, Benjie always thought. Chalk his face white and give him a red nose and he would be a perfect clown!

They all went upstairs to the drawing-room, which was as cold as a mausoleum. They stood in a group beside the sulky peevish fire and talked in low grave voices.

Emily Newmark, a heavy stout woman in tremendous black, joined them. It is a temptation for every generation to deride any world that was fifty years its predecessor: Judith, Veronica, Elizabeth, Jane—these were, in their own kind and character, women to be proud of. They were generous, humorous, courageous and idealistic without priggishness. No period that was their background could conceivably be a period to be mocked. But Emily Newmark was frankly a pity, and was one, among others, responsible for providing our satirists with a living. She believed that Politics and the Services were the only polite careers, and the Land and the Funds the only springs of wealth that could be called decent. She was a snob and a toady. If a gentleman smoked in front of a lady he was insulting that lady's morals. She was always ready to be insulted. She looked absurd in her gathered flounces, draped skirts, and hair-plaits at the back of her head, but thought she was magnificent. She approved of the Queen in retirement and was preparing to be shocked by the Prince of Wales. (She *wanted* to be shocked.) She considered *all* foreigners (including—very much including—Americans) false, obscene, dangerous and unwashed. (Her own ablutions were neither so constant nor thorough as you would suppose.)

She approved of archery, croquet and painting in water-colours for young girls, but thought that that was enough excitement for them. She was an exceeding prude with a passionate private curiosity in sexual matters. She believed in good works, Missions to the Heathen, and patronising visits to the slums. She was, in fact, *all* wrong, being hypocritical, snobbish, unkind to servants, a worshipper of wealth and a devout believer in a god whom she had created entirely after her own image. She was not a typical woman of her period— only typical of the section of it that was the easiest for after-generations to caricature.

She disapproved, of course, entirely of her brother Barney; she thought his novels 'horrid' with their racing, gambling, and loose women. Sometimes he brought men like Mortimer Collins to the Newmark home, and they smoked and drank together in Barney's sanctum. Now that both Phyllis and Stephen were gone, that Horace lived in Manchester, that Mary was dead, and Katherine married, Emily took charge of the Newmark remnants, Phyllis (named after her mother) who was a weak character, Barney who was not, and Stephen who was a lazy ne'er-do-well. She thought that she dominated all three, but Phyllis agreed with her in order that she might get what she wanted—new hats, novels from the library and a succession of silly young men; Stephen stole money from her, and Barney laughed at her. But Emily, in her blind self-satisfaction, arrogant patriotism and hypocritical prudery, learnt nothing. She had, however, her effect on others . . .

She had her effect on this particular and very important evening, for had she not entered the Hill Street drawing-room just when she did she might not have exasperated Barney to his point of later recklessness.

'What's this I hear, Barney?' she cried. 'You are surely staying indoors this evening?'

'I am not,' said Barney.

'Well, of course,' and her voice was of a sepulchral gloom, 'it is not for me to say, but father has only been buried two days——'

'Father won't mind,' Barney said. 'He has other things to think of.'

Emily had but just sat down on the sofa. She rose.

'I will not hear such blasphemy. Nor shall this poor child. Benjamin, come with me.'

'Benjie is my guest to-night,' Barney remarked. 'He is to share my humble chop in some decent quiet place where we can think reverently of the past and pray hopefully for the future.'

Emily was aghast. She was truly and honestly aghast. This

seemed to her a horrible thing. She broke into a flood of oratory in which their poor father, their poor mother, their poor sister Mary, all looked down from heaven in an agony of distress, in which childhood and vice, innocence and nasty men of the world, insults to herself and Lady Herries, all confusedly figured.

'Ellis will at least support me in this.'

'Ellis is coming with us,' said Barney.

She burst into tears.

'Oh, dammit, I can't stand this!' Barney cried. 'Come along, Benjie.' And Benjie rather sheepishly followed him out.

Down in the hall they found Ellis.

Ellis, waiting, looking up to the staircase, down which they were descending, had then the oddest hallucination. He was not an imaginative man, but, staring in the rather dim gaslight, he saw this: Barney had vanished. Benjamin, not a boy but a man of mature years, had halted on the stairs. Behind him stood a very beautiful lady in a white evening cloak with a high white collar. There was a Chinese clock at the turn of the stairs, a tall, thin clock brilliant in gilded lacquer. He noticed the time on its round face. It was twelve-thirty exactly. He was conscious of a violent, suffocating rage, and he heard his own voice, high, shrill, convulsed: 'Get out, both of you! Get out! Get out!'

As quickly as it came, it was gone.

There was no clock. Benjie jumped the last two steps.

'Hullo, Ellis!' he cried.

This only meant that Ellis was tired and had a headache. When one had a headache one did not know what one was seeing or what one was hearing. These last few days had been trying, with so many members of the family in and out of the house. But he always felt a little queer with Benjamin, never quite at his ease. He was not perhaps comfortable with small boys, and you could never be sure whether they were not laughing at you. But it was more than that. Ever since that day, ten years back, of the Heenan and Sayers fight, he had had an almost nauseating impression of Walter Herries. He could see him now, wandering, lost, drunk, you might have said, a disgusting old man, and also his own half-brother. He hated to think that he had any link with him. And here was the man's grandson. They said that Walter's life in Cumberland was a disgrace. That horrid man's son had murdered this boy's father. Everything that was abnormal, fantastic, revolting—cruelty and illicit passion and madness—were in the strain of that branch of the family. And he was himself mixed in it, he who loved everything to be proper and sane and wholesome and virtuous. He had a passion for virtue! But old Walter and he had the same father. He would have cut all that off as he would have cut off a diseased arm, and so he would have been able to do were it not for this boy. The boy seemed normal and decent enough. But he was young yet. You could not tell what the future would be. And just as something in that branch disgusted him, so something attracted him. He had insisted that the boy should be invited to Hill Street. He tried to be friendly with the boy, but he was not clever at friendliness, poor Ellis. He wanted to be so many things that nature prevented him from being.

'All right,' said Barney. 'Shall we go?'

They found a cab in Berkeley Square and, on the way, Barney enlarged to Benjamin on the delights of London life.

'You shall have a night out, young 'un. We'll have dinner at Duke's. No, be quiet, Ellis. It's my evening. What are you, Benjie? Fifteen? Dammit, you look seventeen anyway.' He'd like to give the boy a week. He'd take him to the Café Riche, Sally Sutherland's, Kate Hamilton's, Rose Young's, Mott's. Cafés were open all night. Pity he hadn't been with Barney at the fight between King and Heenan, driving across London Bridge three in the morning with a pork-pie in your pocket. Mott's, too, where old Freer kept guard. None of your tradesmen let in there—not that Barney minded tradesmen. 'You're in the City, Ellis, yourself, aren't you, my boy?' But still a gentleman was a gentleman when it came to eating together. It was at Mott's you could have seen 'Skittles,' famous for her ponies, or lovely Nelly

Fowler. And Kate Hamilton's—well, Benjie was still at school so he'd say no more. But you should have seen a raid at Kate's—carpets turned up, boards—under which bottles and glasses were hidden—raised, all in the twinkling of an eye. Or the 'Pie,' where you were positively bound to have a row before the night was up and where you tipped the Kangaroo so that he shouldn't knock you down.

Barney wasn't a bad fellow; he was warm-hearted, generous, a famous friend, but to-night three things drove him on—the thought of his sister Emily, Ellis' air of wanting 'to be a sport' and wanting, too, to go home to his comfortable bed, and Benjie's excitement. He really loved the boy that night as he sat there, a proper little gentleman, his high hat tilted a trifle, his lips parted with his eagerness, his fresh colour, his sparkling eyes, his laugh, his readiness to trust anyone, his impulse to throw himself into whatever adventure was forward. 'I'll look after him,' he thought. 'I'll see that he comes to no harm.'

Duke's, near St. Alban's Place, was half-hotel, half-hostelry. In the bedrooms the beds were cleanly enough, and most of the residents slept in them all day because they were out and about all night. A number of the residents may be said to have never been sober.

Excellent joints could be had for dinner, and the best of eggs and bacon any time of day or night, but the establishment *did* exist mainly for drinking—no one pretended other. Brandy-and-soda, rum and milk all day, sherry and bitters before breakfast, and a glass of brandy for tea.

A later generation might have thought Duke's eating-room a little on the stuffy side. Everything was a trifle close, smelly, thick with tobacco and brandy fumes, linen and under-linen not quite clean, a strange air of rooms littered with feathers from an old bed, warm with the odour of unwashed bodies, cats furtively picking at fish-bones on a sanded floor, and the Chairman banging with his hammer on the table in the smoke-thickened distance. Stuffy! That was the word for the night-life of the London of the 'sixties.

But for Benjamin, Duke's room was Paradise. He gazed with eyes of wonder and admiration at old Charles, the presiding deity, who shuffled about in a shiny snuff-coloured tail suit and slippers, who—Barney told him—was never known to sleep, for at any moment of day or night he was ready to assist a drunken gentleman from a cab, or part two combatants. There were two chuckers-out, Jerry and Tom—men, it seemed, of almost legendary strength. It was nothing, Barney said, to see a long wooden coffin come down the stairs into the middle of the diners. One of the gentlemen had died upstairs, of delirium tremens. No one thought anything of it at all.

Dinner went well enough. Ellis was quiet. He seemed even to be enjoying himself and watched a young swell with an eye-glass and long moustaches drink one brandy-and-soda after another. 'Marvellous, isn't it?' he said in his precise careful voice. 'Can't think how he does it!'

But it was here and now that Benjamin had the first brandy-and-soda of his life. He had tried gin up in Cumberland, but had not liked it. Cherry-brandy had been an adventure at Rugby. But this brandy-and-soda was different. It may be said, in a way, to have changed his whole life. He was ready for it. In many ways he was old, very old; in others he was a baby. But the recklessness, the urge to do something simply because it was forbidden, the bravado that led him again and again to challenge anybody at anything, the absence in him, not of a sense of good and bad, but altogether of a sense of right and wrong, all these were pledged by him that night in that glass of brandy-and-soda. As he drank it down he may be said to have whispered to his familiar spirit the words that were to be his Creed all his days: 'I'll do what I want. I'll see all that I can see. I'll love and enjoy with all my heart. I'll do no one harm but nothing shall stop my adventure.'

To be fair to Barney it was true that Benjie *looked* seventeen. There was something in his hard blue eye, in his confident carriage and his air of assurance that made him seem, even then, mature. But he was not; in one meaning of the word, he would never be. After that brandy-and-soda he was ready for anything and he thought that it would be amusing to tease Ellis.

Ellis was twelve years older. He was staying in Ellis' house, and Ellis had been kind to him. For all these reasons he should have been polite to Ellis. But he was happy, he was reckless, he liked old Ellis even though he *was* a bit of a woman and even though Ellis didn't like him. So, on their way to the 'Paragon,' he broke out:

'I say, Ellis—what relation are you to me really? Ought I to call you Uncle?'

'No, of course not. What an idea!'

'But *what* are you? My grandfather is your brother, ain't he?'

'My half-brother,' Ellis answered stiffly.

'Oh, so you're my half-great-uncle! What a funny thing to be to anybody!'

'All right,' said Ellis, yet more stiffly. 'We'll forget it!'

'Oh, I shan't forget it! I say, Barney, isn't that funny? To be someone's half-great-uncle?'

He hadn't a notion that Ellis was minding. All life was rosy and golden. Never, never had he been so happy before. He loved Barney and would do anything in the world for him. The streets were a glory of light and splendour. Wouldn't it be fine to be going to the Opera in the Haymarket—and then, all in a moment, they are out of Piccadilly and walking down a street where the gas is flaring over coarse scraps of meat, where linen-drapers are still, at this hour, invaded by poorly dressed women wanting pennyworths of needles or farthingsworths of thread, where there are little open dens, reeking with the odour of fried fish and sausages, where a lady in a mob-cap is instructing a sailor in the mysteries of the famous dance 'Dusty Bob and Black Sal,' where a huge negro, his teeth gleaming white under the gaslight and his brown chest bare, is turning somersaults for pennies!

Then, as suddenly, they were in broad lighted streets again and passing through the wide painted doors of the 'Paragon.'

'We'll walk about,' said Barney. 'We can see just as well from here.'

Benjie had never been to a real theatre before. It was a while before he could take all the dazzling brilliance into his system. First the stage with its blaze of light held him. A group of young women in low green bodices and wide skirts were dancing while two gentlemen in evening dress, one at each corner of the stage, waved flags. A large box, protruding over the stage, contained a crowd of gentlemen, very elegant and noisy, smoking cigars and leaning over to shout encouragement to the girls. At the back of the theatre everyone was walking about, talking and laughing. There were little tables at which ladies and gentlemen were drinking. Men stood up in the pit and shouted at one another.

'Hullo, Connie!' Barney said. 'Never thought I'd see you here.'

'Oh, didn't you? Well, where were you last Friday night? I was waiting an hour and a half and wouldn't have had no supper at all if a gentleman hadn't taken pity on me. Nice treatment, I call it!'

Benjie thought that, save for his mother and Veronica, he had never seen anyone so beautiful. She was fair with bright blue eyes, ringlets and a dress the colour of primroses, gathered into great festoons at the back. She was angry, anyone could see, but Barney was not at all discomforted, only more like a clown than ever, his hat on one side of his head, grinned and stared over his shoulder to see who else might be there. Benjamin feared that she was about to do something desperate, she looked so angry, but her eyes fell on himself. She smiled, a lovely, entrancing smile.

'Hullo, baby,' she said. 'Where's your mother?'

He smiled back, and murmured something with proper bashfulness.

'Isn't he a pet? What's your name, dear?'

But Barney was, in an instant, the guardian. He put his hand on Benjie's shoulder.

'Now then, Connie, enough of that.'

Her voice was soft. She stared at Benjie as though she could eat him.

'All right,' she said quietly, 'I shan't hurt him.'

There were two chairs near to them. She sat down in one and motioned Benjie to the other.

'There! Now we are at a proper distance. Is he your guardian or something?'

'No,' said Benjie.

'What's your name then?'

'Benjamin Herries.'

'Well I never! Do you often come here?'

'It's the first time,' said Benjie.

'But not your last, I'll be sworn. Here! you want a flower in your button-hole. Take this.'

She had two small white roses at her waist. She took out one and gave it him. Very proudly he stuck it into his button-hole.

'You're the prettiest boy I've *ever* seen!' She drew her chair a little closer. 'Like to come and see me one day?'

'I should very much,' said Benjie. 'Only you see——' He was about to say that to-morrow he would return to school, but that seemed to him childish, so he altered it to 'I don't live in London.'

'Where do you live then?'

'In Cumberland.'

'Where's that?'

'Up in the North.'

'Oh, never mind where you live. Here, see, I'll give you my card and then——'

But it seemed that Ellis, who had been standing awkwardly by himself, was now remonstrating, in great excitement, with Barney, for Barney broke out:

'Come on, young Benjamin. We'll go and visit the Captain. Ta-ta, Connie. See you again.'

Benjamin had to go. He had just not courage enough to demand that he should stay, but as Ellis and Barney turned ahead of him, the lovely Connie, coming so close to him that his nose was suffocated in some scent that seemed to contain a whole garden of flowers, caught his neck in her fair hand and kissed him.

He ran after the others, his heart hammering, his cheeks flaming, and his mouth tasting of some sweet powder. Who had ever dreamt that life could be like this?

They went behind the stage to a large room in which ladies (performers evidently) were drinking with bearded and high-hatted gentlemen, while a funny little man in a very light waistcoat and bushy side-whiskers claimed Barney as his most intimate friend, bowed gravely to Ellis, and asked them all to have a drink.

But Benjie saw and heard nothing. He sat in a dream of happiness. Oh! what a lovely lady! How kind, how generous, how amusing! It was always his first thought when he met anyone whom he liked that he wanted to make his new friend a present. What could he give her in return for his rose? He had the ten shillings that Ellis had bestowed on him—or, at least, he had some of it. He could buy her flowers or fruit. Barney would tell him where she lived. He would go to visit her . . . Into the middle of these charming dreams Ellis gruesomely plunged.

'Benjamin, we are going home, you and I.'

'Going home?' he gasped.

'Yes. You must not be up late. You are returning to Rugby to-morrow. I myself am tired.'

'But of course I am not going home!'

He hated Ellis, who had the sad long face of a horse pining for its stable.

'This is no proper place for you,' he said.

'Why not?'

'Well—it's plain—you are only a boy——Places like this——'

To do Ellis justice, this was one of the most difficult things that he had ever had to do. He did not wish to preach, to improve others; on the contrary, his desire was that he should be a jolly companion, a merry wit, a Prince of Good Fellows. But nature is too strong for us. Good fellows are not made, they are born. His capacity for finding life shocking was abnormally large. It was not his fault that it was so. It was simply his destiny. He did not want to spoil Benjamin's fun; he only thought it dreadful that Benjamin should be finding this fun at all.

'You are to come with me,' he said, his voice trembling. He looked out of place, absurd, in that room.

Benjie saw it and, unhappily, Benjie laughed.

'You don't know how funny you look, Ellis!'

Then Ellis hated him. One thing he could not forgive—mockery that seemed to him unjust. It was his misfortune that all mockery of which he was the victim seemed to him unjust.

He caught Barney's arm.

'Benjamin and I are going home.'

Most regrettably Barney was by now drunk enough to find seriousness a farce and gloomy faces a pantomime. He roared with laughter.

'I say—don't be so sad, Ellis, old buck. Why, dammit—oh lor! look at your face——'

'We are going home,' Ellis, pale, tortured, terrified of a public scene, repeated.

'Well, *I'm* not,' Benjamin cried. 'I'm not, am I, Barney?'

'No, of course you're not. Here, Captain, this is my young friend, *very* young friend. Never been to a Green Room before, never seen a pretty girl.'

'Shame! Shame!' Ellis cried in the best transpontine manner. He caught Benjie's arm.

'You are coming with me!'

'I'm not,' said Benjie, struggling to be free.

Two girls laughed. A gentleman with enormous side-whiskers, holding a glass of champagne rather uncertainly, came forward.

'What's the matter?' he said.

'Let me go!' Benjie said indignantly, wrenching himself from Ellis' hold.

Ellis let him go, and in that moment hated his half-great-nephew with all the hatred that a shy, self-conscious, awkward man feels for anyone who makes him the centre of a scene. Lowering his head, picking up his hat, he slipped away.

Benjamin was invited to sit at a table. Several ladies talked to him. Somebody said: 'You can have four monkeys to one if you like.'

'Put it down,' said someone else.

'By Gad,' some voice cried, 'if you can put me on to a good thing, Gordon, I'll be eternally grateful.'

He drank some champagne. He felt a little sleepy. The ladies were kind to him, but they were nothing, nothing at all because Connie had kissed him. Then he heard the Captain, the gentleman with the flowing whiskers and very light waistcoat, say:

'What about Victorine's, Barney, old boy?'

'I'm agreeable,' said Barney.

'What about the boy?'

'I'll look after him. We shan't stay long.'

Benjamin found himself accompanying the Captain, who confided to him as they went into the street:

'I've got a boy just your age. What are you? Seventeen?'

'Yes,' said Benjie, lying proudly. 'And a half.'

He felt about forty, or what he supposed that forty would feel. Nothing excited him like something new—something he had never done before, the company of someone whom he had never seen before, a new place, a new trick, a new risk, a new danger. Now, feeling like a knight of old, he strode through the streets, trying to keep pace with his two friends so that they should not discover how short his steps were. He did a little trot, then a long step, then a little trot again. Where were they going? Would Connie be there? Victorine's! That sounded exciting. They came at length to a barren waste surrounded with railings. In the centre of the waste was an equestrian statue. Here were oyster rooms, public-houses, night-houses. Here was Jerry Fry's Coffee House and there a small theatre with a large lady in black tights painted on a crimson ground over the doorway. A four-wheeler, lonely and disconsolate, wandered from darkness into darkness.

They turned into a narrow, intensely dark street, found their way cautiously down a kind of tunnel.

'Here we are,' said Barney.

Behind the door, through a little window, two janitors were watching. They recognised both Barney and the Captain; the door swung back. As they passed in, the barren waste of Leicester Square seemed to follow them, bringing with it the 'Shades,' one of the wildest eating-houses in London, where the spoons and forks were marked 'Stolen from the Shades' as a delicate hint to its patrons, and the 'Tableaux Vivants,' a festive hall almost next door to Victorine's, where, for a shilling, you could listen to more filth within half an hour than in any other place in London.

'Victorine's,' however, seemed as respectable as a church-service. Barney, Benjie and the Captain seated themselves in a corner and brandy-and-sodas were ordered from a benevolent-looking old man with a hare-lip and snow-white hair. It was not a very big room. In the far corner was a billiard-table at which several gentlemen were playing. The centre of the room was cleared for dancing and there was a shabby piano decorated with two dusty ferns in pots wrapped in green paper; at the piano a large ringleted lady in a crimson dress was playing. Two staircases vanished into upper regions. Several ladies were drinking at little tables with several gentlemen. But the great glory of the place was Victorine herself, a huge woman weighing over twenty stone, who sat at a raised desk near the piano. It was said that she drank champagne all day and all night. Her countenance was hideous, for her nose was flat, she had a scar across her upper lip and a number of chins. Her little eyes were wrapped in fat.

Benjie gazed at her with excited fascination. Her bodice was cut very low and her enormous bosom shook with every movement. He had never seen anyone so ugly and he felt that he would like to talk to her. The gentlemen at the tables embraced the ladies, and one stout female balanced herself precariously on a stout gentleman's knee. Benjie was always a great observer; he missed very little, and was capable of a detached non-moral attitude that permitted him to see life steadily and, unless his own emotions were aroused, with great fairness.

His emotions were not aroused now except that he was greatly enjoying himself—for had not Connie kissed him and given him a white rose? He was still, in the back of his mind, considering what sort of a present he should give her. He had better wait, perhaps. Christmas-time he would be in funds.

Then Victorine noticed them and beckoned Barney over to her. After a while he returned and said to Benjamin:

'Ma wants to speak to you. She won't eat you. Come along.'

Benjamin went over to her, feeling rather self-conscious as he crossed the floor, but he was ready for any adventure. He stood on the raised platform beside her, laughing. She spoke in a deep husky voice. She held out a large dirty hand.

'How are you?' she asked.

'Very well, thank you, ma'am,' said Benjie.

'How do you like my place?'

'I think it's very nice,' said Benjie.

'First time you've been here, isn't it?' she asked him, suddenly bending towards him, and he thought that he had never known anything so terrifying as that great round soiled, misshapen face with its little eyes, its flat nose, its grotesque mouth coming so close to his own.

'Yes, it's the first time.'

'You can see for yourself how quiet it is.' Her little eyes stared into his. 'There isn't a quieter house in London. It's these —— who come with their —— interference who make all the trouble. Take my word for it.'

It was astonishing to him, the quiet friendly manner in which she used words of a terrifying impropriety. They were not, it is sad to say, new to him, because boys at Rugby, or anywhere else, understand many words that would frighten Billingsgate. Not that they had ever done Benjie any harm, these words. They were simply counters in a normal day's play.

'You see,' Madame Victorine continued, her voice lower than ever, her manner extremely confidential, 'I am a mother to all the boys and girls who come here. You wouldn't believe all that I do for them. Saved their lives again and again. Mother I am and Mother they call me. I'm a widow, you know,' she added unexpectedly. 'My late husband was a Captain in the Army and he died in the West Indies of a yellow fever.'

'I am sorry,' Benjie said. He could think of nothing else to say.

'Yes. It was a tragedy.' There was a tear in her eye. Her vast bosom heaved. He thought that she was going to cry, but instead, to his great surprise, she banged with her fist on the desk and yelled in a voice of thunder, 'Here, you dirty ——. Get out of here! Didn't I tell you last Thursday not to show your —— face in my place again? Here, Cormey, put him out! Knock his —— face in if there's an argument!'

Benjie turned to see a very mild-looking little man, bearded, in a dirty sack-coat and pepper-and-salt trousers talking with a big man in his shirt-sleeves. The little man gave one glance round the room and vanished through the door. At the same moment Barney came and rescued Benjie, bringing him back to their table.

Barney was never so drunk that he did not know what he was doing. Now he preached Benjie a little sermon. 'You see, my boy, I've brought you here to show you life a bit. But never do anything you'd be ashamed of your mother knowing. You're young yet, but how are you to know what to avoid if you don't look round a bit?'

'I say, Barney,' said Benjamin. 'I want to give that lady a present. I'm going back to Rugby to-morrow so there isn't much time. Do you think you could give her something from me? I'll pay you back when I get my pocket-money. I've got a bit now that Ellis gave me, and with two weeks' pocket-money——'

'Here you are, my boy,' said Barney, diving confusedly into his pocket.

He produced two golden sovereigns.

'I don't know what you are talking about, but if it's money you're wanting——'

Two sovereigns!

'Oh, I say! But, Barney, I shan't have two pounds for months!'

'Oh, never mind! Keep them.'

'No. If I give her something, you see, I want it to be with my own money——'

He kept a sovereign. With luck he could pay that back by Christmas. A sovereign! He could buy her something fine—a scarf, a pin, a brooch . . . And it was then that the fun began. Over the silver image of his divine Connie he saw, rising as it were from the floor, a thick-set squat fellow, very hairy, very unkempt, very drunk. He wandered, as though he were describing with his feet a geometric figure, towards one of the little tables, raised a glass of champagne stationed there in front of a gentleman and drank from it. At the same time, grinning amiably, he knocked off the hat of the gentleman. Then, turning, he began to orate to the room:

'In the name of our Queen, of Mr. Disraeli and little Lottie Heever, down with the French! Down, I say, with the French! Are they eating dogs in Paris? Poodle-dogs? And is elephant their one luxury? Right and right again! To hell with the French!'

But he proceeded no further, for the two strong men, who had been watching the billiards, were across the room, had the man by the legs and were trundling him towards the door. At the same time the gentleman whose drink had been abstracted—stout, plethoric, with a beard of the colour of jet— cried something in a kind of frenzy and rushed towards one of the staircases. Benjie, looking in that direction, saw that two young ladies, most scantily dressed, were peering over the stair-rail. One of them, seeing the bearded gentleman, vanished with a scream, the gentleman after her.

Then everything happened together. The victim of the strong men wriggled from his captors and, his trousers tumbling towards his knees (for the strong men had burst his buttons), lurched toward the piano; there were shouts and cries from the upper floor which drew Madame Victorine, panting, upwards; some gentlemen ran in from the billiard table; the lady at the piano stayed with her back to it, cursing at the height of a shrill soprano; a large tortoise-shell cat crept from nowhere and began to feed eagerly upon a sandwich that had dropped; a table fell, glasses and bottles crashing with it; and the Captain, who had been dancing very solemnly with a stout lady in green, left her where she was and reeled (for he was very drunk) towards Barney.

'Here,' said Barney. 'We must be out of this.'

And then a fantastic thing occurred. At the end of the room there was a long mirror hung with yellow and green papers. Reflected in the centre of this mirror was the old waiter with the white hair and the hare-lip. He seemed to Benjie to swell and lengthen. As he grew in size, another figure, long and thin, spread out behind him, caught him from the back, in the neck, and began to twist his head round. The mirror grew ever more unusual, for now it was swinging, slowly swinging on its nail, and the two men reflected in it increased to three, to four, to five. They all struggled together, and behind them and around them the room swayed with them, tables and chairs, Madame's desk, the coloured portraits of the Queen and the Prince Consort, the piano, overturned tables, all swaying, swinging, swaying again.

Someone threw one of the flower-pots and it struck the mirror in its centre: a great crack like a spider's web struck the bodies, faces, furniture . . . Someone turned out the gas.

It was then, in that strange darkness, smelling of spirits, dust and tobacco, filled with cries and shouts, that Benjie felt a great exultation and a wild spirit of enterprise.

'Here! Benjie! Where are you?' he heard Barney crying.

But nothing could stop him. He plunged forward into the

darkness, tumbled over a recumbent body, was up again, had found the piano, was enveloped by large female arms. Some woman held him to her. She was crying, sobbing.

'Oh dear, oh dear! . . . And I had a nice supper at home waiting . . . ' And then, in a whisper over Benjie's head, 'Mr. Archer, are you there? Are you there, Mr. Archer! Oh dear, and if it hadn't been for the five shillings he promised me——'

'It's all right,' Benjie said, feeling real wet warm tears dropping on his cheek and, in sympathy, patting with his hand what was, he imagined, a huge naked arm. 'Only a moment and they'll have the lights——'

But the lady murmured, sobbing as she spoke, 'Don't you move, Charlie, my darling. You'll be killed for certain if you move a step——'

She planted a wet kiss on his cheek. She began to croon in a drunken kind of lullaby, her vast arms now tight about him, and then surprisingly, in the middle of her crooning, in a sharp business-like voice as though she were giving an order at a shop: 'Where are you, Mr. Archer? I'm here, Mr. Archer, by the piano.'

He ducked his head, slipped to his knees and had escaped. Everything was wild now. Fighting was on all sides. He could hear blows struck, bodies thudding to the floor. Women were screaming, it seemed, from earth and air. Someone again embraced him. This time it was a man—someone fat, paunchy and smelling dreadfully of brandy. They were entangled, intermingled, dragging along the ground together. The man said no word but breathed desperately. He had Benjie by the slack of his breeches, and Benjie had his fist in a handful of beard. The mirror must have fallen, for there was a great crash of shattering glass. Benjie, laughing, shouting he knew not what, tore at the beard, was released like a shot from a catapult, and half flew, half fell through a door, clutched at a wall to save himself and was caught by some hand. He looked up and saw that it was Barney, Barney hatless, his neckerchief torn, but Barney quite sober.

'Thank God!' He held Benjie as though he'd never let him go.

'Here's a piece of luck. Come on, my lad. It's the lock-up for us if we are not speedy.'

A moment later they were in the deserted street, surveyed by an orange-tinted moon and two gas-lamps. Dead silence. Dead, dead silence. A little breeze rose from the pavement and fluttered on their faces. Victorine's was gone. Everything in and around Victorine's was gone. Ahead of them was the desolate waste of Leicester Square with the equestrian statue.

'Walk! Walk!' said Barney. 'Can you walk all right? Have you got your legs?'

'Oh, I'm all right,' said Benjie grandly. 'Are you all right, Barney?'

'Hush!' said Barney, who now that he had found Benjie was, all in a moment, drunk again. 'Hush! We'll wake Emily.'

Benjie's head ached, he thought that he had lost a tooth, his right leg hurt a trifle. But he felt at his button-hole. Miraculous! The white rose was still there! How had it escaped? Was that not of itself a triumph? He was dizzy with happiness, adventure, maturity, first love, the wine of battle, the ether of recklessness, the full, complete, uncensored actuality of life.

'Barney, I've still got my rose!'

But Barney was striding on ahead. Benjie did a long step, a trot or two, a step again.

With a sudden alarm he felt in his pocket. Yes, the sovereign was there. What would he buy for her? A scarf, a chain, a pin, a brooch . . .?

He did a long step, a trot or two, a step again.

BATTLE WITH PANGLOSS

Elizabeth, walking through the dusky afternoon up the hill to Fell House, was stopped by a little man like a ferret riding a large bay mare. She knew at once who it was—Glose, the handyman at the Fortress, her father's handy-man—and, as always when anyone or anything connected with Ireby confronted her, she shivered with apprehension. Glose, who had sharp beady eyes and was always a trifle drunk, thought, as he looked at her: 'That's a pretty piece, although she *has* got grey hair.'

It was generally acknowledged up at the Fortress that Walter Herries' daughter, even though she was nearly sixty, was the most beautiful lady in the County. They liked to tell old Ma Pangloss so, when they dared.

'She'll be back one of these days and send you packing, Mrs. Pangloss, *Madam*,' said a lively carroty-haired girl from Braithwaite who had just received her notice, 'and then we'll have a lady who is a lady.'

Elizabeth had a dark crimson coat with a silver-grey fur collar turned up above her slender neck, and she wore on her grey hair a feather toque with flame-coloured feathers. She was protected from the chill October wind by a thin veil. The twists and bands in which her hair was arranged at the back under the little feathered hat held lovely lights and shadows, so Glose thought. He was something of a poet where women were concerned, and afterwards in the kitchen at Ireby he declared:

'She had on a little hat all flaming feathers, and her hair was silver, you understand, and she has the figure of a girl of twenty, old as she is. Very pretty with the dusk coming on and the leaves blowing down, all the colour of her little hat.'

He was an Irishman, vagrant and worthless. He was in gaol

for trying to knife a man in Keswick three months later.

But he had a letter for Mrs. Herries. He was riding up to Fell House. He touched his cap, leaned down and gave her the letter.

Her hand trembled as she read it by the pale light of the saffron sky above the hill. It was written in a hand so shaky that it was difficult to decipher.

DEAR ELIZABETH—

I am ill and would like to see you.

—Your affectionate father,
WALTER HERRIES.

That was all.

'Thank you,' she said to Glose. 'I will see to it.' She walked quickly up the hill. She was in a turmoil of emotion, but once in the house she told no one anything. She had always been quiet, reserved, by herself; her mother, who had learnt, through suffering, restraint, had taught her.

She peeped in to say good night to Judith, but the old lady was sleeping. Had she been awake Elizabeth might have said something, for although Judith was now ninety-eight and was being preserved as though constructed of egg-shell china, every noise, shock, sudden news kept from her, yet, inside this elegant glass case, she lived, Elizabeth fancied, an exceedingly alive and conscious existence. Judith knew more about Walter than anyone else at Uldale. It was she who had seen him last, who had known him longest. To her, Elizabeth might have spoken. But to Dorothy, who was now as fat as a tub and as contented as a pork-pie, Elizabeth said not a word. Otherwise there was only Jane, for Veronica had been Mrs. Forster now for two years, and Amabel had, of all mad things, gone to be a student at the Ladies' College at Hitchin. She had been there two years and was now at Cambridge, whither the College had just removed

279

under the name of Girton. Ridiculous of Amabel, who was now between thirty and forty! She said, of all things, that she intended to study medicine!

So there were, besides Dorothy, Judith and Elizabeth, only Timothy (who showed no signs of marrying: he was fat, red-faced, cheerful—a proper Squire) and Jane. Elizabeth might have said something to Jane. She did not. Jane was such a dear old spinster, already ringleted and shawled, her face sweet and anxious and kind under her pale-gold hair, her small body *intensely* virginal. No, she would be of little use.

Of course Elizabeth must go to Ireby, and this time she would remain. From the moment that she received the note and read it in the gathering shadow of the autumn dusk she knew that there was only one thing that she must do. But oh! how she didn't want to! Her quiet, reserved, cloistered life, saturated with the memory and actual presence of John, devoted to Benjamin and Aunt Judith, was exactly right at Uldale. She was young no longer. She was nearing sixty. She shrank in every vein and pulse of her body from the roughness, violence, hateful rudeness that going to Ireby meant.

So she fortified herself with Adam and Margaret. On the morning after receiving her father's letter she told Dorothy quietly that she was going to stay at Cat Bells for a night or two.

'Are you sure that they want you, Elizabeth dear?' said Dorothy. 'Adam is just finishing his book, I believe.'

'I don't think that they will mind,' Elizabeth said. And they did not.

On that first evening, sitting by the fire after Vanessa had gone to bed, hearing Will softly singing as he occupied himself with something in the kitchen close by, Adam tranquilly smoking his pipe, they talked it all over.

The two women had a great regard for one another. Margaret had broadened into a maternal and seemingly placid woman, more German now perhaps in type than English. Her love for Adam was so strong that she could not sit with him five minutes without snatching a private glance at him to see that all was well. She knew that he loved her but she knew also, as nine out of every ten wives come to know, that she had not captured all of him; a certain wildness in him had escaped her. He was her friend and she was his, but she knew also that soon he would get up, knock his pipe against the stone of the fireplace, mutter something and slip off to Will—and that then for an hour at least those two deep voices would rumble on beyond the wall, and that they would both be happy together with a kind of happiness that neither of them could find with a woman. So she was glad to have Elizabeth then. They were two quiet, elderly women, sitting together by the fire; they were like hundreds of thousands of other elderly women sitting beside the fire that evening all over England—and the lives of those women contained sufficient courage, unselfishness and loving devotion to fill a Calendar of Saints.

Margaret, beneath her reserve, was frightened. There were many things in the Herries family that she did not understand, and what she understood least of all was that some of them were so very different from others! That you should have Garth and Amery, the Archdeacon of Polchester, Will and Ellis, Judith and Adam, poor John, crazy Uhland and his father, all of the same stock and closely related, seemed to her sober German imagination extravagantly improbable. Yet it was so, and she had long ago realised that the mad strain in the Herries family was not for her. She shrank from it with all her quiet strength because it was that element in her husband—although Adam of course was not crazy!—that prevented him from being entirely hers, and it had been that same element in his mother that had given her all her young married sorrows.

Now she was set, with all the determination of which she was capable, to keep the wildness from Vanessa! Vanessa as yet was as good and obedient and loving as a child could possibly be, but she was impulsive, fantastically generous, and—most perilous of all!—worshipped, increasingly with every year of her growth,

Benjamin Herries. Now Margaret was Elizabeth's friend, but in her heart she was afraid of Elizabeth's son. Young Benjamin was wild; they said that he did wild things in London. He was eighteen years of age, and in another term he would be leaving Rugby. Then, Margaret supposed, he would come to live at Ireby and would be terribly close to Cat Bells. Margaret had to confess that when she was in the boy's company she could not but like him. He looked you straight in the face with his clear blue eye, he was merry, honest, open-handed, the friend of all the world. But he was wild. Margaret was sure that he had no principles, and although Adam sometimes laughed at principles yet he respected them as a good man should. Margaret was no narrow condemner of her fellow but she had acquired the prejudices of her time. She believed in righteousness, and for her own beloved daughter she would fight like a fishwife if need be.

Vanessa would be beautiful—of that there was no question—and she must be guarded against Benjamin, but how she was to be guarded poor Margaret had no idea. Adam only laughed when she spoke to him of it.

And now Elizabeth was going back to that horrible place at Ireby with that drunken old wretch her father and the loose women he had with him. She was going back into all that craziness and wildness and bad living, and she intended to remain there. That quiet, frail woman with her gentle face, shy, retiring way, so perfect and refined an English lady, thought Margaret, would live in a world that must revolt and disgust her at every turn. And, if she did remain, Benjamin would of course come to her there; he was heir, Margaret supposed, to that place, and any money the old man might have if, indeed, his dissipations had left him any. And Benjamin at Ireby meant Benjamin very near to Vanessa. At the thought of her child so peacefully sleeping in the upper room her whole protective fighting maternity was at arms. She felt inclined to cry out to Elizabeth, although she loved and admired her:

'Go away! Please, please go away and let neither your son nor yourself ever return.'

But they sat talking calmly; only once Margaret said:

'Do you think, Elizabeth dear, that it is *worth* going? Can you do anything for him? Is his life not too settled? Can it ever be your life?'

And Elizabeth answered, looking at Margaret:

'I know it's my duty, Margaret.'

Margaret shivered with some quick sense of chill and discomfort. Her German blood gave her an unusual sensitiveness to intangible influences. Many past events touched her moment's consciousness, and future events, linked to these, hung like clouds about her vision. It was as though the cheerful fire-lit room were, at that instant, fogged with smoke.

Elizabeth slept little that night and in the morning she shrank from what she was going to do as she had never shrunk from anything in her life before. After all, she was returning to the house where, it seemed to her excited fancy, Uhland's footstep must have left everywhere an imprint of blood. That was not a melodramatic exaggeration. John's death had been bloody, and, although his murderer had been her own brother, that did not make his ghost more stainless. In every room, at every turn, there would be memories, agonising thoughts, vain, wretched recriminations. But nevertheless, she had no hesitation as to what her duty was.

Two things made the journey easier for her. One was the luxuriant splendour of the day. In October this country is often a fantastic dream, and on this especial morning the fragment of this world contained by the sky, the hills, the water, was a glory. Last night there had been the first frost and the lawn glittered in a dancing fire-fly extravagance under a pale autumnal mist. She stood in the doorway of the cottage and looked out to the Lake and Walla Crag. Near her was a mulberry tree; there were roses, chrysanthemums, currant bushes; someone was drawing water, and the smoke from the cottage chimney went up in a gay, fluttering pennon of thin colour. A squirrel watched her from a branch. She could see into the living-room with the bright-blue cups on the white cloth, rough pottery with a pattern of flowers. All this world at her hand was clear and distinct with a hard edge to it. Then, in the space of the lawn, of a leaping jump, terrestial existence was cut off and mirage began.

The blue cold sky ranged like a sea infinitely high and remote from change: the tops of the larch and birch and fir suddenly, if they were high enough, struck a hard stainless light and were edged like cut paper, but so soon as the feathering vapours of mist rolled curtain-like across the scene colour so rich and varied began that the sky seemed to belong to another infinitely remote existence, unactual and a planet away.

The mist was neither ascending nor descending in clouds; it was not thick enough for form, it only caught the sunlight and transmuted it, and that sunlight, joyfully enclosed, glowed within, an imprisoned fire.

It is the quality of this country that with a structure of rock, naked fell and dark grim water, it has the power of breaking into an opulence of light and colour. So the Lake that could be cold as driving snow, harsh like shadowed steel, fierce with white foam as a bird's feathers are blown angrily by storm, now was streaked and veined with shadows of the grape that trembled, as though a hand gently stroked its surface. This trembling was not cold nor wind-swept, but burned with the sun-filled mist. Above these purple shadows the hillsides were orange clouds, orange in their brighter spaces, but like smouldering, glowing embers where vapour enshrouded them. An isolated field, a blazing tree, a strip of bracken against the dark plum-coloured islands, shone out like the gilt of missals, damascened, exotic, flaming to the eye where all else was mystery, but the mist above the gold was as dim as the white ash of burnt wood.

Because the sky was decisive with its virgin chastity of egg-shell blue, the misted land in contrast took all the colours of purple, topaz, orange, and laid them under washes of pale gold. And yet, with all this dimness the hills were strong, striking deep into the Lake and, where they topped the mist, hard-ridged against the chill sky. And on Skiddaw there was a sudden flame-shaped crest.

Nothing but words of colour could describe this colour, but its final delight for Elizabeth was that it was friendly. The Lake, the cottage, the chrysanthemums, the sparkling lawn, wished her well. She could feel the warm quiver in the air, could think without extravagance that the sun laughed with pleasure as it struck again and again through the mist to touch with the point of its shaking lance the purple shadowy waters, the flaming autumn trees, the sharp dark ridge of Blencathra. She drew in a deep breath of the frosted air as she saw Walla Crag riding into the orange vapour like the bow of a Viking ship. The breath was as though she had leant her forehead against the pure cold of a newly riven stone . . .

And the second thing was that Will Leathwaite drove her to Ireby.

She could not have had a more perfect defence in perilous country. But before she went she had a moment with Vanessa. Vanessa came dancing on to the lawn, flinging her long arms out, running across the frosty grass, breathing in the air that stung the throat like pepper-mint. Her dark hair was in ringlets, her white strong neck bare. 'She will have big strong breasts,' thought Elizabeth, 'she will be very tall. I never saw a child carry her head with such majesty, and yet she is dancing about the lawn like a little pony.' She was going down with Will to Grange to fetch the carriage. They had to keep it in Grange. As she came nearer to Elizabeth the curve of her face from cheek to chin, still the face of a child innocent, open-eyed, fearless, gave promise of an almost startling beauty. You looked again to see whether that curve could be as perfect in shadowed line, in proportion and purity as you had at first supposed. And it was. Her eyes, lit now with happiness, were direct, unequivocal, so honest that they put you on your guard. What base part of myself am I going to betray here? you must ask yourself.

But Elizabeth knew that Vanessa was no perfect paragon. Her impulsiveness was always taking her into trouble; she had a temper. She was irritated often by stupid people; like her father and grandmother, she did not suffer fools gladly. Her mother was always checking her for answering back her elders (which no child was allowed to do), but, as Vanessa said, it was her father's fault because he encouraged her.

She was compassionate and generous, but not at all sentimental. At a time when both young men and young women 'gushed' and the world was on the whole more insincere than usual, Vanessa laughed. She laughed, it is to be feared, at Dorothy Bellairs, and Captain Forster who had married Veronica, and Mrs. Ponsonby and a good many more. In fact Vanessa was not perfect at all. Margaret often shook her head over her.

'I am going down to Grange with Will. We'll be back in a twinkle!'

'Vanessa!' said Margaret.

'Well, but, Mama, twinkle is quite a proper word!'

'And as soon as you are back, Vanessa, you sit down to the German.'

'Oh, bother the German on this lovely day! I'm sorry, Mama; isn't it a pity that I don't like the German language better?'

She came to Elizabeth and said good-bye.

'Please, how is Benjamin?'

'Very well. He plays in the football team this term, and you know Rugby is very famous for football'

'Yes. I am so glad.'

'Now, Vanessa, Will's waiting.'

'When you write to him will you tell him, please, that I asked?'

'Of course I will.'

'Now, Vanessa.'

Elizabeth thought it rather strange that Adam and Margaret should allow their girl when she was only fourteen to go off alone with Will—but then all the family at Uldale, except Judith, thought that Adam treated Will with far too great a familiarity.

Servants were servants, and however good and valuable Will might be (certainly he was a *most* trustworthy man), still it was intended that a member of one Class should not be too intimate with a member of another Class. Emily Newmark, when she heard of it in London, tossed her head. 'Oh, well, we are none of us surprised. Adam Paris was a Chartist for years and would have burnt us all in our beds had he had the chance. Of course he *would* make friends with a common working-man.'

However, when Elizabeth was seated beside Will in the little carriage and they were driving towards Bassenthwaite she could not feel that he *was* 'a common working-man.' He was simply Will Leathwaite, and like most Cumbrian and Westmorland men, sons of Statesmen who have owned their own land for hundreds of years and been servants to none, he held his head high, said nought, and feared no man. But the great thing that Will Leathwaite was was comforting. He was a man of tremendous prejudices, prejudices often based on nothing at all, and he disliked more people than he liked, but if he *did* take you under his wings, then he would see that you were protected. There was nothing he wouldn't do for you, no danger, no strife of tongues (a thing that he greatly disliked) that he wouldn't face. His loyalty was absolute. He had long regarded Elizabeth Herries with a tender protective affection because of John Herries' death. Further than that, she was a member of the Herries clan. He did not think much of several Herries whom he had met, but his friend and master Adam was a Herries and that was enough for him. So Elizabeth was under his wing. As he sat there, staring in front of him, saying 'Gee-up,' cracking his whip, his brow wrinkled a little above his very clear blue eyes, his rebellious lock of hair tumbling out across his forehead from under his old high hat, he said very little—but she *knew* that he was protecting her.

In actual fact he was wondering what he would do when they reached Ireby. He did not want to leave the elderly, delicate lady all alone there. There was every kind of bad story about the

Fortress, and that Mrs. Pangloss was a holy terror. *He* could deal with her—he would like to see any old fat whale of a woman get the better of him—but a lady like Mrs. John Herries, so quiet and soft-spoken, what chance would *she* have?

At last when they were driving along the far end of Bassenthwaite Lake, he said: 'See here now, Mrs. Herries. I don't like leaving you all alone, by yourself as it were, at the Fortress. Please pardon me, Mrs. Herries, if I am saying what I shouldn't.'

By now, poor lady, she was dreadfully frightened and her hands were trembling inside her muff, but Will must not know that.

'No, Will. You can say anything you like, of course. But I shan't need anyone. Sir Walter is my father, you know.'

This made it very difficult for Will, who considered that to warn a daughter against her own father was not at all man's work. Nevertheless, something had to be done. So he thought, looking straight in front of him between the ears of old Bartholomew the horse.

'Yes, Mrs. Herries,' he said at last. 'I do hope you'll forgive me, ma'am, meaning nothing but good intentions and doing as Mr. Adam would wish me to do, seeing that you are one of the family, ma'am.' He cleared his throat, gave a crack with his whip, set back his broad shoulders. 'You see, Mrs. Herries, your father isn't so young as he once was, and there's a woman—Pangloss, they call her—who's no good whatever if the half they say is true. And a lady like you and a woman like her . . . I thought if I was to wait half an hour or so and you wave a handkerchief or some such article out of the window to say that she hadn't done you no kind of harm——'

'She won't harm me, thank you, Will,' Elizabeth said. 'It's very kind of you, and I've met Mrs. Pangloss. I know that she isn't a very nice woman. But I'm not afraid, you know. My father himself has written to me to come and see him, so there is nothing to fear.'

'Yes, Mrs. Herries, I quite understand, ma'am,' said Will.

Nevertheless, he made a private resolve that he would not drive away until he was well assured that all was safe for the poor dear lady.

When they had driven slowly up Ireby Hill and the Fortress came at last into view, Elizabeth drew a deep breath of astonishment. She had seen the chimneys and the two towers, of course, every day from Uldale, but she had never, since her rebuff six years ago, been up that hill. She could not believe what she saw. How could someone as strong, as commanding, as powerful as her father had been, have allowed what had once been his pride to drop into this decay? She had seen the degradation begin in him long before her flight, but the house itself, ugly and forbidding as it was, had been proud, well cared for, the gardens kept, every kind of life and bustle about the place. And now!

She made Will stop the carriage round the bend of the trees so that they could not be seen from the house. In this part the veils of mist were thicker than above Derwentwater, and both Uldale and Skiddaw were invisible. The sun burnt strongly enough for the clouds of vapour to be faintly stained with rose, and here, as on the islands of the Lake, the upper mist was grey above the rose like the ashes of dying fires. But the top of the hill, the trees, the house, were chill and clear, crowning the shrouded valley; their detail was lined with sharpness against the cold bare sky. Elizabeth could see everything, how the trees had grown until they seemed to be throttling one another, how the garden was overgrown with weeds, grass had sprung up between the stones of the garden path, a shutter had swung off a hinge before one of the lower windows, there was an empty pane in the top window of the right-hand tower, stones had tumbled from the wall. There was something especially deserted to-day in the house outlined against so pale and bare a sky. As she looked it seemed to her that the house moved, its walls bulging outwards then sagging in again—an illusion of light.

She caught Will's arm.

'Is there not someone moving in the garden?'

'I don't see no one,' said Will.

'There—moving into the trees—a woman in black. No, it is my imagination. There is no one—not a soul . . . '

She put up her hand to her throat; this was so pitiful, this home of her youth where there had been so much life, now picked bare like a bone, or, to see it the other way, strangled with climbing triumphing vegetation.

'Leave the carriage here,' she said. 'I'll walk to the door. Bring my bag.'

She pulled her coat more closely about her, for it was cold up here, arranged her veil and walked quickly up the road through the gate, up the garden path.

She did not dare to hesitate for a moment lest she should lose all her courage, but it was a reassurance to hear Will's heavy certain tread behind her. Then she rang the bell and it pealed in the air as bells peal through empty houses. She looked around.

'No one has tended this garden. Look at those poor chrysanthemums. I feel as though someone were watching us.'

'Maybe it's the Pangloss woman from behind the window.'

She rang again and while the bell was still echoing the door opened. To her surprise a little girl, very ragged and tattered, wearing a woman's bonnet, was standing there. Elizabeth had thought out her plan of campaign and, taking her bag from Will, she walked into the hall and on into the small room beyond, which, in the old days, had been the gun-room. She knew it very well of course. But now it was quite different: the walls bare save for an old hunting-scene picture; there was a screen with boxing pictures pasted on it, and she remembered that this had been once an ornament of one of the spare bedrooms. There were the ashes of a fire in the grate and a stuffy stale smell of spirits in the air. She put her bag down and stood in front of the fireplace.

She saw that the child, who had large goggly eyes, was in the doorway staring at her.

'What's your will?' the child asked.

It was plain that she had not seen for a long time so grand a lady, for her gaze was rapt by the little dark green bonnet, the green coat with the velvet collar that Elizabeth was wearing.

'Will you please tell Sir Walter Herries that his daughter, Mrs. John Herries, is here and would like to see him?'

The child said nothing but only gaped.

Elizabeth came over to her. She took her mottled red hand in her glove.

'Poor little thing . . . You are shivering with cold. Listen, my dear. Will you find Sir Walter for me and then say that his daughter has come to see him?'

The child vanished; the house was still. A mouse scratched behind the wainscot. She was glad that Will was waiting in the road outside. The door flung open and there stood a fat blowzy woman with a red round face, wearing a faded blue calico dress.

'I beg your pardon, madam,' she said, speaking very quickly. 'The girl shouldn't have shown you in here. This is private.'

All Elizabeth's fear had vanished at the sight of this woman, and she was so deeply filled with pity for her father that she could think of nothing else.

'It is not private to me,' she answered smiling. 'I am Mrs. John Herries, Sir Walter's daughter, and I lived in this house for several years. So you see I know it well. We have met before.'

'Yes, and Sir Walter is not well enough to see anyone.'

'I know that my father is not well because he wrote to me, telling me so and asking me to come and see him.'

'Oh, did he? Excuse me for doubting your word, but he's not able to write to anyone.'

Elizabeth found the note and handed it to her. This brought them nearer to one another.

Mrs. Pangloss read it very slowly, word by word.

'Silly old fool!' Elizabeth heard her mutter. Her great bosom heaved with indignation, but the letter had its effect.

'Well, I'm sorry, Mrs. Herries, I'm very sorry, I'm sure. You're his daughter, as you say, and have a right—although for all the trouble his relations have taken all these years he might have been dead and buried, poor old man, for all they cared. What he *would* have done if it hadn't been for strangers taking care of him it's pitiful to think. However, perhaps you'll call another day, Mrs. Herries, if it isn't a trouble. He isn't quite himself to-day—he's past eighty, you know, Mrs. Herries—and it's the doctor's orders that he isn't to be disturbed by no one—not his nearest and dearest.'

Elizabeth walked back to the fireplace.

'I'm sorry,' she said, 'but I'm afraid, Mrs. Pangloss, I can't do that. You see, I've come to stay. I have brought my bag. I intend to remain here.'

Mrs. Pangloss gasped. Colour slowly mounted into her cheeks and changed them from red into a faintly streaked purple.

'Remain?' she brought out at last in a husky whisper.

'Yes. I have been far too long away. I should have come back years ago and would have done so, had I thought that my father wished for me. Now it is plain from this letter that he does. So will you take me to him, please?'

They stared at one another. This very slender elderly lady was, it seemed, nothing to be afraid of, for Mrs. Pangloss changed her tone.

'No, Mrs. Herries, I'm afraid I can't. Very sorry, but there it is. Doctor's orders, you see, *is* doctor's orders, and those were the doctor's very words. "I trust you to see, Mrs. Pangloss, that nobody disturbs him, not on any account *whatever*—no account *whatever*. I wouldn't like to be answerable for consequences," he said. Those were the doctor's very words.'

'When was the doctor here last?' Elizabeth asked.

'Well, I'm sure, Mrs. Herries, I don't see that it's any business of yours, but if you *want* to know—well, yesterday afternoon.'

'What doctor did you call in?'

'Now really and truly, Mrs. Herries, you are going too far! Here you are, his only child, the only one left to him, poor old gentleman, and you living for years as you might say right at his very door and never so much as asking——'

Elizabeth's delicate face flushed and her eyes flashed—really flashed so that a light, indignant, proud, struck the thick heavy features of Mrs. Pangloss. So, many, many years before, a young Buck in Islington had also been struck!

'I wrote several times,' she said, 'but received no answer. I understand now why I did not. I came once myself—perhaps you have forgotten, Mrs. Pangloss? I did not wish to remind you because you were exceedingly rude and vulgar on that occasion. I admit that after seeing the kind of woman into whose hands my father had fallen I ought not to have left it there, but I was anxious not to drive myself in upon him . . . I was always hoping for a letter——'

'Oh yes,' Mrs. Pangloss broke in. 'I can have you up for libel for that, Mrs. Herries! I can indeed—"kind of woman" indeed—"kind of woman!"—and I the only one all these years who's been good to him. And *that* settles it! I'm a trifle wearied of having all his relations coming round poking their noses in, and it's got to stop! A year or two ago it was that old French Madame who should have been in her grave years back if she'd had any proper decency—and her mother nothing better than a road-gipsy if all they say is true. And now *you* coming worrying! Well, you've no right here, Mrs. Herries—no right at all—and I'll thank you to be off!'

She had worked herself into a splendid temper and, shaking with an anger that had been plainly fortified with both gin and brandy, she advanced several paces into the room.

That was the very thing that Elizabeth desired. It was not very dignified perhaps, but dignity, on such an occasion, must be forgotten. She walked swiftly to the door and then, once outside, ran up the wide staircase, along a passage, up another stair, and through the door into the room that had always been her father's bedroom.

Thank God, it still was! Yes, and there was the same big four-poster with the yellow saffron hangings that, as a tiny child at Westaways, she had looked at with awe and terror, the picture of a hunt with gentlemen in red coats, over the stone mantelpiece, the two old chairs covered in green silk that she so well recollected, a walnut ring-stand, the mahogany cheval glass, the white sheepskin hearthrug, a mahogany wash-stand with marble top and two rosewood pole-screens—all articles that seemed to be part of her very life.

And he, her father, was in the four-poster. From the door she could see only the peaked night-cap but, at the first step forward, he roused himself.

'Who's that!' he called out. 'Alice, you bitch, I told you to bring me a drink. Hours back I told you.'

She came up to the bed. And this was her father whom she had last seen, on the evening before her flight, corpulent, rosy, covered with clothes even too strikingly elegant, master—as he thought—of his world. Now under the night-cap there was untidy grey hair, drawn cheeks with a week's grey stubble; his open nightshirt showed the bones of his throat as sharp and pointed as those of a plucked bird. For him, too, it must have been a striking vision—this very elegant lady with her grey hair, her little green bonnet and her long green coat fitting perfectly her tall slender body. He did not recognise her. He raised himself on his elbow.

'Why, what the devil——?' he said.

She stood close to the bed, smiling.

'Father, don't you know me? You wrote to me and I've come. Elizabeth. I should have come years ago.'

'Elizabeth!' he sat up, and at the same time, with trembling hands, pushed his night-cap straight on his head and pulled his nightshirt about his skinny neck. 'Are you Elizabeth? Dear me! Yes, I wrote that I was ill. But I should not receive you here. Go into another room a moment, my dear, while I dress——'

'No, Father; I've come to stay. You must——'

But she said no more, for Mrs. Pangloss, bursting in, had interrupted her.

'If this isn't *shameful!*' she cried. 'I can have the Courts on you for this, madam. There he was just in his first sleep of the morning and me keeping all the house quiet so that it shouldn't be broken——'

But Walter, sitting up and grinning, said:

'Alice, you old washerwoman, this is my daughter. She has come to pay me a visit.'

'Yes,' cried Mrs. Pangloss with a ripe round oath, for she was now too angry to care what she said (and had also, in the brief interval between the scene downstairs and this, fortified herself with more brandy). 'As she's come so she'll go. I'm mistress here, and the sooner she knows it the better. Forcing herself into a gentleman's bedroom, even if he is her own father!'

Elizabeth had crossed to the window which looked on the road and, glancing down, saw the thick solid body of Will Leathwaite stationed patiently by the gate. He looked up, saw her; she waved her hand.

Turning into the room again, she said:

'Now, Mrs. Pangloss, have this perfectly clear. It is not of the slightest use for you to rant and swear. I am Sir Walter's daughter, he has asked for me—here I am and here I stay—and you leave within the hour.'

At the audacity of this Mrs. Pangloss for a moment could not reply at all. She gasped and stuttered. Then, in jerks, the words came.

'Me! . . . within the hour! You to order me . . . You!' She strode to the door, flung it wide and called: 'Harry! Harry! Where are you? Come here a moment! I want you!'

Walter, meanwhile, found it extremely amusing. He sat there, propped up by pillows, his eyes moving from the one to the other, grinning with his bare gums (his teeth were in a glass by the bed) and mumbling: '*That's* done it! *That's* a pretty thing! Now for a tumble!'

A moment later there arrived a heavy slouching man in corduroys, black rough hair over his eyes. He looked exceedingly sheepish, as well he might. Here was his master in bed in his night-cap, and Pangloss in one of her tantrums, and there, near the window, a beautiful lady in green. He was further embarrassed by the fact that the little girl (the child of himself and Mrs. Pangloss) had crept after him (for although he beat her when drunk, she adored him as truly as she hated her mother) and, sucking her thumb, her old woman's bonnet on the back of her head, looked in.

Throughout the scene he kept muttering: 'Get away, Lucy . . . 'Tisn't no place for you . . . Go on or I'll larrup yer,' but the child paid no heed, and he, Harry Borden, restlessly shifted from heel to heel.

Mrs. Pangloss turned to him. 'Now, Harry, you listen to me. This lady has been asked to go. Master has asked her. I've asked her. If she won't go, well—*you* shall ask her!'

Elizabeth went back to the window. She could see from there all the soft sprawling shoulders of Blencathra above the tops of the golden trees. The whole world swam in light this lovely morning. Inside the room the sun fell in coins and saucers of gold upon the faded ragged carpet. She felt the autumn sun, knew that Will was in the road below, and was conscious of a cheerfulness and high spirits that had not been here for many a day. She thought: 'Benjamin would enjoy this.'

'Well, Mrs. Herries, ma'am, will you have the decency to go? You came uninvited—the sooner you go the better for all parties.'

'I did not come uninvited,' Elizabeth answered quietly. 'And I am certainly remaining.'

'You are not! You are not!' Mrs. Pangloss found a glory of liquor at her heart and the fury of a righteous woman monstrously wronged in her head. 'If you won't go out you shall be put out! I'm in charge here, and so you shall know. Harry, if this lady won't go, you'll please *lead* her——'

But the ludicrous little scene was interrupted from the bed.

'Alice! Do you know to whom you are speaking? And who told

you to bring Harry Borden into my bedroom? And I want my drink—I'm sure it's well past eleven—and the *Times* newspaper of yesterday. You'll fetch me my drink, Alice, and give a poke to the fire before you go.'

But Mrs. Pangloss, all control lost, strode to the bed, stood over the old man and screamed at him. Words poured from her. She flooded the room with her life-story, her virtues as a child, her nobility as a young woman, the criminal errors of Husband One, the positive loathsomeness of Husband Two, her patience in bearing great suffering, a struggle with Husband Two that had nearly lost her an eye, her self-sacrifice in coming to the Fortress, her devotion, generosity in guarding and caring for a gentleman . . . But, most unexpectedly, Walter rose to the occasion.

'Clear out, Alice. Clear out. I'm sick to death of you. I've been sick of you for years. There's been nothing but mess and filth here, and I'm too old to put up with you any longer. An old man wants his comforts, and you've always thought of yourself, you nasty old woman. And what are you thinking of, talking like that in front of my daughter? I asked my daughter to come and I'm glad she's here. So you be off this afternoon. Mrs. Herries will pay you what is due to you. Harry can drive you in the cart. And tell the old hag downstairs to send up my drink. I'm parched.'

The poor woman was amazed. She was stuffed after all only with sawdust, and perhaps, Elizabeth, watching from the window, thought, she had a real affection for him. The look in her face of dismay and chagrin was not only brought there by drink and ill-temper. She stared through her stupid tear-filled eyes. She put out her hand as though she would appeal. 'You don't want me any more? . . . After all I've done for you?'

'I'm sick to death of you, I tell you. I'm sick enough anyway, but I'll spend my remaining days in peace. There, there! . . . I can't bear women to cry. Mrs. Herries shall pay you what's due and Harry shall drive you in the cart . . . '

The catastrophe had been so sudden that she could only look about her, turning her head now this way, now that, large fat tears coursing down her cheeks.

She must care for him or she would not so abruptly surrender, Elizabeth thought. She felt an impulse of pity.

But the woman turned to her, her words almost lost between anger and tears:

'It's you that have done this, Mrs. Herries, and I shan't forget it either.'

Then, blowing her nose and wiping her eyes with a large check handkerchief, she went to the door.

'Come, Harry,' she said. 'They shall suffer for this.'

'Don't forget the drink,' Walter called after her.

When she was gone Elizabeth opened for a brief moment the window, and leaned out.

'Thank you, Will,' she called, waving her hand. 'There is no need to wait. Please tell Mr. Paris that I am remaining.'

Will nodded and started down the road to the carriage.

She closed the window and came to the bed. She took off her bonnet and folded her veil.

'There are a number of things will need doing in this house,' she said.

He looked at her rather piteously.

'You'll be kind to me, won't you? I'm a very old man.'

THE HUNDREDTH BIRTHDAY

As the great day of November 28, 1874, approached ever more nearly it may be said without very much exaggeration that all the Herries all over England held their breath. Would she do it? Could she last the course? Were they once more in their history to touch the Hundred? Or would she perhaps fail them just before reaching the post? A little chill, a window left carelessly open, a hot-water bottle neglected, the wrong food, a sudden shock . . .

Barney Newmark, who had been staying in Cumberland recently with Adam, declared: 'Pooh! She is as tough as an old hen! Not that I speak disrespectfully, for a nicer, jollier old lady you never saw. I had half an hour with her and her brain's as clear as a bell. She's got eyes like a child's. Of course she's *old*. What do you expect at ninety-nine? She looks frail. She was always a pocket-edition but, dammit, she's sporting! *And* got a temper! But sweet-natured, you know, wants everyone to be happy. They all worship her and I don't wonder!'

In August she caught a cold and the news went right through England. Lady Herries in Hill Street (she detested Judith) gave a sniff and said the vain old woman had lived quite long enough, and for once Ellis became quite heated and said she had no right to speak so. She was an honour to all of them and it would be splendid did she live to her Hundred. Garth and Sylvia, pigging it in a little alley off Victoria Street, were genuinely concerned when they heard of the cold. 'Oh, she *must* live to a Hundred. She *must*,' Sylvia cried passionately.

'Perhaps she'll leave us something,' Garth said gloomily. Then added: 'I say, old girl, I lost on that damned horse yesterday. You'll have to pawn that ring again.'

Emily Newmark remarked virtuously that the Lord knoweth His Own Time. What He Giveth He taketh away; but Barney said:

'By gad, Emily, you'd weary a saint.'

All over the country it was the same. In Wiltshire, Carey, coming in from riding, was told by his mother and cried: 'Oh lor! I hope she isn't beat at the post! A cold, do you say? Damn' dangerous at ninety-nine.' Down at Bournemouth, where Jennifer's brother Robert had founded a little family (Robert himself was dead and his son Bradley reigned in his stead), they were greatly concerned, and Ruth, a pretty girl of twenty-two, thought of writing to Dorothy with a cure for colds that a Bournemouth doctor had given her. The Ormerods in London *did* write to Dorothy, and Horace Newmark, now extremely wealthy in Manchester, thought of running up to see the old lady.

However, all was well. Judith quickly recovered.

'Nothing the matter with her whatever,' Dorothy wrote to Sylvia. 'Of course it's very touching that everyone should be so deeply concerned, but Jane and I are *quite* capable of looking after her. And *what* do you think? Timothy is engaged at last, to a Miss Greenacre of Taunton Hall, near Grasmere. She seems a nice girl—quite a beauty but manners a little haughty. Timothy says she'll make a good mother. I trust he won't be disappointed.'

The truth was that the Herries were very ready for a public demonstration of their position. A century or so back they had been nothing at all—and now look at them! A Peerage in Wiltshire (Carey intended to stand for Parliament at the next election); Ellis, young though he was, one of the richest and most important men in the City; Barney Newmark, a famous novelist (famous *enough* anyway); Adam Paris, a well-known writer (well known at least to all the *real* readers of literature); Horace Newmark, one of the richest men in the North of England; Rodney, Archdeacon of Polchester, and his son, a most oncoming Captain in the Navy; Lady Herries in Hill Street, a leader of fashion; the Witherings, and the Bellairs at Uldale, among the first County families of the North; and Judith Paris herself, *really* famous so that all kinds of people asked after her. Mr. Disraeli had known her, Dickens and Thackeray in their day had heard of her, the Bishop of Polchester often asked Rodney about her, and as to the North itself—why, everyone knew her and everyone was proud of her!

So they were determined to make this Birthday of hers a Herries demonstration, just to show the world what a Herries could do were he or she so minded! No other family in England, so far as was known, contained so famous an old lady.

Many of them intended to be present at Uldale for the event. As the day drew near, Dorothy, Timothy and Jane, who were the managers and presenters of the Ceremony, had great difficulty in arranging for what Timothy called the 'horse-boxes.' Where were all the Herries to be put? Fell House itself would have to entertain for the night—Veronica, Captain Forster, Amabel, Lady Herries, Adam, Margaret, Ellis and Vanessa. Quite a problem! Jane and Amabel must share, Margaret and Vanessa; Forster, Ellis and Adam would have to take one of the big attic rooms. The Witherings, who would drive over, could put up Garth, Sylvia and Amery, old friends of theirs. Horace and Barney could manage in the village. Will Herries, the naval son of Rodney, his wife and sister Dora were found rooms in the Peter's House Farm. There were two distant cousins— Rose Ormerod and Sophia Fanchard—who were to stay in Bassenthwaite, and, lastly, Ruth and Richard, the grandchildren of Robert, Jennifer's brother, were young enough and lively enough not to care where they were. The two little rooms over the stables would do for them. How fortunate that Elizabeth and Benjamin were now settled at the Fortress! That left more room for everyone.

When this was all settled there arose the question of the Orders of the Day. It was decided that the procession to Judith's room with the gifts and the little speeches should take place in the morning: that would be less tiring for her. Then there should be a grand dinner at two o'clock. In the afternoon everyone should go their own sweet way, and in the evening there was to be a Ball to which everyone of any importance in the neighbourhood was to be invited.

This all settled, two great questions remained—one, the state of the weather, and two, the state of Judith's health. Were it to pour all day—to come down a regular 'posh' as so easily it might—why, then we must all put up with it, smile, and say that we liked rain rather than not. Nevertheless, it would be provoking. All the afternoon the house would be unpleasantly crowded, for these Southerners were not accustomed to Cumberland rain and had not acquired the good Cumberland habit of going out in all weathers. Tempers would be strained and it would be annoying to overhear, as one undoubtedly would: 'Of course in the Lakes it always rains.' . . . My dear, what do you suppose you came for? Here it never *stops* raining.'

The other question—of Judith's health—was the most serious of all. Of late she had had her bad days: how at her age could you not expect it? She was often dreamy, far away, lost in some other world. Sometimes she was cross and peevish when her digestion worried her. Sometimes she was very deaf and could hear nothing, although Dorothy always declared that she could hear perfectly and affected this deafness simply to give herself a rest. But her heart was her real trouble: any excitement was bad for her, but how could she enjoy her Hundredth Birthday *without* excitement?

And to make everything worse, she insisted upon taking the greatest personal interest in everything. She wanted to know exactly who was coming, *where* everyone was staying, what everyone would do. Her brain was often of an astonishing clarity. 'My dear, don't be a fool,' she would say to Dorothy. 'Of course the Herries woman must have a room to herself.' Or 'Dora? That's Rodney's girl. I remember. Her brother was at the opening of the Exhibition. In the Navy. A prig.'

It was a delight to her that Adam, Margaret and Vanessa

were to sleep at Fell House. It was a long time since they had done so. It became clear, as the day approached, that almost all her anticipation was centred round Adam. It was *his* coming, that *he* should be present at her Hundredth Birthday, that gave her the keenest pleasure. Had she had the strength she would have gone herself to see the attic where they were putting Adam and Forster.

'Is the wardrobe large enough? Adam is very untidy, you know, Jane. He throws his clothes all about. Is there a nice cheval glass?'

But of course she could not move farther than to the armchair by the fire. If she had one of her bad days she must not leave her bed and they must make their speeches as quickly as possible.

But on the great morning of the Twenty-Eighth all was well. It was neither a good day nor a bad day as to weather, but at least it was not raining. Clouds shaped like ram's horns twisted above the hills, whiter than other grey clouds behind them. It might be that they held snow, for it was cold enough. The larch trees were pale gold—like gold beaten very thin—against a background of rolling hills, grey and thick like flannel, and from this vast sprawling bed a point on Blencathra, palely lit, stuck up like an old man's nose. Nevertheless it was not a bad day.

By nine o'clock of the morning they thronged the downstairs and passages. The Ceremony was to be at ten. All the women were in their loveliest dresses, and there was no question but that Veronica outshone them all. Matrimony had improved her. She knew—and dear Robert, her husband, knew—that she was to have a child; as yet there was no sign of this, but the knowledge of it (for now she loved her Robert dearly) gave her an added colour and excitement. Her dress, too, admirably suited her, with its corsage like a cavalryman's tunic, the draped back, the innumerable narrow flounces. At the back of her head her dark hair was piled in masses of curls, and she wore a little hat, very small indeed, pushed forward over her forehead. The colour of her dress was rose. She wore broad ribbons of rose on her hat. So she was the queen of the party, and Robert Forster was intensely proud of her. No one else was beautiful (Elizabeth had not yet arrived from the Fortress). Lady Herries was painted and affected, Sylvia's dress had too many flounces to suit her age, Dorothy was too stout, Amabel too masculine, Jane was just a dear old maid, Rose Ormerod was a pretty little thing, Ruth Cards—grand-niece of Jennifer—was by far the most charming of the younger ones. She had a slight slender figure like a boy's, and the skirts of her jacket, projecting over her bustle, made her look like a boy in fancy dress. She and her brother Richard were rather new events in the life of the Herries. No one had seen them before. They won approval.

Of the men it may be said that Timothy was the most impressive, for he was host; he was large, stout and jolly, and he was but recently engaged to that stiff, haughty-looking girl in a purple dress, Violet Greenacre. He was of the type that the Herries admired, for he looked as though he would stand no nonsense and would live for ever. Barney was in splendid form, laughing with everyone. The Herries liked him because, although he *was* an author, he did not, thank God, look like one! Ellis was grave, dignified and, as usual, alone. They thought him haughty, stuck-up, and did not know that he, in his heart, was longing to be jolly, genial, generous as Timothy was, but didn't in the least know how.

And what of Judith upstairs?

She did not know, she told Jane, whether she had had a good night or no. She *thought* that she had slept well, but she could not in fact be certain because it was hard to tell when she was sleeping or when she wasn't.

She was, however, very cheerful, drank her tea and enjoyed her egg. *Of course* she would get up! She had, it soon appeared, thought out everything. The armchair was to be just here, near the fire but not too near, the small table at her side for her silver spectacle-case, her needle-case, a spare handkerchief and a silver-topped bottle of smelling-salts. She knew the Ceremony was to be at ten o'clock and she was glad that it would be early, because then 'she could have a nice time after talking to one and another.' Dressed, in her chair, she seemed, thought Jane, very small and very beautiful. Judith had never been beautiful, but it may be true to say that she approached more nearly to beauty on this her Hundredth Birthday than ever she had done before.

Her white lace cap had the brilliance of a jewel, the soft folds of her black silk dress shone in the firelight, her cane was at her hand, and on her black shoes were the diamond buckles that she wore only on very great occasions. The white lace at her wrists emphasised the fragility of her hands. Her only ring was the plain gold one that Georges had given her. Around her neck was the long thin gold chain that ended with a small gold watch in a pocket at her waist.

But it was her snow-white hair (once so brilliantly flaming) and the small face crowned by it that caught any observer's attention. That small face was wrinkled across the forehead and at the corners of the eyes and was pale ivory in colour—yet its outlines were as firm as ever they had been. The mouth had not the weak indecision of the mouths of so many old people. The lips were firm, now parting in a smile, now ironic, now commanding and sometimes bitter, for all old ladies are bitter sometimes. The eyes, though, were never bitter. Their light was astonishingly bright for so long a history, shining, penetrating, merry, questioning and, above all, loving: never weak nor sentimental unless she suffered unexpectedly some childish disappointment, when she could look like a little girl not out of the nursery.

It would be idle to pretend that she was not feeling the fullest satisfaction in this her great day. What is more, she felt that she deserved every bit of it. Very few people lived to be a Hundred and it needed a lot of doing! She was proud of herself and proud of England. She had been thinking a great deal about England during this last year, not with any weak sentiment nor any boastful patriotism. She thought, it is true, of the Queen because she was another woman like herself and had suffered a bereavement just as she once had, but she did not otherwise think of any special events or persons—neither of Mr. Gladstone nor of Mr. Disraeli, nor of Oxford undergraduates breaking stones in the road for Mr. Ruskin, nor of Cardinal Manning advising the Irish working-man to be temperate, nor of the Monday Pops, nor of the famous new Ladies' Golf Club at Westward Ho, nor of the great bicycling race from Bath to London. Even in the mornings now when Jane read her the newspaper she did not listen very much and often fell asleep.

The England that preoccupied her now was her own personal England which seemed, when she looked at it, to spread all about her, a bright, coloured, lovely country, infinitely gentle and infinitely kind. The England of the wild life at Stone Ends, of Uncle Tom Gauntry and Emma Furze, of the fireworks at the Lake's edge, of that moment in the hall at Stone Ends when Georges had proposed to her, of mornings and evenings and nights at Watendlath with the Tarn black under the hill, the fresh smell of the new bracken, the early-morning calling of the cows, the sight of Georges coming up the path with the crimson bird in the cage, Braund Fell and Armboth, Rosthwaite and Stockley Bridge. The England of London, of the cobbles and the sedan chairs, the Ball at poor Christabel's, Mrs. Ponder and the Southeys and Jennifer, the hour at Rosthwaite with Warren. The England (her happiest England of all) of Watendlath and young Adam and Charlie (dying so foolishly after of a little silly chill), of Adam above Hawkshead laughing at Walter, running up the hill with her to see the sun rise . . .

And later than that England did not seem to go. After that many things had happened to England, she supposed, and Adam had grown, married, and had a child; the hills, her beloved hills, had darkened and been lit again by the sun, had taken on every colour and been blinded by the rain—but in this later England movement had ceased. Someone called Judith had lived there, but the real Judith by then had slipped away. And yet the real

Judith was still here and Adam was here. He was coming this very morning to see her have her Hundredth Birthday. She had every reason to be happy.

She smiled at Jane, who was seeing that everything in the room was right.

'I think England is very nice, dear,' Judith said.

'What, darling?' said Jane, who thought that she had not heard aright, but that Judith had been talking about her breakfast.

But Judith did not bother to repeat. However, she said something else.

'Will Walter be coming?' she asked.

Jane was startled. 'Oh no, dear. Poor Walter is much too feeble. But Elizabeth and Benjie are coming, of course.'

'Walter!' thought Jane; 'what an idea!' He was now quite a foolish, brainless old man, and although Elizabeth had done wonders so that the Fortress was now clean and alive and wholesome again, the thought of Walter coming into the middle of this happy Birthday was most distressing.

'That's a pity,' said Judith.

'What, dear?' asked Jane, who was busy all over the room, as she loved to be, dealing with trifles.

'I said "That's a pity,"' said Judith. 'You are growing a little deaf, Jane dear. I've noticed it before.'

Jane said nothing.

'It's a pity, because Walter and I once had a quarrel and I should like to tell him that it's ended.'

'He knows that,' said Jane. 'The last time you ever went out you drove up to the Fortress and made it up. Don't you remember?'

'Of course I remember. But to-day would be a nice day to end it all up—a very nice day. Is Adam come yet?'

She had asked that already fifty times. Jane went to the window.

'Why, yes. There he is now. Driving up.'

Judith smiled.

'Very good. I'm very glad.'

307

* * * * *

Meanwhile downstairs, Adam, Margaret and Vanessa had arrived and mingled with the family. Vanessa's beauty startled everyone. Many of them had never seen her, and for others she had been still a child. Now, although she was only fifteen, her slender height, her rich colouring, her black ringleted hair behind her little dark blue hat, her girl's dress with the white flounces, the bustle only just pronounced enough to give her waist its perfect shape, her modesty and quietness mingled with the evidence, almost impossible to control, of tremendous happiness and high spirits, created a great impression.

'That's a stunning girl!' said Captain Will to his sister Dora. 'She's Madame's grand-daughter, you know. Yes, her mother's a German. Her father married a German. That's him—that brown-faced bearded fellow over there. Writes fairy-stories, books for boys—that sort of thing.'

Adam and Barney were delighted to see one another.

'I say!' cried Barney, 'that girl of yours is growing into a Beauty. 'Pon my word, she is! Regular Beauty!'

Adam laughed, pleased and proud.

'She's as good as she's beautiful, my boy.'

'Not *too* good, I hope,' said Barney. 'Don't like 'em too good, you know.'

But it was Ellis who was stricken as though by lightning. Standing by himself, near the staircase, hating it all, wishing it over, wishing that his mother would not make a fool of herself, intensely proud at the same time, saying to himself: 'You couldn't find such a set of people in the whole of England,' proud of his relations and despising them, longing to be friends with them all, hating it if any of them came up to speak to him; it was Ellis who, seeing Vanessa for the first time in his life, as she waited a little shyly behind her father, just out of the crowd, received a blow at the heart from which all his life he was never to recover. It was not that he fell in love with her at first sight; it was, more simply, that he had never known what life was before, that he moved, at that instant, into a new world of colour, light, sound. He stood there, staring. He gazed and gazed. He did not know who she might be. He turned and found Garth, already a little gay with morning brandy, at his side.

'Tell me, Garth, who is that?'

'Who is what, my boy?' said Garth, who had already borrowed a considerable amount of money from Ellis and intended to borrow a lot more.

'Why, there—over there! That young girl with the black hair—in the blue hat.'

Garth followed his directing hand.

'Oh, that! Why, she's Adam Paris' daughter, the old lady's grand-daughter . . . Damn' pretty child, if you ask me.'

Ellis said no more. He stood back against the wall, gazing.

* * * * *

There then occurred the great sensation of the day. The clocks pointed to twenty minutes to ten, and the party from the Fortress had not yet arrived.

Dorothy was distressed, anxious. She moved about like a great green whale, saying to everyone: 'Very strange! Elizabeth is so punctual! I hope that nothing has occurred. Very strange indeed! I hope that Walter has not died, this morning of all times!'

There was a stir by the door. They *had* arrived. All was well. Dorothy hurried forward. The door opened and Elizabeth, bringing the cold November air in a gust with her, came in. Leaning on her arm, looking about him in an interested but rather aimless fashion, was her father, Walter Herries.

Walter Herries! The news went round the company in a flash. Walter Herries, who was, they all supposed, a doddering old idiot whom Elizabeth had splendidly rescued from destruction and was now nobly devoting her remaining years to succouring! Walter Herries, once the villain of the Herries piece, now a harmless old imbecile—actually he had come to Judith's Birthday!

It was a real sensation that gave way presently to a grave and general satisfaction. This was well. This was indeed most fitting! The Feud that had distressed for so long all the Herries, that had had its climax in a terrible tragedy, was now, on this splendid occasion, to be finally closed. This was Elizabeth's doing, Elizabeth who had suffered more deeply from that Feud than any other. Could anything be more proper? Soon everyone was delighted. A chair was found for Walter in the parlour and down on it he sat, looking kindly about him, smiling, seeming quite happy, yet plainly without any idea as to where he was.

'Elizabeth's smartened him up!' said Lady Herries to Amery. He looked indeed quite elegant with his snow-white beard, a handsome blue frock-coat and a dark blue neckerchief.

And that brown-faced, healthy-looking young man with the bright blue eyes was Benjamin, Elizabeth's boy. Yes, the son of poor John . . . A bit of a rascal . . . He had left Rugby now and was looking after his grandfather's land, or *should* be . . . But they said he couldn't stick to anything, was a great anxiety to his mother. Yes, he was eighteen or nineteen, just kicking his heels . . .

Benjamin himself heard none of these whispers nor would he have cared if he *had* heard. He was enjoying himself outrageously as he always did enjoy everything. Where was Vanessa? His first thought was for Vanessa. What a rum lot of old codgers these relations were! How ridiculous old Lady Herries in her paint and powder! Garth he could see had already been at the bottle. By Jove, was not Veronica a picture? *There* was a woman! Beautiful figure and what a pair of eyes! What fun bringing Grandfather into the middle of all this! It had been the old man's own idea. In a lucid interval he had grasped that Judith was having a grand birthday. He had hunted round and found a brooch that had belonged to his wife, a pretty little gold thing with three pearls and a ruby. He would give her that and he would present it himself. He explained to Elizabeth that he and Judith had not been the best of friends—but that was all over now, quite finished. Much too sensible a woman to cherish a grudge. And his excitement had been tremendous. He had got out of bed himself at about four that morning to find a box to put the pearls in. He sat in the parlour now, clutching the box in his hand, patiently waiting until he should offer it. Rum old boy, thought Benjamin, rejoicing in his own youth and strength; but he rather liked him. He was just like a child, and Benjie played draughts with him most evenings. Not that the old boy could play. He just moved the counters about, but it gave him pleasure. And there the old man sat, clutching his parcel.

However, Benjie had not come there to look at his grandfather. He moved about looking for Vanessa. And then, of course, he knocked against Ellis, the last man in the world he wanted to see.

He had encountered Ellis only briefly since that rowdy night in London four years ago. He was aware, without any question, that that evening had made a breach between himself and Ellis. Not that they were ever the kind to get on well together, Ellis so solemn and proper, and himself—well, *not* so solemn and proper! But he could not know with what profound distaste Ellis now regarded him nor the deep shudder of disapproval with which Ellis had seen Walter's entrance. What did they want to bring that old man for? He had a wild fantastic notion that it had been done in some way to insult himself. As with all egoists and men unsure of themselves, like all men sensitive to an unpopularity that they would give their lives to alter, most things in life seemed to Ellis to be directed against himself. This doddering, wandering old man was his brother! Did they not know that? Well, then . . .

It would be, he suddenly thought, just like young Benjamin to have arranged this—maliciously, simply to distress him. Ever since that night at the 'Paragon,' Ellis had thought of Benjamin as wild, malicious, reckless—all the things that he hated!

'Hullo, Ellis!' said Benjamin.

They made a strange contrast, Ellis, long-nosed, pale-faced, grave, in his official dark clothes; Benjie, snub-nosed, brown-faced, in a long brown sack-coat and a dark red tie caught with a gold ring.

'How do you do, Benjamin?' said Ellis, offering his hand.

'Have a good journey up?'

'So-so. Cold, you know.'

'Yes, I suppose. Well, we'll be moving up to the old lady shortly. Quite a gathering of the clans, ain't it?'

'Quite,' said Ellis.

Benjie moved off. He had no intention of wasting his precious life over Ellis!

Where was Vanessa? He tumbled into Adam. Dear old Adam, the man he liked best in the world and Vanessa's father!

'Why, Adam! Isn't this grand? I say, where's Vanessa?'

'Somewhere,' said Adam, who was rejoicing in every minute of this great day that was to do his mother honour. 'How are you, young Benjie?'

'So-so,' said Benjie, dropping his voice and grasping Adam's arm. 'I say, this sort of thing makes a fellow restless. Ever feel restless?'

'Sometimes,' said Adam.

'Well, *I* feel restless up at the Fortress. If it weren't for mother I wouldn't stay.'

'Why, where would you go to?'

'I don't know. The sea perhaps. Or America.'

'Take my advice,' said Adam, 'and stay at home. There's no place like home.'

'You didn't always think so?'

'No.'

'Nor do I. When I'm your age, Adam, I'll settle, but as it is——'

He went off, laughing, poking Barney in the ribs, bowing ceremoniously to Lady Herries whom he detested, seeing little Ruth Cards for the first time in his life and thinking, 'That's a pretty girl. I wonder if she'd mind being kissed.' He did in fact kiss someone a moment later, for he wandered through the green-baize door at the back of the hall and there, in the passage leading to the kitchens, was Hannah, carrying a tray.

'Why, Hannah!' he cried.

'Master Benjie!' She smiled. They all adored him.

'Here, give me a kiss! No, there isn't a moment to lose! Here, I'll hold the tray!'

'No, Master Benjie, you're not to!'

But he put his arms round her, held her close to him, kissed her full on the lips. Then, laughing, ran off.

But where, oh, where was Vanessa?'

* * * * *

All the clocks struck ten. Everyone began to move upstairs. There had been a change in the arrangements. A very handsome volume in blue leather and gold had been provided, and in it every member of the Herries family who could be found had signed his or her name, agreeing that they from the bottom of their hearts congratulated Judith on her Hundredth Birthday and wished her health and prosperity.

It had been Barney's idea, a very pretty one. It had been intended that Adam should present this, but after Walter's unexpected arrival it had been thought that it would be excellent if Walter, the senior of them all, should make the Presentation. At first there had been some difficulty. He wanted to give his *own* present. He had come all that way to give his *own* present . . .

'But so you shall, dear,' Elizabeth whispered. 'You shall give them both. Only this is from all of us and the other is your special one . . . '

But he wanted to give his *own* present! However, at last he had consented to hold the blue leather book in one hand and his own precious little box in the other. Elizabeth guiding him, they headed the Procession up the stairs.

And up the stairs they all crowded, laughing, joking, excited, feeling that this was really a *great* Herries occasion, that, as it were, the eyes of all England were upon them.

On the way up Barney said one thing to Amery in a chuckling whisper:

'Very fitting, you know, old Walter making the Presentation. Closes the Feud. He and Judith were enemies for years. That's the end of *that!*'

At that same moment Benjie caught sight of Vanessa just ahead of him. He brushed forward, almost, in his haste, knocking someone over.

He did not know (nor would he have cared if he *had* known) that that someone was Ellis.

'I say! Vanessa! Vanessa! Where *have* you been?'

She turned. She was a stair or two higher. Her face was lit with delight as she turned her head and saw him.

'Oh, Benjie! I've been looking for you everywhere!'

Ellis stared at her. The staircase seemed to rock beneath him.

'Hush!' Timothy said. 'We go in now, three at a time. Sir Walter, you're first. Thank you. Elizabeth, if you wouldn't mind!'

* * * * *

Judith sat looking at the door, Jane standing beside the chair. She was quite calm, very dignified, extremely proud and happy.

The door opened and Walter entered, led forward by Elizabeth.

Jane gasped.

'Oh, Aunt Judith—it's Walter Herries!'

But to Judith it seemed perfectly natural.

'There, Jane, I said he would come. How extremely attentive of him!'

Walter had no idea of anything save that it was Judith's birthday and he was giving her a present. But he realised, as he wandered, gazing about him, across the floor, that that was

Judith sitting in the chair. He knew Judith well enough. He had known her all his life. But why was he in a bedroom? He stopped, mid-way, and looked at the bed.

'Walter,' said Judith, smiling. 'How are you?'

That brought him to himself. This was, in any case, Judith, and this was her birthday. He found himself by the chair. Elizabeth was beside him.

'Well, Judith,' he said, his eyes still roving about the room. 'They tell me it's your birthday, so I've come and I've brought you a present.'

He pushed the little parcel into her lap and dropped the blue book. Elizabeth picked it up and put it into his hand again.

'Father, dear. You know what you are to say. You are to give Aunt Judith this. It's from all of us, and you are to say that all our names are here and that we all wish her a lovely birthday and many more birthdays.'

'A lovely birthday and many more birthdays,' said Walter, dropping the volume into her lap. Then, quite of his own accord, he bent forward and kissed her. Elizabeth had to steady him because his knees were very shaky.

Judith was delighted and greatly touched. She took her handkerchief from the table and wiped her eyes.

'Thank you indeed, Walter. Thank you, thank you. I am very glad you have come, because once we were not friends, were we? And now we are. I want to be friends with everyone to-day. And most especially with you, Walter.'

Walter began eagerly: 'And you must open *my* present, Judith.'

With very firm fingers Judith undid the parcel.

'Oh, isn't that pretty? *Isn't* that pretty? Do you see it, Jane? A lovely brooch! Walter, how *very* good of you——'

'Yes,' he said, immensely satisfied. 'It's a very pretty thing. I've had it a long time . . . ' His eyes began to wander. 'Uhland would have come to-day, only—only—I don't know why—but——'

Elizabeth gently took his arm.

'Now, father, you must make way for the others.' She led him to the window.

And Judith, now with her eyes bright and eager, was staring at the door. The great moment of her life had come. Adam would be next. Surely, surely Adam *must* be next!

She saw that they had all crowded to the door, and, all their faces smiling, were staring in.

A figure detached itself from the crowd. Grinning all over his face, moving his heavy body in his own rambling, comfortable way, Adam came forward.

At the sight of her son Judith's eyes and mouth broke into the loveliest smile that any member of the Herries family, here present, had ever seen.

Now her Hundredth Birthday was indeed a Triumph!

Christmas Eve, 1930.
November 1, 1931.

FOOTNOTES:

[1] *Dandy Grimmett*, by Barnabas Newmark. 3 vols. Suller & Thome, 1863.

[2] *The Dwarf with the Purple Comb, And other Stories*; by Adam Paris. Harris & Sons. 1865.

NOTE

It is hoped that the fourth and final volume of the 'Herries' chronicles, entitled *Vanessa*, will be published in the autumn of 1933. It will be chiefly concerned with the lives of Vanessa Paris and Benjamin and Ellis Herries.

Printed in Great Britain
by Amazon

28750058R00179